HOWARD BARKER

HOWARD BARKER

COLLECTED PLAYS

VOLUME THREE

THE POWER OF THE DOG
THE EUROPEANS
WOMEN BEWARE WOMEN
MINNA
JUDITH
EGO IN ARCADIA

CALDER PUBLICATIONS · RIVERRUN PRESS
Paris London New York

First published in Great Britain in 1996 by
Calder Publications Limited
179 Kings Cross Road, London WC1X 9BZ

and in the United States of America in 1996 by
Riverrun Press Inc
1170 Broadway, New York, NY 10001

ISBN 0 7145 4279 2

British Library Cataloguing in Publication Data
A catalogue record of this title is available from the British Library.

Library of Congress Cataloging in Publication Data
A catalogue record of this title is available from the Library of
Congress.

Set in 9/10 pt Times by Pure Tech India Ltd, Pondicherry
Printed in Great Britain by Redwood Books, Trowbridge, Wiltshire.

For Charles Lamb

CONTENTS

page

THE POWER OF THE DOG
Moments in History and Anti-History

CHARACTERS

McGROOT	A Comedian
POSKREBYSHEV	A Secretary
STALIN	A Politician
MOLOTOV	A Politician
CHURCHILL	A Politician
ENGLISH INTERPRETER	
RUSSIAN INTERPRETER	
DIPLOMAT	
ILONA	A Photographer
VICTOR	A Photographer
ARKOV	A Russian Officer
SORGE	A Russian Officer
MATRIMOVA	A Russian Infantrywoman
NEESKIN	A Russian Infantrywoman
TREMBLAYEV	A Russian Infantrywoman
MELANKOV	A Russian Infantryman
GASSOV	A Russian Infantryman
GLORIA	An SS Officer
MADAME DONKIN	An Intellectual
ZDHANOV	An Intellectual
LASHENKO	An Official
BUBER	A Tradesman
TOSHACK	A Town Councillor
PROKASH	A Citizen
MAN IN OVERCOAT	
WAITERS	
WORKMEN	

'Deliver my soul from the sword,
My darling from the power of the dog.'

Psalm 22

A Great Man Hallucinates

A banqueting hall in the Kremlin. Waiters laying cloths. A clown practises juggling.

McGROOT: The mon tells me this is an honour. Wha' kind of honour, says A, A ha' spent ma life avoidin' honours — the honour o' servin' wi' His Majesty's forces, the honour o' makin' a wooman decent in the eyes o' God, the honour o' buyin' the boss a drink, cheers, but honour's somethin' A can do wi'out. He says, the honour o' bein' the furst Scotsman to appear in the Kremlin. A pretended ta think aboot it — well, ye gotta look serious, haven't ye — an' then A said, wi' all respect, A'm perfectly happy wi' the circus, A've noo great ambition to play the Kremlin, it's noo a billin' A'm so desperate for. But he's very persistent — they can be persistent, can't they — he tells me this is one honour A canna refuse, there's noo exactly a glut o' Scots entertainers in the USSR. A was put on the shortlist — in fact, A was at the top of it — in fact, there was only one name on it — an' he showed it to me, an' there it was — Archie McGroot. A looked at it a minute. Archie McGroot, ma name's Vladimir Galoshev — (STALIN *enters, with his aides.* McGROOT *drops the balls*) — fuck — (*He scrambles after them.*) A will noo survive this . . . A will noo see the streets o' Paisley underneath ma boots agin, A'm a doomed mon — (*He drops the balls again.*) Christ . . . ! (*He retrieves them.*) He does noo laugh, it's like flashin' yer bollocks in the convent — (*He walks on his hands to where* STALIN *is idly tasting food.*) **Wha' did the Emperor say to the clown?** (STALIN *ignores him.*) **Wha' did the Emperor say to the clown?** (STALIN *drifts away.*) Fuckin' hell, A should ha' stayed in the clubs, but A'm an idealist . . .
MOLOTOV: What did the Emperor say to the clown?
McGROOT (*flipping onto his feet*):   **Lend us yer trousers, Harry!**

MOLOTOV: Lend us your trousers . . . ?

STALIN: Does Churchill find Scotsmen funny?

POSKREBYSHEV (*reading from a list*):   He enjoys cheese on toast, playing draughts, and a singer called George Robey. We could not find George Robey.

STALIN: This is a Scotsman.

MOLOTOV: Yes, but I'm afraid he isn't very funny . . .

McGROOT: **Noo funny! Who says a'm noo funny!**

POSKREBYSHEV: There are very few Scottish clowns in Russia.

STALIN: I will sit here, and they will sit there.

McGROOT (*to* STALIN):   Hullo, Jock! A luv yer whiskers!

STALIN: Molotov will sit on my right . . .

McGROOT   If every whisker was a kulak, how many barbers wud ye need?

POSKREBYSHEV: The General Secretary is not enjoying your performance.

McGROOT: He is, but he woon't admit it — A've cum across that before, A been booed offstage because they were so pleased wi' me —

STALIN: Tell him I will kick his arse . . .

McGROOT: Thank yoo! (*He rolls into a ball.*) It is a fact that the more resistance you encounter, the more effective yoo are bein'! A take a kick in the bollocks as a positive sign o' favour, it's all part o' bein' a radical comedian — (*He wiggles towards* STALIN, *arse rampant.*) Goo on, kick it, A've noo pride in tha' particular region, A doona keep ma brains there like sum people — (STALIN *goes to kick it.* McGROOT *tumbles under a table.*)

MOLOTOV: Churchill wants to thank you for Stalingrad.

POSKREBYSHEV (*with a bowl*):   The roses have just arrived from the Caucasus! Smell that!

MOLOTOV: He has a present for you, I warn you.

STALIN (*smelling the bowl*):   I haven't a present for him.

MOLOTOV: What is there to thank him for?

STALIN: I only give presents for killing Germans.

POSKREBYSHEV (*sniffing*):   Marvellous . . .

STALIN: I wish I was in a better mood all the same. Does he have someone to taste his food? Tell him I understand if he wants a food taster, I will not interpret it as bad manners, though it must be obvious it is in the interests of the Soviet Union to keep him alive, his party is full of Nazi sympathizers.

McGROOT (*poking his head out from under a table*):   There was a Socialist, an Anarchist, and a Communist, an' they all wanted a new pair o' trousers —

STALIN: I feel miserable, why?

McGROOT: So they went to this Capitalist trouser-maker, and the Socialist said, if ye make me a pair o' trousers, A will give ye thirty roubles. Thirty roubles, says the Capitalist, tha' will noo pay the wages o' ma worker, nor the cost of th' electricity, nor the rent of ma factory, let aloon ma profit, so you stuff yer thirty roubles, A will noo make ye a pair of trousers for less than a hundred —

STALIN (*sitting disconslately*):   Why? Is somebody against me?

McGROOT: So the Socialist thinks for a minute, and then he goes to the bank an' he takes oot a loan, goos back to the Capitalist an' gives him the hundred roubles. An' the Capitalist gives him a pair o' trousers. And then the Anarchist comes along, an' he says, if ye make me a pair o' trousers, A will give ye thirty roubles. Thirty roubles, says the Capitalist —

STALIN: Somebody is . . . against me . . .

POSKREBYSHEV: Not necessarily, it may be just a headache . . .

McGROOT: Tha' will noo pay the wages o' ma worker, nor the cost o' th' electricity, nor the rent o' ma factory, let aloon ma profit. A will noo make ye a pair o' trousers for less than a hundred. So the Anarchist thinks for a minute, an' then he goos to the bank, an' he robs it, an' he goes back to the Capitalist, an' he pays him the hundred, an' the Capitalist gives him a pair o' trousers . . . are ye still with me?

WAITER: The English are coming!

McGROOT: Fuck the English, A have n'a finished yet! (*The WAITERS take up their positions around the tables. POSKREBYSHEV goes to a gramophone. STALIN does not move.*) So then the Communist comes along an' he says, if ye make me a pair o' trousers, A will give ye thirty roubles. Thirty roubles, say the Capitalist, tha' will noo pay the wages of ma worker, nor the cost o' th' electricity, nor the rent of ma factory, let aloon ma profit! A will noo make ye a pair o' trousers for less than a hundred. So the Communist thinks for a minute, an' then he goes away an' starts a revolution to abolish trousers. (*Pause, then MOLOTOV bursts out laughing.*) Ye got to tell a joke agin yersel' sometimes . . .

POSKREBYSHEV *puts the needle on the record. The sound of 'Land of Hope and Glory' echoes through the Kremlin.* CHUR-CHILL *enters with a* DIPLOMAT *and two* INTERPRETERS. *He stands for a few bars, quite rigid.* POSKREBYSHEV *lifts the needle off, abruptly. Pause.*

CHURCHILL (*to his* INTERPRETER): Tell Generalissimo Stalin, that it brings tears to my eyes to hear the music of my country echo through the chambers of this august edifice . . .

ENG. INTERPRETER: Prime Minister Churchill wishes you to know it brings tears to his eyes to hear his country's music playing in this place . . .

STALIN: Tell the Prime Minister it is a sign of his greatness that he cries out of love for his people . . .

SOV. INTERPRETER: Generalissimo Stalin says it is a sign of the Prime Minister's greatness that he —

McGROOT: Oh, fuckin' hell, yoo compliment me and A'll compliment yoo —

CHURCHILL: The great Soviet people, and the great English people —

McGROOT: Never mind the Scots, they're just cunts —

CHURCHILL: Join hands in this epic struggle —

ENG. INTERPRETER: The great Soviet people and the great English people —

McGROOT: A do love you. Oh, A do love you!

ENG. INTERPRETER: Join hands in this epic struggle —

CHURCHILL: I bring you from my master —

ENG. INTERPRETER: He brings you from his master —

CHURCHILL: The great King George, by grace of God —

ENG. INTERPRETER: By grace of God —

CHURCHILL: This weapon, forged of English steel —

ENG. INTERPRETER: A weapon made of English steel —

CHURCHILL: The sword of Stalingrad —

ENG. INTERPRETER: The sword of Stalingrad. (*Pause*)

CHURCHILL: Give it to me, then. (DIPLOMAT *removes it from a case, hands it to* CHURCHILL.) Does he want it or not? (*They look at* STALIN, *who moves towards* CHUR-CHILL *and takes it. Then he kisses it.*) Why is he crying? Don't translate that.

DIPLOMAT: They lost three-quarters of a million men.

CHURCHILL: No . . . it is because of the King. It is the power of monarchy . . .

McGROOT: Fuckin' hell it is . . .

CHURCHILL: I ask Generalissimo Stalin, would he care, for my erudition, to propose a definition of History?

ENG. INTERPRETER: Mr Churchill asks Stalin, how does he define History?

MOLOTOV: I propose a toast!

SOV. INTERPRETER: Mr Molotov requests a toast —

MOLOTOV: To the Collective Farms!

SOV. INTERPRETER: The Collective Farms!

CHURCHILL, ETC: The Collective Farms . . .

STALIN: History? (*He stands, leans on his table.*)

CHURCHILL: No doubt we are about to hear something of the dialectical mumbo jumbo of the communist mind . . .

STALIN: History? (*Pause*) The incredulous overwhelmed by the incredible . . . (*Pause. He sits.*)

SOV. INTERPRETER: Er . . . the unbelievable . . . er . . .

ENG. INTERPRETER: The unlikely . . . triumphing over . . .

McGROOT (*emerging*):   History! A will tell ye wha' history is, it's a woman bein' raped by ten soldiers in a village in Manchuria . . .

CHURCHILL: I see entertainment has been laid on, of a most succulent kind . . .

ENG. INTERPRETER: The unbelieving meeting the . . . er . . . (*He looks to the* SOVIET INTERPRETER.) dyoksavna . . . ?

CHURCHILL: My love of Scottish comedians has been noted, but alas, not satisfied . . . Tell Mr Molotov, I drink to the Red Army.

ENG. INTERPRETER: Mr Churchill drinks to the Red Army —

MOLOTOV: The Red Army!

CHURCHILL: The robust Ivan, fearless in battle and loyal in heart — translate —

ENG. INTERPRETER: The er . . . wonderful Ivan . . . er . . . unafraid . . . and . . .

McGROOT: Wha's the difference between history and a hysterectomy? One's done wi' a bayonet and the other wi' a scalpel —

STALIN: I drink to the appearance of the English army . . .

SOV. INTERPRETER: The General Secretary toasts the coming of the English soldiers!

STALIN: Are the English afraid of the Germans?

CHURCHILL: What's he say?

ENG. INTERPRETER: Er . . . he wonders if . . . er . . .

STALIN: To fight a war, you must first get near the enemy . . .

CHURCHILL: What's he say?

ENG. INTERPRETER: He says . . . er . . . you have to . . . he implies the British are . . . er . . . unwilling to —

STALIN: You cannot fight a war with banks. Tanks, yes, but not banks! (MOLOTOV *laughs*.)

ENG. INTERPRETER: He says the banks are all very well, but —

McGROOT: There was an Englishman, a Scotsman, and an Irishman, and they were all scared o' the Germans! (STALIN *laughs, applauds*.) Christ! A goot somewhere! Shall A say it agin? (*He goes to a* WAITER.) Hey, have ye heard this?

CHURCHILL: I have not travelled across the seas and the great land masses of this continent, tell him —

SOV. INTERPRETER: Mr Churchill has not come all this way —

CHURCHILL: In order to submit to a calculated and unjust reprimand —

McGROOT (*doing a headstand*): If all politicians were liars, would anything be any different? Correction! If they all told the truth, would anything be any different?

STALIN: I would give up all the authority I possess to meet a beautiful woman on a train . . .

McGROOT: Like hell ye wuld . . . .

ENG. INTERPRETER: Stalin says . . .

CHURCHILL: . . . that he cast aspersions on the honour of the English people . . .

ENG. INTERPRETER: . . . he would give anything to meet a woman on a train . . .

STALIN: It is a sad fact I cannot meet a woman on a train unless both the woman and the train are commandeered for me. But of course that entirely removes the significance of the occasion. Accident, which is the essence of experience, has been eliminated from my life . . .

ENG. INTERPRETER: He says, such opportunities don't . . . come his way that often . . . .

STALIN: Has Churchill ever met a beautiful woman on a train?

ENG. INTERPRETER: He asks — the connotations are humorous — if you, Churchill, have encountered a lady in a railway compartment —

CHURCHILL: I have met my wife.

SOV. INTERPRETER: Churchill says he has met Mrs Churchill — (MOLOTOV *bursts out laughing*.)

CHURCHILL: What is so amusing about my wife?

McGROOT: In Manchester a geezer is lookin' at a woman in a train. In Manchuria they are cuttin' a woman's breasts off wi' a bayonet, ye gotta laugh, noo, ye gotta laugh!

MOLOTOV: I propose a toast —

SOV. INTERPRETER: Molotov toasts —

MOLOTOV: Mrs Churchill!

CHURCHILL, ETC: My wife.

McGROOT: The woman in Manchester says to the woman in Manchuria, this geezer keeps starin' at me, wha' shall A do?

CHURCHILL: Tell Stalin, if he wants to meet women in trains he should be a clerk —

McGROOT: So the woman from Manchuria says, ye call tha' a problem, A got ten soldiers here are gonna murder me! Ooh, says the woman from Manchester, but they're beasts, a'nt they? **Noo funny! Tha's noo funny! Tha' is a fuckin' disgrace!**

CHURCHILL: The great man endures his loneliness with few compensations but the certain knowledge of his immortality . . .

ENG. INTERPRETER: Er. . . . it's . . . a lonely life in politics . . .

MOLOTOV (*taking a glass*):   To the Red October tractor plant!

ENG. INTERPRETER: Red October Tractor Plant . . .

CHURCHILL: I wonder if we should not move to the question of the future of the European peoples. Translate . . .

ENG. INTERPRETER: Mr Churchill would like to talk about . . . the post-war settlement . . .

CHURCHILL: The British Government cannot concede that the social systems of the countries liberated from the heel of Nazidom shall be dictated by the colour of troops who stand upon their soil . . .

MOLOTOV: Especially since the English soldiers persist in standing on their own soil. Well, it is a very understandable point of view . . .

ENG. INTERPRETER: Molotov says . . . observes . . .

CHURCHILL: What does Stalin say? I do not listen to the puppet, only the puppet master. (STALIN *is fixed, absent.*)

McGROOT: Wha' is it, Joe? Cum on, son . . .

MOLOTOV (*raising his glass*):   The Black Sea torpedo boats!

ENG. INTERPRETER (*standing, shakily*):   The Black Sea . . . Christ . . .

MOLOTOV, ETC: The Black Sea torpedo boats!

McGROOT: There was a great mun, an' he chopped half the people's heads off to make the other half better, an' when he got to the pearly gates, he said to God, didn' A do well, A only killed half the people, an' God said, yoo are a merciless bastard, an' A will put yoo in hell. An' then another great mun arrived at the pearly gates, an' he didna chop anyone's head off, but he never made 'em better either, an' he said to God, didn' A do well, A never killed noobody, an' God said, yoo are a complacent bastard, an' A will put yoo in hell too. An' the two great men looked at one another in the flamin' furnace, an' said, wha' the fuck does God want, then? And there came a terrible roar out o' Heaven an' a voice said **charity**. (*Pause*) Do ye get that? A doon't . . .

STALIN: What does Churchill want to see in Greece . . . ?

ENG. INTERPRETER: He asks what you would like in Greece.

CHURCHILL: Tell him I should like, if there is a monarch available, to install him there . . . A kingdom of the Hellenes would delight me profoundly —

STALIN: He can have Greece, but not Bulgaria —

ENG. INTERPRETER: Greece is okay, but we can't have Bulgaria —

CHURCHILL: What about Italy?

ENG. INTERPRETER: Italy?

STALIN: I do not care for Italy.

ENG. INTERPRETER: Italy's all right —

CHURCHILL: A Polish king would be a nice thing, too —

SOV. INTERPRETER: What about a monarchy in Poland?

MOLOTOV: There are two million dead Russians in Poland!

CHURCHILL: I cannot see the objection to a monarchy . . .

MOLOTOV: We will have preponderance in Poland.

CHURCHILL: Who's got a bit of paper?

ENG. INTERPRETER: I've got an envelope . . .

DIPLOMAT: What about Roumania?

MOLOTOV: Fifty per cent.

SOV. INTERPRETER: Fifty per cent . . .

DIPLOMAT (*scrawling*): Hang on . . . Bulgaria, no . . .

CHURCHILL: Italy, put Italy . . . (*As they huddle over the paper*, STALIN *rises suddenly to his feet.*)

STALIN: What is that man doing?

POSKREBYSHEV: Where?

STALIN: That man!

POSKREBYSHEV: He is a waiter.

STALIN: He is rubbing my face with a pencil . . .

POSKREBYSHEV: Sorry . . . ?

STALIN: **A waiter you call him!** (MOLOTOV *looks round. The* WAITER *is aghast.*) Why is he rubbing my face with a pencil? If he's a waiter? Go on, explain that.

POSKREBYSHEV: Er . . .

STALIN: If he's a simple, common or garden waiter, why is he rubbing me out?

MOLOTOV: Rubbing you —

STALIN: **Yes!**

POSKREBYSHEV: Could you — expand on what —

STALIN: **I don't have to expand anything, it's obvious what's going on!**

POSKREBYSHEV: Yes —

STALIN: **Stop it, then.** (*Pause*)

POSKREBYSHEV: Yes . . . (*He goes to the* WAITER, *whispers to him, and the man starts to leave.*)

STALIN: He has scissors in his hand.

POSKREBYSHEV: Scissors?

STALIN: **Do I have to repeat myself? It's scissors he's got!** (CHURCHILL *and his aides look up.*) For cutting me out of the films . . . the man with the miniature paintbrush is turning my face into sky . . . a lifetime's work, painting Stalin out of every frame . . . one idle moment, dreaming of cunt in the archives, and I slip by — there, I saw him, behind Lenin, don't blink! It was Stalin!

MOLOTOV: Ask him if he's tired . . .

POSKREBYSHEV: You ask him.

STALIN: **I don't trust one of you! There is the only one I can trust!** (*He indicates* CHURCHILL.) Because he is my enemy . . .

CHURCHILL: What's he saying?

ENG. INTERPRETER: It's Georgian . . . dialect stuff . . .

CHURCHILL: Is it bawdy?

ENG. INTERPRETER: I think it is, yes . . .

STALIN: My picture has been reproduced more than any man's . . . when the wind blows I drift down in gardens and parks . . .

POSKREBYSHEV: Yes . . .

STALIN: . . . the waiters are planning to wipe me away . . .

POSKREBYSHEV: I don't think —

STALIN: Shh! Millions of waiters will go around Moscow, removing my face from the walls. Waiters are like that. It's time for a purge.

POSKREBYSHEV: Yes.

STALIN: Ask Churchill, what will they do to him when he's dead?

SOV. INTERPRETER: Stalin asks, what will they do to Churchill when he is dead.

CHURCHILL: Honour me.

STALIN: There are no mirrors to Stalin. Only his portrait sycophantically done . . . (*He turns.*) **Who will know me when I'm dead!**

POSKREBYSHEV: Me . . . ?

CHURCHILL: Tell Stalin there is nothing like the truth. It is the steel that cuts the Gordian knot of autocracy . . .

ENG. INTERPRETER: Er . . .

CHURCHILL: Translate it . . .

ENG. INTERPRETER: Churchill says there is nothing like the truth . . . when it comes to . . .

STALIN: Tell Churchill he can go now . . .

CHURCHILL: Honour and truth are the twin gryphons of proper authority . . .

ENG. INTERPRETER: Oh, fuck . . .

CHURCHILL: Bearing in their horny claws the shield of munificence . . .

ENG. INTERPRETER: I really cannot . . . translate this fucking . . .

CHURCHILL: It is the eagle swooping from the clouds of darkness . . .

ENG. INTERPRETER: Stuff . . .

POSKREBYSHEV: Stalin has finished talking. (*Pause.* CHURCHILL *etc stand unsteadily.*)

CHURCHILL: Is it not an awesome power, ask him, that no one in this continent, no child nor woman, shall live without our caveat?

DIPLOMAT: He doesn't mean caveat . . . he means . . .

CHURCHILL: No medieval prince, howsoever unrestrained, could reach down as we do —

DIPLOMAT: Not caveat — surely —

CHURCHILL: — into the lives of the as yet unborn, and stir their entrails . . . history . . . history . . . my hand . . . hold my hand . . . (*He extends it in a drunken passion to* STALIN, *who does not reciprocate*.) **Is anybody translating this?** (*People are drifting away*.)

MOLOTOV: Good night! Good night!

CHURCHILL (*withdrawing his hand*): Good night, you foul genius . . . Good night . . .

The English go out. The WAITERS *stand by the tables.* MOLOTOV *pours himself a drink.*

STALIN (*at last*): Somewhere in the Polish desert is a little photographer. Bring him to Stalin. (*Pause.* POSKRE-BYSHEV *looks to* MOLOTOV.)

POSKREBYSHEV (*taking out his notebook*): You wouldn't happen to know the name . . .

STALIN: No, I don't know the name . . .

POSKREBYSHEV: We will round up all the photographers. Did you say little?

STALIN: Littler than Stalin.

POSKREBYSHEV: What . . . under five feet? (*Pause*) Five-feet-six inches? (STALIN *just stares at the* WAITERS, *who, on a signal from* MOLOTOV, *have started clearing the tables.*) Five-feet-six . . . (*He writes it down.*)

STALIN: We must wipe out the waiters . . . (*The* WAITERS *stiffen.*)

POSKREBYSHEV: What . . . in the restaurants . . .

STALIN: Not in the fucking restaurants. Do you take me for an idiot? He thinks I am an idiot. He thinks I am intuitive —

POSKREBYSHEV: No, I —

STALIN (*to* MOLOTOV): Who are they?

MOLOTOV: They are lieutenants in the NKVD.

STALIN: Quite . . . (*Pause*)

POSKREBYSHEV: Ah . . .

STALIN: He understands . . . (McGROOT *appears from under a tablecloth.*)

McGROOT: Is it okay if A goo now? (*No one replies.*) Where shall A collect ma fee from? Is it the geezer doon the corridor or . . . (*Silence*) A'll see masel' oot . . . (*He starts to leave, stops.*) The gag aboot the women, A meant to say . . . (*Pause. He turns to go.* STALIN *suddenly bursts out laughing.*) Wha' did A say? (*and laughs*) Noo, noo, hang aboot, wha' did A say? A'll say it again, shall A? (*He walks backwards.*) Where was A? (*The lights fade.*) McGroot's the name, Archie McGroot — (STALIN *laughs again.*) Fuck me, A'm doin'

well all of a sudden — (*It is black.*) Noo, noo, ye're overdoin'
it, yoo are, yoo make me feel embarassed ... thank yoo ...
thank yoo ...

The Banality of Yet Another Murder

*Somewhere in the Polish Plain. A dead woman is hanging from
a rope. A* YOUNG WOMAN, *chic but dirty, stands underneath.
A* PHOTOGRAPHER *underneath a cloth adjusts a tripod
camera. The* WOMAN *strikes a pose.*

ILONA: Her stockings are quite clean. Why did she put clean
  stockings on? And brush her shoes? She did, look ... Are
  you ready? I look up, I — (*She breaks the pose.*) Would you
  object if I removed the stockings? No, not for the photograph, silly. I will do, if you don't mind. (*She strikes the pose
  again.*) I interpret silence as approval. (*A protest from under
  the cloth.*) You took a wallet! Yes, you did! You took a
  snakeskin wallet from the dying officer! (*She poses.*) I look
  up, I — (*A protest.*) What is wrong with my expression!
  (*Muffled voice.*) No I wouldn't touch her underwear! Silk
  notwithstanding I — (*She lifts the dead woman's skirt quickly.*) Anyway, it's not, so — (*She poses.*) I look up, I — (*A
  protest.*) **This is my human condition face**. (*Murmurs*) You say
  it's stockings, I say it's human condition — (*Protests*) Yes, I
  know you are looking through the lens and I am not —
  (*Protests*) **It is not stockings it is lachrymae rerum, all right?**
  It is — Weltschmertz ... (*Moans*) All right, I will — (*She
  abandons her pose and begins unhitching the woman's stockings. The* PHOTOGRAPHER *appears from under the cloth.*)
VICTOR: There is the photograph I ought to take ...
ILONA: Who's stopping you?
VICTOR: The dead thighs robbed. The knees offended.
IONA (*stuffing the stockings in her pocket*): Do you want to
  carry on? There is a perfect sky. (*Pause*)
VICTOR: You haven't put her shoes on ...
ILONA: Never mind, she says ... (*Ignoring her,* VICTOR
  retrieves the shoes.) Shall I tell you what I believe? I believe

that every murder is an acquiescence, and every victim possessed the means of her escape. I believe in your eyes and in your mouth you own the means of your salvation, whether you want to be loved, or whether you want to be saved. At the door of the restaurant, or the gate of the camp... (*Pause*) She thought so, too, which is why she put her best things on...

VICTOR (*throwing down the shoes*): **They won't go on...!**

ILONA: You walk through History... in polished shoes... you dance on tanks... you don't refuse... and if you die ... you may not feel it... arbitrary, you can't conceal it... but only if the shot comes from the back... if you can catch his eye... you're all right, Jack... (*She sits, takes out a map and studies it.*)

VICTOR: I wish I was a camera... I would have no feelings ... my shutter wouldn't jam with shock... like eyelids which shut tight and lock... my lens would stay all hard and glassy... (ILONA *stands up suddenly.*) If I was staring at a ditch of murder...

ILONA: Shut up...

VICTOR: Or a tart whose tits were classy...

ILONA: **Shut up**. (*She goes to the hanged woman, stares at her.*) I think that is my sister... (*A* RUSSIAN OFFICER *enters.*)

ARKOV: The German is not a beast.

The German is not a beast.

The German is not a beast. (*Pause*)

Human nature is not fixed but fluid, is not a granite monolith but a blank sheet of paper on which is written the social and political conjunction of its time. Man is neither good nor bad but an infinity of possibility waiting to be chosen. Have you certification entitling you to photograph in a combat zone? (*They are silent.*) My brother died in Byelorussia, my mother was murdered in Kerch. But we do not talk of private losses. How can you reconstruct if you are undermined by grief? Everyone has lost and who would benefit from competition in suffering? All right, you can go. (VICTOR *makes to move.*) Did you show me your certification? (*Pause*)

ILONA (*quickly*): Yes. (*They move swiftly to go.*)

ARKOV: You must think I am silly. I am letting you go because you are a woman.

ILONA: Yes...

ARKOV: I must say that while objectively I am unable to regard the German as a beast, I do abhor the fact he kills so many women.

ILONA: Yes . . .

ARKOV: Not that my regret is of the slightest significance in the scales of History.

ILONA: No, indeed . . . (*She signals* VICTOR *to pack up more quickly. They start to go.*)

ARKOV: I mean, women are love. (*Pause*) Not that love is of the slightest significance, either. I regret it all the same. Will you take my photograph and never mind the combat zone certificate? (VICTOR *nods agreement.*) May I stand close to you as if to indicate we are acquainted, if not intimately, then at least —

ILONA: **That is my sister on the rope**.

ARKOV: I do understand that. I do not mind a smile which is thoroughly enigmatic . . . (*He poses, close to her.*)

ILONA: Quick . . . .

ARKOV (*as* VICTOR *sets up*): That is an ancient camera. I have a Leica with apertures from 1 to 22.

ILONA: It was my father's.

ARKOV: Is that so?

ILONA: He carted it through Europe on his back.

ARKOV: Ah.

ILONA: In the last war. In the last slaughter. From Lemberg to Caporetto —

ARKOV: You are not smiling . . . .

ILONA: From the Isonzo to the Prut —

ARKOV: But never mind . . .

ILONA: He left five hundred plates of dying Austrians. His best were scenes in dressing stations. Later on, he specialized in bowls of fruit — (VICTOR *takes the photograph.*) **Who is going to bury my sister . . .**

SORGE *enters in a long overcoat. He walks to the hanged woman and takes her gently by the ankles.*

SORGE: This is a wonderful century. (*Pause. He looks at them.*) I hold her ankles and I say **this is a wonderful century** . . .

The Soldiers Fictionalize Their History

Shouting soldiers.

MATRIMOVA: The student Georgina Matrimova of the
  School of Film and Poetry of the University of Sverdlovsk,
  temporarily attached to the Support Unit of the 72nd Motorized Division, presents her innovatory Celluloid-Free film
  entitled WAR ... ! (*The soldiers punctuate her statement
  with a roar of battle.*) In this celluloid-free film the battle
  sequences achieve a degree of realism never before encountered in the history of the cinema! (*They roar.*) Un-
  flinching detail of a night attack against the Fascist lines
  renders all previous examples of the genre artificial and
  redundant. **Roll!**

*The lights go out. In the darkness the actors simulate a battle of
great ferocity. They stop dead when the lights come on. One of
them walks forward holding his boots.*

MELANKOV: The Story of the Boots. (*The rest groan.*) If
  only these boots could talk, what a story they would tell ...
MATRIMOVA: Close up boots ... !
MELANKOV (*mechanically*): Because these are not ordinary
  boots, these are not — (*He dries.*) Shit ...
MATRIMOVA (*prompting*): Covet ...
MELANKOV: Sorry?
MATRIMOVA: Covet ...
MELANKOV: Thou shalt not covet thy comrade's boots ...
MATRIMOVA: Stock film of Soviet infantry!
MELANKOV (*marching on the spot*): Private Shishkin was
  not born to die in socks ...
MATRIMOVA: Zoom feet!
MELANKOV: His mum and dad will never know how Private
  Shishkin's comrades longed for him to stop a shot ...
ALL: **Bang!**
GASSOV (*running forward*): The Hungry Soldiers Find a Pig.
MATRIMOVA: Sound effect!
NEESKIN (*narrating*): Owing to the speed of our advance the
  kitchens have been —
MATRIMOVA: **Sound effect!** (*The soldiers squeal.*)
MELANKOV: Georgina, you have cut my line about the —

NEESKIN: The kitchens are fully fifty kilometres in the rear!

MATRIMOVA: Stock film of tanks!

MELANKOV (*still holding the boots*): Thank you, cunt . . .

GASSOV: Is it a mirage, or is it a pig?

MELANKOV: Any time you want the boots, tell me and I'll just —

ALL: **It's a pig!**

MELANKOV: Say fuck off —

MATRIMOVA: Comic sequence of animal evading capture! (*A tumbling of soldiers.*) And cut to face of outraged NCO—

GASSOV: **'o said you could fall out you!**

ALL (*acting satisfaction*): Munch, munch, munch . . .

TREMBLAYEV (*stepping forward*): A Girl Makes Love. (*Boos and groans.*)

MATRIMOVA: Shh!

TREMBLAYEV: A Girl Makes Love.

MATRIMOVA: Close up Startled Peasant.

TREMBLAYEV: Language is no barrier. In war the simplest communication will suffice . . .

MATRIMOVA: Close up eyes . . .

TREMBLAYEV: He is shy and so is she . . .

MELANKOV: Bollocks . . .

MATRIMOVA: Sound effect of wind in trees . . . (*They susurrate.* TREMBLAYEV *slowly unbuttons her tunic,* ARKOV *goes towards her. Suddenly, as he goes to touch her, she shrieks.*)

TREMBLAYEV: **Not to touch me!**

MATRIMOVA: Cut! (*Jeers and boos.*)

TREMBLAYEV: **I said not to touch me didn't I?**

MATRIMOVA: **Cut!**

TREMBLAYEV: You promised me he wouldn't and he —

MATRIMOVA (*distraught*): **Cut! Cut!** (SORGE, *still in his overcoat, walks forward from where he has witnessed the exercise.*)

SORGE: The war film which merely dispenses pity does not help anyone. The experience of war is very narrow — hence the proliferation of clichés. The proper war film asks, did the soldiers die for something, or did they die for nothing? It is a revolutionary question. So the proper war film is not actually about the battle, it is about the reasons for the battle. What are the reasons for the battle? Arkov?

ARKOV (*getting up*): It's eleven o'clock and I want to write a letter.

SORGE: You write too many letters.

ARKOV: Yes, it's what I'm good at.

TREMBLAYEV: Answer the question.

ARKOV: Must I?

TREMBLAYEV: You must participate in group discussions!

ARKOV: I do participate in group discussions.

SORGE: No. You are present at group discussions. You don't participate in them. (*Pause*)

ARKOV: What was the question?

MATRIMOVA: What are the reasons for the battle? (*Pause*)

ARKOV (*routinely*): The liberation of the homeland.

TREMBLAYEV: No!

ARKOV: Oh, Sonya, please . . .

TREMBLAYEV: The liberation of the homeland is not sufficient reason for the battle!

ARKOV (*shrugs, gets up to go*): It's good enough for me.

TREMBLAYEV: Liberation for whom? That is the question, surely? Liberate for landlords, or liberate for peasants? Examine liberators closely!

ARKOV (*going to her*): You have lovely tits, but you bore me to the marrow of my balls . . . (*Laughter as he goes out.*)

TREMBLAYEV (*turning on* GASSOV): What's funny about that! You don't really think that's funny, do you? (*She looks to* NEESKIN.) Do you think that's funny? I don't, I think it's absolutely pitiful —

MELANKOV (*leaping out*): **I kill the Germans! I kill the Germans!**

TREMBLAYEV (*to* SORGE): Can we have that censured, please?

MELANKOV: **I creep to the rim of the machine gun pit!**

TREMBLAYEV: Can we?

SORGE: Yes.

MELANKOV: **The night is black and so am I . . .**

MATRIMOVA: Sorge, one day I will make a film, and it will tell the entire truth. It will contain every political truth and every personal truth. It will contain the whole of reality. I will call it **wholefilm**. I hate partiality, I hate bits!

MELANKOV: **I wait . . . in less than thirty seconds they will be dead . . . under the stars they snore their final sleep . . . !**

SORGE: It is easy to satirize the bourgeois film but difficult to cut free from its principles. For example, the principle of courage —

MELANKOV (*clutching his face in horror*):   **Aaagghh! I, a boy from Uzbekistan who drove a tractor I will kill four Germans sleeping, aaagghh!**

MATRIMOVA: I do not like the principle of courage.

SCORGE: I think it is the principle of individual courage that you do not like.

MATRIMOVA: Yes.

SORGE: Courage in whole peoples you do like.

MATRIMOVA: Yes.

SORGE: So we must represent artistically a new form of courage, mustn't we?

MELANKOV: **I hop! I hop! I have no legs I am so springlike and so coiled! I spring! and I am in the pit and they are sleeping, they are sleeping, oh, they did not think and they are sleeping!** (*He leaps.*)

SORGE: And this courage will not consist of sacrifice but will celebrate survival.

MATRIMOVA: Yes.

SORGE: It will be the opposite to bourgeois courage.

MATRIMOVA: Yes.

MELANKOV: **I stab them in their throats, I stab them in their throats, their throats! one, quick! and then! and then! quick, quick, oh, quick!**

SORGE: Not heroics, but endurance. Not bravery, but cunning.

MELANKOV: **And run! run! my back is big, is such a big back bounding through the night, don't shoot me, I am only seventeen!**

MATRIMOVA: Thank you. You see, I am only satirical because I have such a longing to be — incredibly serious.

SORGE: Yes.

MELANKOV: **And down! down in the soft, safe earth, my love, my dearest, oh, my fucking love, I stuff the snow into my gob and taste, and taste! I live! you see, I live and they don't!** (*Pause*) **They don't . . . they don't . . . they don't . . .** (*Pause*)

SORGE: Don't let me keep you up . . . (*The soldiers wander off, except* TREMBLAYEV.) Did you want something? (*He looks at her. Pause.*)

TREMBLAYEV: I can't sleep because of you. (*Pause. He wanders a little.*) Did you hear me?

SORGE: Yes.

TREMBLAYEV: It is not worth going to bed because all I do is think of you —

SORGE: Comrade —

TREMBLAYEV: Sighing and so on, turning over all the time I keep the other women up, I —

SORGE: Listen, Comrade —

TREMBLAYEV: Please don't patronize me, will you! (*Pause*) I was a secretary before the war. Earrings, nail varnish, giving the eye in corridors and rotting my bras with desperate little sweats, I wouldn't care if I was killed tomorrow, I have lived more in the last two years than all my —

SORGE: I wonder if you shouldn't —

TREMBLAYEV: **I haven't finished yet.** (*Pause*) You cannot just do this to me — alter my life — drain me, wash me out and fill me up again when —

SORGE: What?

TREMBLAYEV: **I think you have a responsibility.** (*Pause*) You deliberately set out to undermine my personality — you did — to demolish everything I was — for which I am entirely grateful — and to exert a power over my emotions which —

SORGE: Comrade, I am going to recommend you take special leave —

TREMBLAYEV: **You did, you know you did, why are you such a liar?**

SORGE: It is my primary function as political officer with this regiment to carry out instruction —

TREMBLAYEV: Shut up.

SORGE: In the materialist conception of history and the —

TREMBLAYEV: Shut up or I will slap your face. (SORGE turns to go.) I am fucking with Roy, have you noticed? (*He goes out.*) **Liar, you have!** (ILONA *enters*).

ILONA: Someone has pinched my sister's body. Where is it, please? (TREMBLAYEV *looks at her*.) They put her under a tarpaulin. Now she's gone. So has the tarpaulin.

TREMBLAYEV: I am not responsible for bodies. I am a rocket instructor. (*She goes out. GASSOV passes. ILONA accosts him.*)

ILONA: Have you seen it?

GASSOV: What?

ILONA: The body.

GASSOV: Which body? I have been in action continuously since Stalingrad. Which body do you mean?

ILONA: I have a sister. Her name is Hannela. I found her hanging over there. They took her down. They covered her in a tarpaulin. Now she's gone. So has the tarpaulin.

GASSOV: I expect they put her in a hole.

ILONA: On whose authority?

GASSOV: It's not a question of authority. It's an instinct.

ILONA: She's been stolen.

GASSOV: It is one of the major achievements of the Red Army to have disposed efficiently of twenty million murdered people. Some say a hundred million. I don't know. But that is a lot of holes. And the tanks go very quickly, leaving fields of dead behind . . .

ILONA: I have been robbed.

GASSOV (*as* VICTOR *enters*): Sometimes they dig up bits from other wars. In Prezymsl, under all the shattered concrete, they found a Teutonic knight still upright on his horse. I didn't see it. And a Swedish pikeman whose blue eyes were pickled in a bog. But the sanitary squads are obsessive liars, perhaps because the work is boring. Are you sure you had a sister? (ILONA *stares in disbelief.*) I only ask because there are so many people claiming they're bereaved. Some invent whole families and go around in mourning. My mother starved to death in Leningrad. Now, that is true, but I haven't got the papers proving it. And that's another thing, you can't claim pension unless you have the documents. The party is aware of the tendency to fabricate dead siblings, and —

ILONA: **I had a sister!** (*Pause*)

GASSOV: Yes. (*He goes out.* ILONA *looks at* VICTOR.)

ILONA: Not that I knew her. I think of all the people I have known — and God knows I have known some — I knew her least. When I was dangling from the other tit from birth you'd think I'd know her, wouldn't you, you would think so, but I don't believe in intimacy, it tells you nothing, does it, I have never actually been close to anyone, she was more beautiful than me, **I don't understand how she got herself hanged**. (*Pause*)

VICTOR: I don't want to change the subject, only — (ILONA *looks at him.*) Do you mind if I change the subject? I have this feeling — do you mind this — I think we're going to be shot.

ILONA: Why?

VICTOR: I think we've run out of luck.

ILONA: We never had any luck.

VICTOR: I know that, only —

ILONA: We never wanted luck, or asked for luck, or even entertained the possibility of luck. I hate luck — it's what hope shits in a panic —

VICTOR: Yes —

ILONA: If we'd relied on luck we wouldn't have eighteen boxes of historic photographs —

VICTOR: Of course, I'm only saying — what am I saying — I am saying we have the most comprehensive collection of documentary suffering in the history of photography. We have hanged and murdered people from the Adriatic to the Barents Sea, which is marvellous, which is — excellent — but it is also a terrible responsibility and I — I want to go to America. (*Pause*)

ILONA: We used to go dancing together. She went to fall in love. I went to be educated. (VICTOR *puts his hands in his pockets.*) I used to tell myself the education I shall get in the dance hall will be greater than the assembled libraries of the world. Of all the howling deserts of philosophy, none will teach me so much as a strange man's kiss. So I go in and wait, angling myself favourably to the floor. You may have noticed I have not got very perfect legs . . .

VICTOR (*routinely*): No . . .

ILONA: You haven't? And I wait until I see a man who wants to kiss me —

VICTOR: With or without perfect legs —

ILONA: And there are hundreds!

VICTOR (*pacing*): I do not want to disappear, I earned my biography so dear, sometimes to get a picture I have sweated blood, don't let some bastard with a rifle push my mouth into the mud . . .

ILONA: But eventually one shows more persistence than the others. Because he shows persistence doesn't make him the best man. It is quite possible I shall learn more from the man who is not persistent. But how can I persuade him to be competitive? It's impossible! So I end up with the persistent one.

VICTOR: I have a route worked out. It goes through Ankara and Kabul.

ILONA: And we go to a room. Not my room. His room. You cannot be educated in your own room. And we undress. And when we undress I begin to feel sad. Well, education is sad,

obviously! And while his mouth is searching me I think —
this was not the man. I have the wrong man again.

VICTOR: The advantage of this route is that it runs contrary
to the flow of refugees.

ILONA: And I open my eyes. They hate you to open your
eyes, but I cannot keep them shut, they will watch what is
happening, they will witness it! My strange posture . . . my
dear clothes on the bed —

VICTOR: **I have this feeling I will end up in a ditch!**

ILONA: They shout, and then — (*Pause*) that silence, oh, that
lake of silence no words can cross! (*Pause*) He shuts the door,
and I am in the snowy street, the wonderful snowy street,
under the cold and happy stars, and on the tram which rocks
me, lovingly takes my buttocks in its gentle seat . . . and I am
educated, in the beauty of the ordinary, lifeless thing . . .
(VICTOR *turns to go.*) You are not going to America, Victor.
You are sticking with this squirming old, dirty old, European
place. We will find my sister, and ask her how she died. Now
go to bed. (*He goes out.*) To anyone who thinks it is a
mystery, how we cope with so much history, I say the answer
lies in pain, what my mother went through I can again.
Swallow the monster and don't strain, murders from the
Bosphorous to the Hebrides render all complaints absurdities.
Don't ask what makes the system, if it is a system, work,
cover your indignation with your foot, don't think that black
stuff is burned bodies, really it is only soot . . .

Blackout

The Limitless Absurdity of Another's Love

A room in the Kremlin. STALIN *is asleep on a couch.*
POSKREBYSHEV *enters, looks, listens, hovers, is about to
steal out.*

STALIN: I'm not dead, I'm only pretending . . . (POSKRE-
BYSHEV *stops.*) **I'm not dead, I'm only pretending!**

POSKREBYSHEV: I thought — he is still sleeping — I
thought —

STALIN: **Am I?**

POSKREBYSHEV (*confused*):   Are you . . . ?

STALIN: **Dead yet?** (*Pause*)

POSKREBYSHEV: No . . . no, you were only pretending . . .
(STALIN *sinks back with relief.*)

STALIN: I mustn't die, Poskrebyshev.

POSKREBYSHEV: No.

STALIN: History will never forgive me for dying at this
point.

POSKREBYSHEV: Indeed not.

STALIN: Watch me more closely. Come in every two minutes
instead of every five.

POSKREBYSHEV: Very well. (*He turns to go.*)

STALIN: If I appear to be in difficulties, what do you do?

POSKREBYSHEV: I am to press the red button —

STALIN: **No!**

POSKREBYSHEV: No —

STALIN: **You stupid bastard no —**

POSKREBYSHEV: I remember, I remember —

STALIN: **You are a —**

POSKREBYSHEV: I know I am, I know I am —

STALIN: What, then?

POSKREBYSHEV: I am to shoulder the tommy-gun.

STALIN: No doctor enters here unless covered by the
tommy-gun.

POSKREBYSHEV: I was thinking I would press the button
and then shoulder the —

STALIN: **No!**

POSKREBYSHEV: No, of course not —

STALIN: **Of course not! Why not!**

POSKREBYSHEV: Because in the panic I might forget —

STALIN: **Yes!**

POSKREBYSHEV: Then the doctor won't be covered and —

STALIN: **Yes!**

POSKREBYSHEV (*counting on his fingers*):   Tommy-gun,
button, guard-alert, door —

STALIN: And if the bastard acts suspiciously —

POSKREBYSHEV: Shoot —

STALIN: There will be another one outside.

POSKREBYSHEV: Of course. (*Pause*)

STALIN: I am not afraid of death. I only want to post-
pone it as long as possible. Don't laugh. It isn't the same
thing.

POSKREBYSHEV: I wasn't laughing —

STALIN: I am bound to die eventually —

POSKREBYSHEV: Oh, I don't know —

STALIN: **Of course I will die eventually!**

POSKREBYSHEV: Eventually, I suppose —

STALIN: But when? There must come a proper moment, a moment when History will say, it was right that Stalin ceased to exercise the dictatorship of the proletariat then, but when? The problems seem to get worse, not better. Imagine if I died now, it would be a disaster! I have four hundred divisions on the Oder, this is a crucial moment in the history of the world!

POSKREBYSHEV: Absolutely. On the other hand, you are a Georgian.

STALIN: That's balls.

POSKREBYSHEV: Is it? But we have publicized the graphs of longevity in the Baku district!

STALIN: It's balls, I said. I arranged the publicity to dampen the enthusiasm of anyone anticipating my early death. There are no more centenarians in Baku than Berlin. (*The slightest pause.*)

POSKREBYSHEV: Brilliant!

STALIN: There are only two classes of person able to be unreservedly themselves, to follow the absolute dictation of their personality. The supremely powerful and the utterly insane. It is the power of Marxism-Leninism that prevents me sliding from one to the other. (POSKREBYSHEV *turns to go.*) Do I have an aura, Poskrebyshev?

POSKREBYSHEV: An aura?

STALIN: I believe the man who has emptied the cupboard of his personality creates around himself a powerful magnetic field. Do you see it?

POSKREBYSHEV: Er . . .

STALIN: Well, look, then!

POSKREBYSHEV: It isn't so much a question of actually seeing — yes, I can see it! I can see it, yes.

STALIN: What does it look like?

POSKREBYSHEV: It's —

STALIN: What? (*Pause*)

POSKREBYSHEV: I can't see it. (*He lifts his hands apologetically.*) I can't actually see it, Comrade Stalin. (*Pause*)

STALIN: All right. We will find a phenomenologist. Let him investigate it.

The Poet Can Be Trusted to Castrate Himself

A table and chairs. SORGE *is holding* ILONA's *photographic plates up to the light.*

ARKOV: You are not to censor my letters.

SORGE: There is too much death in them. Write more about victory and less about death.

ARKOV: I am not interested in victory.

SORGE: That is a most peculiar sentiment for an officer of a storm battalion.   ·

ARKOV: Make a note of it.

SORGE: Well, I shall, only I was thinking more of your wife. She will think you are morbid.

ARKOV: She knows all about my morbidity.

SORGE: She will fret. She will think you have had a premonition of your death. She will upset her neighbours on the factory bench. So the factory will produce less, and the army will be ill-equipped. The war will last longer and there will be more deaths. So you see, you contribute to the very thing that gives you most pain.

ARKOV: I detest your facile reasoning.

SORGE: You detest reason altogether. (*He shuts the box of plates.*) Put your death interest in some poems. The letter, you see, has too much authority, the poem none at all. Later, the poem will have the authority and the letter none at all, but by then it won't matter. Do it that way, will you? I let all poems through.

ARKOV: How would you know a poem from a letter?

SORGE: They rhyme, don't they?

ARKOV: You must pretend you are a philistine.

SORGE: It shortens interviews.

ARKOV: You are in terror of your sensitivity. You are in terror of your soul. (*He leans on the table, secretively.*) One day your soul will burst out of its servitude. What then?

SORGE: It's gone eleven o'clock . . . .

ARKOV: And run screaming through the empty galleries of your mind. It will send the doors of your conscience flying back on their hinges, your brain will shudder with the sound of crashing doors, I pity you, you will have no sleep . . .

SORGE: All right . . .

ARKOV: **I will not leave until you promise not to cut my letters up.** (*Pause*)

SORGE: Very well, I promise.

ARKOV: **You only promise because promises mean nothing to you!**

SORGE: Really, Lev, you are impossible to please . . .

ILONA (*entering*): Have I come too soon?

ARKOV: Everything he says — everything — is utterly untrue —

SORGE: Captain Arkov is leaving . . .

ARKOV: Things are relatively true or relatively false — but nothing is absolutely true and nothing is absolutely false — **what are you to do with a mind like that?** (*He turns to leave, stops.*) In the Ukraine, they ran out of trees, so they manufactured mobile hanging racks. We captured one outside Lvov. It had wheels on, and the maker's name, G. FABEN OF ESSEN. There was a rush of anger, and we brought up hammers to smash the rack, but a counter-barrage drove us into cover. When we returned, the rack was gone. Later, I saw the rack again, not in the Ukraine, but in Galicia, hitched behind one of our trucks. It was going back again, like the plough over Europe. G. FABEN OF ESSEN. (*Pause*) The womb knows no ideology. The womb is innocent. The enemy is ideology. You tell him. He'll listen to you. (*He goes out.* SORGE *walks.*)

SORGE: During the battle for the Pripet Marshes there was a panic in the regiment. Vital positions were abandoned, and the enemy rolled up the whole left flank. It was decided to execute, as an example to the others, every seventh man who fled. I was given the responsibility for this, and I did it by choosing every soldier whose christian name began with K. This yielded more than the number we required, so I excluded those whose christian names ended with Y. I chose these letters randomly from a lexicon. This struck some as arbitrary, but was it any more arbitrary than the falling of the enemy's shells? The struggle we set ourselves is to overcome the randomness of nature, which we accept with pagan resignation, and replace it by the ordering of man, which can be random too, sometimes. How have you survived the fascist occupation?

ILONA: I have an aura.

SORGE: Really? Do you mean you have a light round you?

ILONA: Yes.

SORGE: I can't see it.

ILONA: Where is my sister?

SORGE (*sitting*): Let's talk about photography.

ILONA: She went to Czernovitz.

SORGE: For example, the problem of selection.

ILONA: I couldn't understand why she had gone to Czernovitz. Perhaps she was in love with someone.

SORGE: It's an art of selection, is it not?

ILONA: She would travel five thousand miles to be with
someone. She crossed frontiers for love the way armies cross
them for murder.

SORGE: So the art is not in the picture but the frame.

ILONA: I was on the Black Sea and she was in Galicia. And
then I got a postcard. This postcard followed me from
Dedogatch to Bratislava. What is it about a postcard that it
passes through wars with no more than a dog-ear when every
ditch is full of people whose faces have been crushed? I felt
such affection for this postcard that could slip through wars
and politics. But it was readdressed so often I couldn't read
what she had said, only the name of this place, Czernovitz.
And I thought no more about it, until, without knowing it,
we came to Czernovitz. Only it isn't like the postcard any
more. Where is she, please? (*Pause*)

SORGE (*standing*): I've looked with great interest at the
photographs. Technically, they can't be criticized. (*Pause.
She concedes.*) It's not in the technical area I have reserva-
tions. It's in the content. Would you care to discuss this?

ILONA: Yes.

SORGE: Because I feel sure you will agree the idea of a
neutral art is utterly redundant. Yet these images strive for
neutrality. Or, to be more precise, they form a background
for your face.

ILONA: I like my face.

SORGE: Your face is perfectly all right.

ILONA: It's more than all right.

SORGE: That's the matter of —

ILONA: Oh, come on! (*Pause*)

SORGE: What do you wish me to say? You tell me and I'll
say it.

ILONA: No, you say it. (*Pause*)

SORGE: You have a beautiful face. (*Pause*) I merely won-
dered why you choose to decorate these pictures with it.

ILONA: I was a fashion model. We wanted some different backgrounds. Of course the clothes aren't up to much —

SORGE: It costs us half a million soldiers in this war for every hundred miles! (*Pause*) We will find the collaborators and we will punish them. It is a duty and a debt. **Are you aware how perilous your position is?** (*Pause*)

ILONA: Yes.

SORGE (*sitting, with papers*): What is your nationality?

ILONA: Hungarian.

SORGE: How old are you?

ILONA: Twenty-seven.

SORGE: Where are your papers?

ILONA: In the handbag of the person who is pretending to be me.

SORGE: They were stolen?

ILONA: Yes.

SORGE: When did this happen?

ILONA: 1943.

SORGE: Why have you not applied for fresh papers?

ILONA: We haven't been near Budapest.

SORGE: You have travelled without documents since 1943?

ILONA: Yes.

SORGE: Impossible.

ILONA: It happened.

SORGE: How did it happen? (*Pause*) A Hungarian fashion model and a Roumanian Jew wander round Europe casually photographing atrocities. They are still alive after four years. (*Pause*) Go away and think about it. Then come back and tell me how it happened. (*Pause.*) People say to me — people like Arkov say — where is the honour in the secret police? Be a soldier, cluster round the turret of a T34, kill Germans and grin black-faced from the newsreels! Thrill your sister! Make your mother weep! (*She looks at him.*) He must have killed a hundred Germans! Simple, clean and honourable, face to face! But me? An officer of NKVD? I must be evil because I work by stealth! (*He gets up.*) What sort argument is that? (*Pause*)

ILONA: Ludicrous. (SORGE *walks up and down.*)

SORGE: I hate simplicity. The intellectual laziness, the posturing of so-called simple men. They float through the world like icebergs, one tenth of sunlit ice . . . but what about the nine-tenths in the dark? (*He turns.*) The contradictions? The counter-arguments? The necessary and the expedient? What about them?

ILONA: Quite. (*She starts to go.*)

SORGE: If, when all the smoke has blown away, and Arkov has gone home to his wife, the old black rats of Europe shake the brick-dust from their fur and creep out into the light, what was it all worth, Arkov's blood? What was it worth? (*Pause*)

ILONA: I think you knew my sister . . .

SORGE: I have stood in doorways in the drizzle, watching a guilty lightbulb throb through dirty curtains, Mayakovsky in one pocket, a Sitka .45 in the other, and hour after hour kept warm from knowing there was a child somewhere whose life would, but for my vigilance, be spoiled like all his ancestors had been spoiled until Comrade Lenin got his fingers round the mad dog's throat . . . (*Pause*) First, there is rebellion, which is easy, and then comes service, which is hard . . .

ILONA: She said that, didn't she? History is a mad dog, I know that's her . . . (*Pause*)

> When the mad dog comes for you
> Don't run, you'll only stumble.
> Instead, lie down and show your throat,
> Some dogs don't bite the humble . . .

SORGE: You have a dirty face.

ILONA: She had clear eyes, eyes which made lying impossible.

SORGE: I can give you soap.

ILONA: And a smell like apples. Not like me. My bad breath is legendary. I think your smell comes from your soul, don't you? You blame the bowel, but really the bowel is only —

SORGE (*tossing a piece of soap*): Wash yourself. (*Pause. The chanting of the soldiers in darkness.*)

ALL: Party card, party card, Number twelve million, six hundred and sixteen thousand, four hundred and twenty eight, all your power, all your power, lend us at this hour — (MELANKOV *tosses down his party card.*) Uncle Joe, Uncle Joe, guarding us wherever we go . . . (*A photograph of* STALIN *is added.*)

MELANKOV: The Great Teacher . . .

GASSOV: The Great Leader . . .

NEESKIN: The Great Gardener . . .

ARKOV: The Great Pilot . . . (*Pause*)

MELANKOV: Matches.

NEESKIN: Oh, God . . .

MELANKOV: Matches!

NEESKIN: I'm not lighting it . . . !

GASSOV: Who asked you to?

NEESKIN: We could get twenty-five years for this, and twenty-five consecutive —

MELANKOV: Sonia, we are releasing the power of the party. It must be burned, all right?

NEESKIN: Couldn't we just —

MELANKOV: What!

NEESKIN: Rub it, or something . . .

MELANKOV: Rub it . . . fucking hell . . . rub it . . .

ARKOV: Hurry up . . . (MELANKOV *strikes a match, ignites the papers.*) Begin.

GASSOV (*adding something from a small bag*): Bit of Private Shenko's jerkin, splashed with brain . . .

NEESKIN (*similarly*): Grease off the wheels of the hospital train . . .

MELANKOV: Tuft of hair from a murdered cossack . . .

ARKOV: Body of the lizard we squashed with the half-track . . .

GASSOV: Letter from a widow in Novgorod . . . (*The rhythm is broken.*) Sonia . . .

ARKOV/MELANKOV: **Sonia!**

GASSOV: Letter from a widow in Novgorod . . .

NEESKIN: Nazi padre's model of God . . .

MELANKOV: Menstrual blood from the typing pool . . .

ARKOV: Bone splinter from the machine gun school . . . (*Pause*)
          Bone splinter from —

GASSOV: Oh, fuck! Fuck! (*He recollects.*) Tooth of a priest strung up by the river . . .

NEESKIN: Little bit of the mascot's liver . . .

ARKOV: The mascot's liver?

NEESKIN: I didn't get it, he did —

GASSOV: So that's what happened to —

MELANKOV: Shut up, you're spoiling the atmosphere!

NEESKIN: You don't think I'd cut up a bloody dog, do you?

MELANKOV: Look, do you want an atmosphere or don't you?

ARKOV: I am very cold, can we —

MELANKOV: It will be fucking cold if you don't concentrate! (*Pause*) Any more interruptions, just 'and over yer relics and fuck off, all right? If you want to meet the dead, respect the dead.

ARKOV: I'm sorry, she —

MELANKOV: I didn't eat the dog, all right? Where were we?

NEESKIN: Mascot's liver . . .

MELANKOV: Right. (*He concentrates.*) Syringe used in the treatment of syphilis . . .

ARKOV: Part of a stocking of the adjutant's mistress . . .

GASSOV: Page of the Bible printed in Lapp . . .

NEESKIN: Specimen of Field Marshal's crap . . .

ALL: Party card, Party card, Number Twelve million, six hundred and sixteen thousand, four hundred and twenty eight, all your power, all your power, lend to us at this hour . . . (*Pause. The circle of kneeling soldiers hold hands in the dark. A distant rumble of artillery.*)

MELANKOV: What's it like to be dead? (*Pause*) Please, is it — (*Pause*) I shoved a cloth in my gob and went down 'ead-first in my sleeping bag, is that what — (*Pause*) It was black an' I was suffocating, then Festoff saw my boots twitching and pulled me out. 'ow was it when I cut your throat? Did you know you were dying and hate it? (*Pause*) If I 'adn't been there, an' you 'adn't been there, it wouldn't 'ave 'appened, would it? But I was there, an' so were you. Now, was that coincidence, or was it gonna 'appen from the moment you was born? From the day you came out bawlin' on the straw, were you goin' to that wood to 'ave your throat cut by a Russian? Or was it all because you silly buggers fell asleep? **Or did you 'ave to fall asleep so I could do it, was it that?**

ARKOV: I don't think this is very —

MELANKOV: **I am goin' barmy tryin' to work this out!** (*Pause, then, invoking the dead.*) Come on, you cunt, come on . . . (*Pause*) Come on!

The concrete slab on which they have made their offering begins to move. NEESKIN emits a stifled gasp.

GLORIA: Ich habe kein festuchen, nicht . . . (*The slab is pushed back. The head of a blonde WOMAN appears. NEESKIN flees in a surge of panic, joined by GASSOV. MELANKOV, overcome, swoons to the ground.*) Was ist gedanken, russ? (ARKOV *stares at her, as with an air of extreme exhaustion, she clambers out of the hole and sits with her head in her hands. She is wearing a dirty SS uniform.*) Ich habe nicht, was tot . . . (*Pause.* ARKOV *looks swiftly over his shoulder.*)

ARKOV: Throw your uniform away. (*She looks at him.*) Get rid of it. (*Pause*) Before they hang you. (*He looks round again.*) Quick, get it off! (*She stares, not understanding. ARKOV goes to her, tugs at her tunic to indicate his meaning. With the resignation of the defeated, she starts to unbutton. Thinking she is submitting to her fate, she lies on the ground. ARKOV slowly comprehends.*) I don't mean that. (*Pause*) Get up. I don't mean that. (*Pause*) **I hate that**. (*Terrified, thinking to please him,* GLORIA *loosens her hair.*) **Nein! Nein! I don't mean that!** (*Mad with despair, he drags his pistol out of its holster.* MELANKOV, *revived, sits up, sees it.*)

MELANKOV: Oi! (GLORIA *hides her face.* ARKOV *thrusts the barrel of the pistol down his trousers. There is a shot. He sways.* GLORIA *opens her eyes.* MELANKOV *is horrified.*) **Help! Mick's shot 'is cock off! 'elp!**

GLORIA (*astonished*): Was ist gesocht . . .

ARKOV: Trust now . . . trust . . .

The Spontaneous Nature of Historical Decisions

A gramophone is playing in the Kremlin. The symphony ends. MME DONKIN *claps.* STALIN *walks.*

STALIN: The artist's head is a boiled egg. You do not slice it off. You tap it gently with a spoon . . . (*They look at him.*) I have yet to meet an artist who did not benefit from being tapped. They think they live on their own, but they're mistaken, they live among us, and they have to learn they aren't the only birds on the lake. If they want to sing out of tune, by all means let them do so, but to expect us to construct music halls and pay the wages of the orchestra! No, sing in tune or shit in your own nest. (POSKREBYSHEV *claps.*)

MME DONKIN: I think the section praising you is most — appropriate.

STALIN: Which section's that?

MME DONKIN: The third movement.

STALIN: Is that in praise of me?

ZDHANOV: It says so in the notes.

STALIN: Of course it says so in the notes. It would do, wouldn't it? I don't read notes. When I'm dead he'll say it was a trick to get past the censors. No, they are ruthless, artists, we have a terrible struggle with them. (*He shrugs.*) I've mixed feelings about it . . .

ZDHANOV: It's better than the sixth.

STALIN: That was a bottle of piss!

ZDHANOV: Yes.

STALIN: He was up the wrong street there.

ZDHANOV: Yes.

STALIN: But we tapped his egg, and you see, he has got better!

MME DONKIN: He nearly committed suicide.

STALIN: Did he! Did he really? Never mind, he didn't, he became a better composer instead! If they cannot resolve the contradictions, they are better off dead, they know that, they do know that, however much women of special sensitivity pander to their souls . . .

MME DONKIN (*going to place a new record on the gramophone*): Khachaturian's fugue for strings and bass.

STALIN: How do they tap their eggs in the West?

ZDHANOV: They don't. A gang of musical idiots play in one another's rooms.

MME DONKIN: Khachaturian's fugue for strings and bass . . .

STALIN: Are there any American composers?

ZDHANOV: No.

STALIN: Do you think socialism would produce some?

ZDHANOV: That is a very difficult question.

STALIN: It is a difficult question. What are material origins of culture?

POSKREBYSHEV: The Commissar for Nationalities is here —

STALIN: I'm not against him coming in — (*He turns back to* ZDHANOV.) No, we must admit, mustn't we, that the individuality of cultures is only partially dependent on differences in economic relations, or how else should we explain, for example, the peculiar rhythms of the Kirghiz dance — which I cannot bear, incidentally — but which you must admit, is at least their own? (LASHENKO *enters.*) It is insufficient, I should have thought, to say that tribal patriarchies invariably produce eight beats to the bar, and feudal oligarchies twelve —

MME DONKIN: Fugue —

ZDHANOV: Changes in musical form follow the rise of certain classes, which alone explains the stability of primitive music —

MME DONKIN: — for — strings — and —

STALIN: I understand that, of course, but I am sceptical that the introduction of the collective economy to the United States would produce a Shostakovich —

MME DONKIN: — bass —

STALIN (*silencing them with a lifted finger*): Khachaturian. (*They are silent for some bars. He removes the needle from the record.*) I played Khachaturian during the three days of disasters. While the Germans shattered our defences, I lay down on the floor and listened, and he told me you have made mistakes, now you must correct them. That is what the music said. It didn't soothe me. It instructed me. (*He looks at* LASHENKO.) What?

LASHENKO: The landlord question in Estonia.

STALIN: There is no question music has a moral content, but how? How was it Khachaturian restored me at the very moment I felt I had betrayed Lenin and the entire people? I was mad with guilt, I saw their ghosts crowding round the room, and yet in three days I was able to emerge and take control, to restore a situation everybody thought was lost — myself included! How is it moral, Zdhanov? I don't understand.

ZDHANOV: There is a theory that certain melodic structures —

STALIN: He knows! He knows everything! Listen to him!

ZDHANOV: Relate in a very material way to stimulate emotional responses —

STALIN: I'm not talking about emotions, I'm talking about morals —

ZDHANOV: I was coming to that —

STALIN: He was coming to it!

ZDHANOV: And that the emotional responses can be placed in fifteen categories, each of which —

STALIN: Shift them to Transcaucasia. (*Pause*)

LASHENKO: Transcaucasia . . .

STALIN: They know about cattle, don't they? Stick them on collective farms.

LASHENKO (*holding a notebook*): There is a small problem of transport . . .

STALIN: **There are always problems of transport, there is a war on!** (*Pause*) Send them in empty ammunition trucks. (*Pause*) If the Red Army can travel in cattle trucks, I'm certain twenty thousand landlords can. (*Pause*) No, there are so many absurd theories being put about in musicology, but of all the arts it is the least susceptible to materialist orthodoxy. I keep an open mind on it. Someone should compose a symphony to cattle trucks. They have reconstructed Europe.

POSKREBYSHEV: Shall I make a note of that?

STALIN: If I have time I should like to write a paper on it.

POSKREBYSHEV: On —

ZDHANOV: I should be fascinated to read it . . .

POSKREBYSHEV (*confused*): On . . . ?

STALIN: You know, there will never be such a movement of peoples again . . . (POSKREBYSHEV *looks at* MME DONKIN.) I think sometimes of a stranger on another planet, fixing his single eye to the lens of a powerful telescope, and bringing Europe into view. Imagine the sheer frenzy that will greet his eyes! An ant-heap kicked into activity, every road and track jammed with civilians or armies jostling one another as they pass, some marching East, some fleeing West, some wandering South, some lost, some under orders, some with guards, some unaccompanied, some crooks, some murderers, the killer and the mother of the killed tramping in opposite directions on the same rutted road, his sack of loot jostling her bag of baby clothes, his curse and her groan. Who knows where he will find himself, by what gate a child will be born, or in what ditch an old woman breathe her last? Is it chaos? Or is it a building site? A building site, to the uninitiated, is the essence of chaos, but to the foreman, merely the first stage of the plan. I am the foreman, and Lenin made the plans. Of course, if you are sitting in a puddle with raw, bloody feet, it is hard to appreciate the beauty of the structure. I understand that! I am perfectly human.

ZDHANOV: No one misses History. Whether he sees its purpose or not.

STALIN: That's perfectly true. Neither monks nor beautiful women . . . (*Pause*) What has happened to my sex drive, Lena?

MME DONKIN: How should I know?

STALIN: You are a bio-chemist, aren't you? (*Pause, She shrugs.*)

MME DONKIN: You don't see enough skirt. (ZDHANOV *laughs.*)

STALIN: I see your skirt. . . . (*He laughs again.*) What about you, Poskrebyshev?

POSKREBYSHEV: I'm all right, thank you.

STALIN: Lying bastard.

POSKREBYSHEV: No, I'm not, I —

STALIN: You rub yourself. I've seen it. (ZDHANOV *laughs.*) He does! I've seen it! Up against the furniture like a dog.

MME DONKIN: There is something about Comrade Poskrebyshev that leads you to think he prefers to be doing it on his own . . .

STALIN (*laughing*): You see, she can tell! Poskrebyshev, what an indictment! How can you tell?

MME DONKIN: His eyes . . .

STALIN: His eyes! Poskrebyshev, look into my eyes!

MME DONKIN: No, that won't —

STALIN: Look into my eyes! (ZDHANOV *laughs.* POSKREBYSHEV *looks at* STALIN.) They are rather watery eyes . . .

MME DONKIN: You cannot possibly tell. You are not a woman.

ZDHANOV: Mystification.

MME DONKIN: Of course it's not.

ZDHANOV: Obfuscation.

MME DONKIN: A man cannot look into a man's eyes the way he looks into a woman's —

ZDHANOV: Feminine obscurantism —

MME DONKIN: It's true, something happens to the retina —

ZDHANOV: If he desires her, of course, but —

STALIN: Poskrebyshev, she says you hate her cunt. (*Pause*)

POSKREBYSHEV: I can't say I feel very drawn to . . .

STALIN: Do you? Hate it? (*Pause*)

POSKREBYSHEV: Yes. (*They all laugh.* ZDHANOV *and* MME DONKIN *leave.*)

Pause. Then POSKREBYSHEV, *in bitter despair, attacks* STALIN, *hammering him on the chest. They move, absurdly, round the room, until* POSKREBYSHEV, *exhausted, falls into a chair.* STALIN, *unhurt, goes out and returns with a glass of water.* POSKREBYSHEV *takes it, sips.* STALIN *replaces the needle on the record.*

The Indignation of a Mass Murderer

A MAN *seated in a chair, guarded.*

MATRIMOVA: The concept of Wholefilm in the developing theory of cinema, by Galina Matrimova. (*Pause. She adjusts her tommy-gun.*) Wholefilm discards the fundamental contradiction of the bourgeois film — the autonomy of the director. Until now, all film has been warped by the interpretation of the single eye. The representation of reality has been incomplete. Wholefilm entails a spectacular and democractic innovation — three screens in a dialectical relationship, producing an artistic experience which maximizes the audience's grasp of reality and at the same time offers the prospect of genuine socialist development. The screens are numbered one, two, and three. They may also be titled Psychology, History and Possibility.

BUBER: What 'ave I got to 'ave my picture taken for? I ain't done no wrong.

MATRIMOVA: The screen numbered one relates the subjective view of the event, perceived from the viewpoint of the individual mind. The bourgeois phase.

BUBER: **I wanna talk to somebody!**

MATRIMOVA: Screen number two places the event in the context of its historical causality. The Marxist phase.

BUBER: **Please**.

MATRIMOVA: Screen number three, which is the synthesis, offers the alternative prospect available given the conditions described in one and two, and for the first time places responsibility on the audience, which escapes its passive role and becomes itself the focus of the new realism!

BUBER: Excuse me, if I 'ave been liberated, what 'ave I got to 'ave my picture taken for?

MATRIMOVA: This is the screen based on the proposition 'if' —

BUBER: **Nobody talks to me!**

MATRIMOVA: Whereas the first and second screens are based on the propositions 'how' and 'but' . . .

ILONA *and* VICTOR *enter, carrying boxes of photographic plates.*

VICTOR: I tell you it's gone.

ILONA: You are looking in the wrong box.

VICTOR (*kneeling by a box*): How can it be the wrong box? This is the final box, look, there is the desecrated crucifix — (*He removes the plates one by one, holding them out to her.*) There is the doll on the rusty bayonet — (ILONA *looks cursorily.*) The cattle killed by shellfire —

BUBER: I want to lodge a protest.

VICTOR: The abandoned ambulance — **where is it, then?**

ILONA: All right, it's missing.

VICTOR: They are going to kill us.

ILONA (*looking at a plate*): That beret really suited me . . .

VICTOR: Why do you have to lie, and posture like that? When you are as scared as I am, why?

ILONA: I am not as scared as you are.

VICTOR: You are! You are!

ILONA: No. When it comes to being scared, you are in a class of your own.

BUBER: There are people walking about who've got a lot more explaining to do than I 'ave. I don't see them 'aving their pictures taken —

VICTOR: Clinging to your dirty little bit of dignity, your dirty little scrap of sex —

ILONA: You always get abusive when you're frightened, have you noticed that?

VICTOR: You're as petrified as I am, you haven't got a hope, why don't you admit it —

ILONA: **Because I'm not going down on my knees yet.** (*She stares at him. Pause.*) Where are the lens hoods? (*She goes to the camera.* VICTOR *gets up, sorts through a bag.*)

VICTOR: I said to him, I am an innocent photographer. He said there is no such thing as an innocent photographer, only photographers with varying degrees of guilt. What does that mean? It's a death sentence. (*He screws the lens hood on.*)

BUBER: What am I supposed to do, smile? I 'aven't got my teeth in —

VICTOR (*as* ILONA *focuses*):   I can't follow the arguments. With the Nazis it was easy, either they liked you or they didn't, and if they didn't, they smashed your jaw, but these . . .

ILONA: You are getting positively sentimental —

VICTOR: Everything is argument, and I can't follow arguments. If I could follow arguments, I wouldn't be a photographer.

ILONA: Don't be afraid of the argument. It's just their way of saying if they like you. Just look in their eyes . . . (*She adjusts the tripod.*)

VICTOR: I can't. I've never looked anyone in the eyes.

ILONA: Don't despise the eyes,
          They don't tell lies, the eyes,
          When the pupil shrinks to nothing
          It's the bullet or a fucking,
          Be wise, forget the words
          And watch the eyes . . .

BUBER: That's very good, that's very fucking true that is . . .

ILONA: He likes it.

BUBER: I fucking do . . .

VICTOR (*getting out the drape*):   I believe we have no sensitivity in our souls at all, and we are paying for it . . .

ILONA: Oh, dear . . .

VICTOR: I believe we have systematically trodden down our feelings until we no longer know the difference between casualness and cruelty . . . I think I would rather not survive than survive the way we do . . .

ILONA: Rubbish . . .

VICTOR: I think we are going to die and we deserve it! (*He turns away from the camera in despair.* ILONA *goes to him.*)

ILONA: Victor, you've got the eyes of a sick dog . . .

VICTOR: Yes . . .

ILONA: The eyes of old men who have sunk down and can't get up again . . . the eyes we've seen on every road in Europe . . . the eyes that beckon rifle butts . . .

VICTOR: I know . . .

ILONA: Victor . . . don't be the left-hand corner of an atrocity. (SORGE *enters briskly.*)

SORGE: Good morning —

BUBER (*jumping to his feet*):   Everyone did business with the Germans, I wasn't the only one, I made it perfectly clear I would prefer to manufacture for the civilian market, I submitted memoranda on twelve separate occasions saying my factory was not competent to supply synthetic rubber for military purposes —

SORGE: Is it light enough in here? I'm afraid we are rather short of equipment . . .

BUBER: Don't take my word for it, ask my foreman, ask Harry Wilkoska, 'e saw the memoranda, ask 'im —

ILONA (*trying to focus*): He keeps moving . . .

SORGE: Ask him to retain his seat . . .

BUBER: Far from being a collaborator, I supplied inferior equipment —

MATRIMOVA: Sit down —

BUBER: I initiated a policy of sabotage, not one of the tyres supplied by me was in usable condition, ask Harry Wilkoska —

MATRIMOVA: Sit down —

BUBER: I will sit down — (*He sits.*) Why isn't 'e 'ere, if I am, why isn't Harry Wilkoska —

ILONA: Can we bring that light in just a — (VICTOR *moves the flood.*)

BUBER: — all the products coming out of my factory were substandard — always 'ave been for that matter —

SORGE: Tell him to shut up.

BUBER: Ask anybody, ask Stefan Pillowitz, 'e knows my tyres caused innumerable accidents, so far from —

MATRIMOVA: Be quiet.

BUBER: So far from 'elping the Nazi war effort, I made a significant contribution to their defeat, all right, take the fucking thing — (ILONA *presses the shutter.*)

MATRIMOVA: Next! (*She shoves him out.*)

SORGE: I hope the photographs have been returned to you in proper order?

ILONA: Yes.

VICTOR: No. (SORGE *looks at them.*)

SORGE: Are you complaining that some damage has been done —

VICTOR: Yes.

ILONA: No. (*Pause*) I never had a sister. I don't know why I said I had a sister. I am an only child.

SORGE: Yes. It's obvious you are an only child. Me too. (MATRIMOVA *hurries in another man.*)

TOSHACK: I cannot see any excuse for the arrests of officials of the Peasants' Party, this is an outrage and I refuse to have my photograph taken!

SORGE: I think we both believe the world belongs to us, which is untrue, of course . . .

TOSHACK: The policy of the Peasant's Party with regard to the Nazi occupation was not one of collaboration but Negative Accommodation, as laid down by the party congress of 17th August, 1943. This was defined as resistance in principle but accommodation in practice, **I will not sit down**, there's no truth whatsoever in the calumny that we supplied the names of communists to the Gestapo **if I sit down I am admitting guilt** —

SORGE: Then you have your photograph taken standing up. (*As* ILONA *adjusts the camera.*) They say the single child is not happy. I think I was happy. Perhaps I might have been happier with a sister, how can I ever know? How happy were you with your sister?

ILONA: I haven't got one. (*Pause.* SORGE *looks at her, then turns to* MATRIMOVA.)

SORGE: Take the chair away. Everyone is to be photographed standing up. (*He looks at* TOSHACK.) You see, you make everything worse for everybody. (ILONA *presses the shutter.* MATRIMOVA *hurries* TOSHACK *out.*)

ILONA: When this is done, is it all right if we go? (*Pause*)

SORGE: Go?

ILONA: Yes.

SORGE: Go where? (*She shrugs.*) You see, I don't think people will be just going — any more. That is archaic. That is very pre-war, like Cook's tours of the Danube Principalities. Like beggars, and caviar. Just going. Just coming. What does 'can I go' mean? It means 'can I avoid', doesn't it? I think we should say, rather, 'Can I serve?' (*They look at one another.*)

ILONA: That's what I meant . . .

MATRIMOVA *enters with the German SS woman,* GLORIA.

SORGE: Once there was a necessity for self, for being **me**, for being the opposite of **you**, and the terror of **them**, for wearing yellow trousers and baring your arse on the top of the bus. When the world makes men dead-eyed with servility, and girls weep on the table tops of clubs, **me** is something to get hold of. In the scream of angry night-life, the dirty cocktail of poverty and exotic fucks, yes, you need **me** badly. But the war's killed that. We are all the same now, we all wear the

same costume of dirty European mud. No me now. Strip the
armour off the tanks, get history in our hot little fingers . . .
plasticine . . . plasticine . . . (*Pause.*   MATRIMOVA   *applauds.*) Galina likes a speech . . . (*He turns to go, stops.*) The
unit photographer trod on a mine. Would you do the
photographs until he is replaced?

ILONA: Yes . . . (SORGE *smiles, goes out.*)

MATRIMOVA: When I hear Sorge, I think I will go mad
because art fails so much! It settles for so little! There is no
point in it, no point at all, unless it is the entire truth! **How
can you get the entire truth?** I shall go mad! (ILONA *slides
in a new negative plate.*)

VICTOR: They are using us. And killing us later.

ILONA: Victor, somewhere in the rubble of Europe is a silver-
framed photograph of me sitting on Heydrich's lap . . .

VICTOR (*horrified*):   Will you shut up . . . ?

ILONA: The Spanish fascists with the female circumcisions in
their caps . . . the Italian bomb aimer who wore mascara . . .

VICTOR (*hurrying to the flood-lamp*):   This could do with a
reflector, couldn't it?

ILONA: The Greek police chief with initialled underwear . . .

VICTOR: What about a reflector in this!

ILONA: The Captain of the Papal Order of White Cavalry
who made me swallow piss . . .

VICTOR: Ilona . . . (*He turns away, shaking his head.*)

ILONA (*smiles at* MATRIMOVA):   The wallets of Europe are
stuffed with pictures of my face . . . heavily powdered to
conceal the bruises I got for being unsatisfactory in bed.

GLORIA (*to* ILONA):   Do you speak German?

VICTOR: I am going to New York. I am going to sit in a bar.
That's all. Sit in a bar in New York.

GLORIA: I want to tell you who I killed and who I didn't.

VICTOR: For the rest of my life. Just sit in a bar in New
York.

GLORIA: Listen, will you? I took part in the massacre at
Gorshin.

ILONA: Which Gorshin?

GLORIA: On the Dneiper. I shot half a dozen children in the
neck.

ILONA: Keep still, please.

GLORIA: I beat a woman to death in Monasterzhiska.

ILONA: That's lovely . . . (*She presses the shutter.*)

GLORIA: I assisted at the gassing of the gypsies at Hyak.

ILONA (*removing the plate*):   Why are you telling me this?

GLORIA: Two hundred and forty-seven individuals.

ILONA (*turning away*):   All right, she can go. (MATRIMO-VA *goes to push her out.*)

GLORIA: But not the woman in the overcoat. (*Pause*)

ILONA: What woman?

GLORIA: He says the woman in the overcoat. I did not touch the woman in the overcoat.

MATRIMOVA: I think we need to move a little quicker —

GLORIA: My name is Gloria Hertfeldz, Jugenfrau SS. I did not touch the woman in the overcoat. (MATRIMOVA *escorts her out.*)

VICTOR: Got to get out, Ilona. Before they shut the garden gates on us.

ILONA (*absently*):   Yes . . .

VICTOR: **I don't ask a lot from life**. (*She looks at him.*)

ILONA: Don't you?

VICTOR: To be left alone . . .

ILONA: You don't think that's a lot! He say that's not a lot to ask from life!

VICTOR: **It's not!** (*He strides, desperately, stops.*) You've changed.

ILONA: Have I?

VICTOR: You know you have.

ILONA: No, I don't know, how have I?

VICTOR: It's obvious.

ILONA: What's obvious about it? What? If it's obvious why don't you tell me?

PROKASH (*propelled into the room*):   Michael Korvash says I spoke to the Germans! So I spoke to the Germans! Didn't Michael Korvash speak to the Germans? They were living in my house for four years, what was I supposed to do, have my tongue out?

VICTOR: You are in love. (ILONA *stares at him.*)

Blackout.

She Did Not Die for Love, But for Its Impossibility

A field at night. The sound of shovels.

GASSOV: I have a theory about God. Do you want to hear
it? (*There is no reply.*) I'm not claiming it's original. Anyone
who claims to be original's a fool. How do you ever know if
you're original? All you're saying is you've never heard it
said before. Somebody has almost certainly thought your
thought but hasn't had the vanity to express it. So I don't
say that. I only say I have a theory. (*Pause*) According to my
theory God is neither good nor bad. He is stupid. Once you
accept that He is stupid, all questions of belief fall into place.
For example, the question, does He exist or not, becomes
irrelevant, like the question or responsibility. We say of Him,
as we say of an insane murderer, He is responsible for the
crime of which He is accused, but not guilty of it. God is
responsible for the world, but not guilty of it. This is a God
you could get very fond of. Now, I don't say He was always
stupid. That is a theological question. He was driven stupid,
in all probability, by the spectacle of His works. (*Pause*) Butt
in if you want to . . .
SORGE (*entering*):   Why do you talk religion so incessantly?
All this metaphysics, but the hole is not getting any deeper.
MELANKOV: 'e started it.
GASSOV: I never stopped digging, did I? I can think and dig.
MELANKOV: You call that thinking? That is the wanderin'
of an unhinged mind.
SORGE: All pain leads to metaphysics. It's a problem for the
party. I could not help noticing, as we advanced, how our
soldiers grew in superstition in direct ratio to the numbers of
the dead.
GASSOV: Oh?
SORGE: But the opposite should be the case! The greater the
pain, the greater the demand for reason. Didn't I love her
enough? Why should they hang her? Please leave me.
GASSOV (*shouldering his shovel*):   Give us your pistol.
SORGE: My pistol? Why? (*Pause*) Oh! (*He laughs.*) He thinks
— I say I loved her and he thinks —
GASSOV: I know it's silly but —
SORGE (*sarcastically*):   **Just in case**. (*Pause, then* SORGE
removes his holster and gives it to GASSOV. *The soldiers go*

out. SORGE *stands by the dead woman's body*.) I am not
unforgiving. I forgive everything. Accusing, forgiving, under
the junk of wasted wars the words lie rotting **love is not to do
with truth** if it was there would be none I am not shouting it
is you who shouts yes you you shout because you don't
possess the arguments it is a matter of correctness not of
volume if you cannot solve the contradiction you will
become not the maker nor the collaborator in the making of
your time but the mud in which the feet of passing armies
left their print your flesh is oh your flesh is do not look at
me with pity I hate that no one to pity me your arrogant
curled lip in wilful incomprehension goes even in death goes
(*He sees a figure in the gloom*.) Yes? (TREMBLAYEV *looks
at him. Pause*.) You shouldn't wander in uncleared fields,
they're full of unexploded things. Did you know the cham-
pagne in the cellar was booby-trapped?

TREMBLAYEV: I think you must be stopped.

SORGE: Stopped? Don't tell me you have climbed over all
this desolation just to tell me I have to be stopped. Stopped
from what?

TREMBLAYEV: I believe you are exercizing a personal
hegemony which endangers the safety of the 12th Motorized
Brigade. While the party has reason to be grateful to you you
must know that no one is indispensable —

SORGE (*shaking his head*): No —

TREMBLAYEV: That it is the duty of every one of us to —

SORGE: No —

TREMBLAYEV: Be vigilant in the interests of —

SORGE: What is it? (*Pause*) Nadia? (*Pause*)

TREMBLAYEV: It is impossible to serve the party and to
indulge in personal relationships.

SORGE: I am not aware of any injunction which forbids —

TREMBLAYEV: That isn't the point. There is no injunction
against gardening either, but if the regimental political officer spent the entire day planting onions, there would be
cause for —

SORGE: Nadia —

TREMBLAYEV: Do not use my christian name —

SORGE: Comrade Tremblayev, what is your evidence for
this? (*Pause*)

TREMBLAYEV: I'm not blind . . .

SORGE: On the contrary, I think you see things no one else
can —

TREMBLAYEV: Do not touch me —
SORGE: I wasn't going to touch you —
TREMBLAYEV: I must tell you I have escaped from you —
SORGE: I am delighted —
TREMBLAYEV: Which she did not. (*Pause*)
SORGE: What are you saying?
TREMBLAYEV: Secret burial is —
SORGE: What are you saying —
TREMBLAYEV: Against the regulations —
SORGE: No, you said —
TREMBLAYEV: The Germans did not hang her. (*Pause*)
   Did they?
SORGE: I have arrested the SS officer responsible for her
   murder —
TREMBLAYEV: Sorge, it is a lie —
SORGE: **I cannot allow the discipline of the unit to be under-
   mined like this. I am charging you**.
TREMBLAYEV: I am simply telling you the truth —
SORGE: Simply telling me the truth! The plea of counter-
   revolution through the ages, the whine of a spurious morality
   drawn like a veil over sinister intentions! When I hear
   someone say I am simply telling the truth I know I am in the
   presence of the enemy. Surrender your pistol.
TREMBLAYEV: No, I won't do that.
SORGE: Very well, I — (*He reaches for his holster. It is
   empty.*) **Gassov is in this with you!**
TREMBLAYEV: In what?
SORGE: **This!**
TREMBLAYEV: What?
SORGE: Conspiracy!
TREMBLAYEV: There is no conspiracy, I only —
SORGE: **No conspiracy, where is my pistol, then?** (*There is a
   crack of a rifle offstage.* SORGE *collapses to his knees.*) All
   right, shoot me! Shoot me!
GASSOV: Sorge! Sorge!
SORGE (*turning to him*):   **Traitor!**
GASSOV: Wha' — Wha's he —
SORGE: What's the matter, Gassov, **got no guts?** You point
   it there and pull the trigger!
GASSOV: Melankov's shot the photographer! (*Pause*)
SORGE: Which photographer?
MELANKOV (*rushing on with his rifle*):   **I 'ate shooting
   people! I 'ate shooting people!**

SORGE (*scrambling to his feet, grabbing* MELANKOV): **Which photographer! Which photographer!**

MELANKOV: Take the fuckin' rifle!

SORGE: **The woman or the man!**

GASSOV: The man. (SORGE *releases* MELANKOV, *who sobs violently*.)

MELANKOV (*to* GASSOV): I shouted three times, you 'eard me, three times, didn't I —

SORGE (*in full possession of himself*): Go and inspect the body. Ascertain if he is dead and —

MELANKOV: **Three times I said —**

SORGE: **Control yourself!** (*Pause*) Take the body to the hospital and write it in the book.

MELANKOV: Can't write.

SORGE: Very well. Wake up a stenographer. Go on. (MELANKOV *slouches away*.) And take your rifle. (*He returns, picks it up*.) Good. (*Pause*) Good.

A Degree of Suffering Is Required

ILONA, *by a bowl of water.*

MATRIMOVA: I think you wash your hair too much.

ILONA: No, if anything, I don't do it enough.

MATRIMOVA: And your back . . . (*She places her hands on* ILONA's *back*.)

ILONA: Spotty as ever . . .

MATRIMOVA: He is coming tonight, and your hair will be wet for his fingers to fasten on. And the next day, you will go about in his jeep, and he will plunder all the shops for you . . .

ILONA: Yes . . .

MATRIMOVA: What a beautiful couple!

ILONA: I have been the half of so many beautiful couples. Plundering this way, and plundering that . . .

MATRIMOVA: When the war is over, I will make a film, and you will be in it, you will be — everything! What was, what is, what should have been! (*She jumps up*.) He's coming! (*She listens*.) The heeltap of the virile boot . . . (*Pause*) And stops . . .

ILONA: Why?

MATRIMOVA: Removes his boots . . .

ILONA: Why?

MATRIMOVA: Comes to your door in socks . . . and says . . . (*She looks up, affectedly.*) Listen to the rain . . . (*She hurries out. SORGE enters. He looks at ILONA.*)

SORGE: Listen to the rain, churning up the mud and beckoning the corpses . . . up they come . . . elbows and knees . . . labouring through fields and gardens . . . by morning there will be a show of clotted heads like crocuses . . . (*Pause*) What do you know about Victor Barbu?

ILONA: He is a left-handed photographer from Ploiesti. He has no special talent, but he's good at judging exposures. He has an eye for light, but none for composition. He drives the Ford. He is clever with engines. I say engines, I mean the plugs. Not the plugs, exactly, the gaps. He once saved fifteen litres of petrol by adjusting the gaps. I never saw him touch a woman. Nor a man either. He gets bad headaches, but aspirin make him sick. (*Pause*) That is all I know of Victor Barbu.

SORGE: He was shot at eleven fifty-three last night, slipping through the compound fence with two crates of photographs. He ignored three warnings. I'm afraid some of the negatives are broken. (*Pause*)

ILONA: Well, of course.

SORGE: It is very hard to shoot accurately in the dark.

ILONA: It was most inconsiderate of him. I think if someone is going to get shot, they ought to present a proper target.

SORGE: I think you are deeply hurt.

ILONA: Victor is dead because he wanted to be dead. New York was just — a metaphor.

SORGE: You are — deeply shocked and so you —

ILONA: I have seen a lot of corpses —

SORGE: But this one you knew!

ILONA: Superficially —

SORGE: Three years and you say —

ILONA: Superficially.

SORGE: Night after night, beneath the stars, mile after mile on rutted roads . . .

ILONA: There are tears in your eyes! I've always said, if you don't cry someone else will always do it for you — (*SORGE grabs her by the shoulders.*) Why do you want me to cry! To reassure you all the old emotions are still knocking around? To show you women are still women — (*He strikes her. Pause.*)

When the man with blood all down his coat
Puts his fingers round your throat,
It's not the prelude to your dying,
You're only the audience for a little manly crying . . .

SORGE (*turning away*): I have to make love to you.

ILONA: What, now?

SORGE: You have no idea how I'm suffering —

ILONA: You are —

SORGE: Yes, terribly suffering —

ILONA: Yes —

SORGE: You must be serious —

ILONA: Yes —

SORGE: And warm —

ILONA: Whatever you say —

SORGE: And giving —

ILONA: You are hurting me —

SORGE: **Must! Must!** (*He pulls away from her.*) When I set eyes on you . . . the mud splashed on your calves and your crushed shoes I felt — how pure she is . . . through all this clamour she walks untouched . . .

ILONA: What do you want me to —

SORGE: Shh . . . shh . . .

ILONA: I am perfectly happy to be your —

SORGE (*waving a hand*): Shh . . . (*Pause*) I felt . . . she is unspoiled by History . . . (*Pause*) I want you to **want** to be my mistress . . . (*Pause*)

ILONA: Well, I do. (*Pause*)

SORGE: No, you see, there is this acquiescence in you which —

ILONA: Yes, I'm sorry, it's a thing I picked up —

SORGE: Not to acquiesce, but to will, and therefore — to suffer . . .

ILONA: Yes . . .

SORGE: For wanting . . . (*Pause*)

ILONA: I do suffer.

SORGE: I expect so much from love.

ILONA: Me, too.

SORGE: **You agree so much it makes me suspicious**.

ILONA: It's a habit, it's, I — real feelings become — after so much — become — impossible to —

SORGE: Perhaps you should resist me —

ILONA: Perhaps I should, yes —

SORGE: **Resist me, then!**

ILONA: Anything that has substance will be snapped, and anything that hasn't, can't be. She had substance, didn't she? So much substance I really hated her —

SORGE: I insist you are yourself —

ILONA: I am trying —

SORGE: No, you are hiding, you are hiding something, no one can be so —

ILONA: I am, I am myself —

SORGE: Let me make some mark on you, what are you, a saint! (*He kisses her violently, painfully. Pause.*)

ILONA: I think she killed herself. She did. She killed herself to get away from you. (*Pause. A* MAN *in an overcoat enters. He is holding Sorge's boots.*)

MAN IN OVERCOAT: I saw your boots! Outside, together. The boots. And I thought, Oh God, he is naked, but. So I came in. You are not naked. Sometimes to catch the lovers naked fills me with. So thank goodness. (*He holds out the boots.* TREMBLAYEV *enters.*)

TREMBLAYEV: You are under arrest.

SORGE: On what charge?

TREMBLAYEV: The charge follows the investigation. You know that very well.

SORGE: I shall extract the highest penalty for this! (*The* MAN IN OVERCOAT *strikes him.* SORGE *is silent.*)

MAN IN OVERCOAT: I hate shouting. He doesn't have to shout to make a point, does he?

SORGE: Comrade Tremblayev is an officer of the NKVD, she has every right to investigate what is probably a routine matter — (*to* ILONA) I love you, do you love me — there will be a cross-examination and I — do you love me? (ILONA *does not reply.* THE MAN IN OVERCOAT *indicates to* SORGE. *They leave.*)

TREMBLAYEV: Your sister is buried by the anti-aircraft trench . . . (*She goes out.* ILONA *is alone.*)

MATRIMOVA (*rushing in*): Sorge has been arrested! They've gone off with Sorge!

ILONA: Yes . . .

MATRIMOVA: Sorge! Why Sorge?

ILONA: **It is very difficult to wash your hair round here!**

MATRIMOVA: He must have done wrong, mustn't he? Mustn't he? It's impossible, but why would they arrest him otherwise? He's arrested, therefore he's done wrong. It's unbelievable! (*She is surging to and fro.*) I don't understand

how you — I mean, if the impossible is true, where does that
leave — how does an artist cope with that? If the absolutely
true is absolutely false, how do you — (*Pause*) It calls for a
fourth screen! A Fourth Screen which says — notwithstand-
ing all that has been registered on screens one to three —
there is always the possibility that — (*She holds her head,
agonized*) I shall never make a film.
ILONA: Oh, don't say that —
MATRIMOVA: No, never make one. (*She stares at* ILONA.)
Don't you even care about the truth?
ILONA: No. (*Pause*)
MATRIMOVA: Please, may I kiss you before you go?
ILONA: If you want to. (*She inclines a cheek.*)
MATRIMOVA: No, your feet . . . (*She kisses* ILONA's *feet.*)
I think you are very near to God . . .
ILONA: Go? (*Pause*) Go where?
MATRIMOVA: Everyone will miss you.
ILONA: **Go where** (MATRIMOVA *shakes out a tape-
measure and holds it against* ILONA's *back, letting the end
fall to the floor. She reads it.*)
MATRIMOVA: Yes! You are under five feet six!

History Encounters its Antithesis

A room with floodlamps. ILONA *is standing by a tripod and
camera.*

McGROOT: There were three hundred and forty-eight photographers, and all of 'em were under five feet six. Which one
had the unmarked grave? (ILONA *drops a film plate.*)
ILONA: Shit.
McGROOT: Correct. The one who shot the emperor. Said
one lens to the other, have ye seen any guid subjects lately?
An' the furst lens says, A seen a weddin', A seen a christenin',
A seen a funeral, an' A seen a donkey fuckin' a woman.
Tha's funny, says the other lens, A seen two people tellin' lies
in a church, A seen a baby dipped in water, A geezer
dropped doon a hole an' a woman carryin' a donkey on her

back, where were yoo? (STALIN *enters*, POSKREBYSHEV *at his elbow. Long pause.*)

POSKREBYSHEV: We came up with three hundred and forty-eight photographers under five feet six. This is Ilona Ferenczy.

ILONA: Good morning, General Secretary. (*Pause. STALIN looks at her painfully and long.*)

STALIN: How did her talent assert itself above the other three hundred and forty-seven, I ask myself . . .

POSKREBYSHEV: There was a short list of ten. Four had relatives serving sentences, three had visited America, and two were party members. The other committed suicide.

ILONA: I was in luck. He cut his throat with a sunlight filter. (*Pause. STALIN sits, stares at her.*)

STALIN: You are to photograph me as I am.

ILONA: Yes.

STALIN: Yes, she says . . . !

McGROOT: She says yes. She cud say maybe, but she says yes! Ye canna blame her, maybe's hanging off a meathook and noo died of electric shocks, I tease, I tease!

STALIN: It is very difficult to photograph Stalin as he is. Who is Stalin? One day he was in the film, and the next they rubbed him off.

ILONA: I —

STALIN: It is fraught with risks.

ILONA: Is it? Isn't it a face like any other? (POSKREBYSHEV *coughs in alarm.*)

McGROOT: Yoo do the coughin', A'll do the shittin', **who said tha'?** (*He pretends to hold his bowels.*) Pass the sugar, how's ye mother, gotta ticket for the Celtic? Come again? (*He cups his ear towards* ILONA.)

STALIN: It is possible I do not actually know my face, and being presented with it, I may become enraged. Have you considered that?

ILONA: No.

STALIN: My skin, for example. Always, they remove the pocks.

ILONA: I shan't do that. Every pock will be included.

McGROOT: Noo pock filters!

STALIN: Why are you so anxious to be agreeable?

McGROOT: Yes, why are ye so anxious to be agreeable, cud it be that this is Joseph fuckin' Stalin, **doon't tell me!**

STALIN: Has she heard that dictators like to be agreed with?

ILONA: I think, when it comes to portraits, you —

STALIN: I do not like to be agreed with. I like the last word. (*Pause*)

ILONA: Yes.

STALIN: Another problem is my shyness.

ILONA: Yes.

STALIN: I despise flamboyance. I despise eccentricity.

ILONA: I can tell.

STALIN: Elegance. Rhetoric. The cultivated gesture. How can you trust the man who thinks himself attractive?

ILONA: Impossible.

STALIN: Trotsky had a cult of personality if anybody did. If I stood on a poor man's toe I would apologize. The handsome man, when he stands on your toe, he expects you to apologize! Since Stalin, there is no smallpox any more. All the children will have lovely skin, but I ask myself if that is necessarily an advantage? How many will be warped by their good looks? (*She looks at him.*)

ILONA: I'll take the photographs, and you do the talking —

STALIN: I must go for a piss. (POSKREBYSHEV *helps him up. They go out.*)

McGROOT: The great man says to his bladder, yoo are a treacherous bastard, yoo are, yoo — (ILONA *drops a glass plate. He looks at her. She puts her hands to her head.*)

ILONA: I'm losing it . . . . I'm losing it . . . (STALIN *returns.*)

STALIN: I had a request from Karsh of Ottawa. He wanted to put me in his album. He wanted me between King George and a horse-faced English actress.

ILONA (*fiddling with the camera*): Karsh of Ottawa . . . ?

STALIN: Does it not show a profound ignorance of art to think you could put Stalin next to George VI? It is not a face I have here, it is a history. (*She photographs him, emerges from the hood.*)

ILONA: But at the same time you are very ordinary!

McGROOT (*horrified*): So the mouse said to the elephant, no, I didn't borrow the saucepan, the squirrel did! What's the weather like in Durban?

ILONA (*undeterred*): I wouldn't look at you twice in the street. I can say that because you are not vain. (*She looks at him, lining up the camera.*) For example, I know you are not happy in that tunic. (*She focuses.*) The epaulettes and so on. You don't spend half the morning at the mirror — stay like that — (*she slides across the plate*) thinking, Joseph — It is

Joseph, isn't it — I will have the white suit, no I won't, I'll
have the black — that's not your way at all — (*again she
drops a plate.*) Fuck. (*A long silence.*)

STALIN: I think she is afraid of me.

McGROOT: Afraid of yoo! Noo, it's no possible, who cud be
frightened of a nice ol' man like yoo? A cud put ma head on
his chest an' say, gi' us a cuddle, uncle! (*He insinuates himself
onto* STALIN.)

STALIN: I enjoy frightening people. Isn't it odd that a man
of my stature should enjoy frightening little girls from
Budapest? Really, Poskrebyshev, it's despicable, isn't it?

POSKREBYSHEV: Well, I suppose it —

STALIN: It is! It is!

McGROOT: It fuckin' is —

ILONA (*reviving*): There's nothing wrong with fear. I've been
frightened all my life. It's panic you have to worry about.
(STALIN *looks at her.*) Stay like that. (*She sets up.*)

STALIN: Give me a kiss. (*Pause*) Give me a kiss. (*Pause, then
ILONA goes to him, takes his hand and kisses it, then returns
to the tripod.*) The idea of intimacy with Stalin is absurd. It
is absurd, even to Stalin . . . (*Pause*) What does she think I
have in my trousers, a brick!

McGROOT: Wha'd ye think he's got in his trousers, a brick!
There was a mon goin' aboot wi' a brick in his trousers, an'
a cock on his head —

STALIN: Must piss.

McGROOT: Okay, that's all, anyway. (STALIN *and* POSK-
REBYSHEV *go out.*)

ILONA (*shutting her eyes to concentrate*): Don't be clever,
don't be shy, don't be vulgar, don't be wise, don't be fruity,
don't be arid, don't be honest, don't tell lies — (POSKRE-
BYSHEV *returns.*)

POSKREBYSHEV: He likes you. (*Pause.* STALIN *returns.*)

STALIN: I have a chill on my bladder. Against the little plots
of nature, even Stalin is not proof.

ILONA (*to* POSKREBYSHEV): Would you remove his cap?
Otherwise, we shall be honouring the cap. (POSKRE-
BYSHEV *looks to* STALIN.) It's a perfectly nice cap, but —
(STALIN *stares at her.*) There has to be a Stalin without the
cap. (*Pause. He suddenly flings it to the floor.*) Yes! (*She
focuses.*) That's just — Yes! (*She is under the drape.*)

STALIN: I understand you are under sentence of death.
(*Long pause. She exposes the plate. Then she emerges.*)

Lieutenant Sorge had evidence that you posed on a mass murderer's lap. (*Pause*)

ILONA: Oh?

STALIN: For some reason the lieutenant neglected to act on the evidence. He continually filed your case to the back.

McGROOT: They do that, doon't they, it's called desire. How do ye knoo when a man loves you? He puts flowers on yer grave. **A've seen it happen**.

STALIN: Why, I wonder? (*Pause*)

ILONA: You should ask him. Now, how about a profile —

STALIN: I don't think we can do that, can we Poskrebyshev?

ILONA: Or three-quarters, turned to — (*Pause, she is drained.*) Why?

STALIN: We can't, can we, Poskrebyshev?

POSKREBYSHEV: No, we can't . . .

ILONA: Can't ask him . . . why . . . (STALIN *looks at her, then goes to get up.*) **Don't get up I haven't finished yet**.

McGROOT (*desperately*): There was a parrot locked in a museum, and the mouse said to the prime minister, wha'd yer want in yer sandwich, Michael, can ye follow this, A'm fucked if A can . . .

ILONA: Save him, please. (*Pause*) Save him. (McGROOT *looks at her a long time.* ILONA *sees her mistake, struggles.*) No, that was silly, where were we? We were doing —

POSKREBYSHEV: Thank you, the session is over —

ILONA: Can't be over, only done four plates, and broke two, so —

POSKREBYSHEV: Four is all that is required —

ILONA: I think with Joseph the profile will be most rewarding and we —

POSKREBYSHEV (*helping* STALIN *up*): Good day.

ILONA (*closing her eyes*): Am I going to die?

STALIN (*turning*): Dying? Who said anything about dying? (*He turns to* POSKREBYSHEV.) Have you been frightening Miss — (*he loses the name*) with tales of dying? I cannot go for a piss without Poskrebyshev taking advantage of my absence to throw his weight about. What are you, a sexual pervert? (*He turns to* ILONA. *He extends his arms. She falls into them.*) There . . . there . . .

ILONA: Are we safe . . .

STALIN: There . . .

McGROOT (*transfixed by the spectacle*): The crocodile says, noo, the alligator, the alligator it was, the alligator says —

ILONA: Are we . . . ?

McGROOT: Listen to th' alligator —

ILONA: Are we . . . ?

McGROOT: The alligator says — says — (*The light dims gradually. Men enter and carry away the equipment.*) **Listen to the alligator, will ya . . . ?** (STALIN *holds* ILONA. *The light goes out.*)

THE EUROPEANS

Struggles to Love

CHARACTERS

LEOPOLD	Emperor of Austria
OFFICERS	Of the Imperial Army
TURKISH CAPTIVES	
THE PAINTER	Of the Imperial Court
STARHEMBERG	An Imperial General
THE EMPRESS	Of Austria
KATRIN	A Wounded Citizen
ORPHULS	A Priest
SUSANNAH	Sister of Katrin
IPSTEIN	An Imperial Minister
HARDENSTEIN	An Imperial Minister
FALLENGOTT	An Imperial Minister
GRUNDFELT	An Anatomist
PUPILS OF ANATOMY	
FIRST MOTHER	Parent of Orphuls
SECOND MOTHER	Parent of Starhemberg
FIRST BEGGAR	
SECOND BEGGAR	
THIRD BEGGAR	
FOURTH BEGGAR	
FIRST WOMAN BEGGAR	
SECOND WOMAN BEGGAR	
SERVANT	To the Empress
SHYBAL	A Common Soldier
McNOY	A Common Soldier
ARST	An Academician
FELIKS	An Academician
STENSH	An Academician
BOMBERG	An Academician
MIDWIFE	
LABOURERS	
JEMAL PASHA	A Turkish Commander
NUNS	

ACT ONE

Scene One

A *plain, following a battle.*

LEOPOLD: **I laugh**
I laugh (*He walks towards some squatting prisoners.*)
I laugh
I laugh
Where's the painter? (*A figure enters with an easel and board.*)
I laugh
I laugh (*The* PAINTER *sketches.*)
This pain which soddens every turf
This bowel which droops from every bush
This crop of widows and orphans
I laugh

OFFICER (*observing*): The Turks! The Turks!

LEOPOLD (*unmoved*): Fuck them. (*Some fire. The* OFFICERS *sheath their swords. The* PAINTER *paints.* LEOPOLD *kneels.*) Oh, God, I thank, Oh, God, I stoop, let all this Muslim flesh manure Christian ground, Oh, God, I bow, let all this scrag of Islam bring forth crops to feed the lowest labourer and he shall situate the crucifix above the lintel of the door and hang his weapon on its hook, and in the frosty fields his child shall kick the Tartar skull that ploughs dislodged —

OFFICERS (*unsheathing their weapons*): The Turks! The Turks!

LEOPOLD: Fuck them — (*Shellfire. The* PAINTER *rises anxiously.*) Are you afraid of dying?

PAINTER: No.

LEOPOLD: You don't mean no.

PAINTER: I do mean —

LEOPOLD: You say no, but you mean yes. You are afraid of
dying, why?

PAINTER: I have this — I am under this — terrible illusion
I am a decent painter and — as yet have little evidence —
so —

LEOPOLD: **I laugh**
                 I laugh

PAINTER: Quite rightly but —

LEOPOLD: You think I am mad but the mad are the spea-
kers of our time —

PAINTER: Yes —

LEOPOLD: Why?

PAINTER: Why —

LEOPOLD: Are they, yes?

PAINTER: I —

LEOPOLD: You say yes to everything I say, how will you
ever be a decent painter?

PAINTER: I don't know —

LEOPOLD: Look at the prisoners, how they tremble like
reeds on the lakeside as soon as their brothers come near,
like a wind they come and go —
                 You lost
                 You lost
No fucking Seljuk lancer will cut you free, Ali! Draw them,
record their bewilderment, they cannot understand why their
god's quit, draw them!

OFFICER: The Turks! The Turks!

LEOPOLD: Oh, fuck your alarums, I am discussing art!
(*Returning to his subject.*) This one in particular, who sports
the topknot of his native land, squats with the distant look
of one who senses execution in the offing, capture that.
Though how you keep a pencil still in fingers that tremble as
yours do, I can't imagine —

PAINTER: It's cold —

LEOPOLD: **It is cold, it is Europe!** (*A general hurrah breaks
out among the* OFFICERS.)

OFFICERS: **Starhemberg! Starhemberg!**

LEOPOLD: Oh, Starhemberg, they do so love the bastard,
they love the bag of bones who showed no terror, who sat
out the siege when emperors fled, this moment I have

dreamed of, I kneel, I kneel to thee who saved Christian Europe, I kneel and lick thy paws and here's a painter will catch my homage for all time and so on, Leopold the stooping, Leopold the supplicant!

OFFICERS: **Star — hemberg!** (STARHEMBERG *enters, goes to* LEOPOLD, *kneels.*)

Star — hemberg!

LEOPOLD: They do go on, they do adore you more than me —

STARHEMBERG: No, never —

OFFICERS: **Star — hemberg!**

LEOPOLD: **I laugh**

I laugh

I slept in lovely beds while you thrust corpses into breaches of the walls, I do most humbly thank you and of course simultaneously hate you for showing the dignity of character I was not endowed with but how was I to know the Europeans would suddenly unite? It is the first and I daresay the last occasion we have managed so fuck you and thank you! (*They embrace, swiftly, and separate.*) Now slaughter this lot. (*He indicates the Turkish prisoners.*) Or their brothers back in Anatolia will say the Christians are merciful and take prisoners, no, this is a spot no Turk will stagger back to but as doormen, dustbin porters, café keepers and the like, **away!** (*The prisoners are kicked offstage.*)

I laugh

I laugh

(*To the* PAINTER.) Did you capture this? I will not embrace the mighty bonebag twice.

PAINTER: Yes —

LEOPOLD: Into Vienna now for all the sarcasm of the survivors.

STARHEMBERG: No, surely —

LEOPOLD: Yes, indeed, and if they toss cabbages —

STARHEMBERG: There are no cabbages in Vienna, we have been eating dogs —

LEOPOLD: Dogs, have you? And not the last time dogs will stand in for pastry, is the palace swept out? If so chuck the rubble back, it's right we should return to chaos, the arms askew, the monograms a shambles etcetera, and cannon holes above the bed, I think Vienna will know the crack of field guns more than once and bury babies of starvation. (*He falls, kneels, as if in a paroxysm of exhaustion. The* OFFICERS *watch, confused. The* EMPRESS *enters, gestures for*

*them to stand away. She goes to him, rests her hands on his
shoulders.*)

EMPRESS: Five hundred disembowelled women are lying in
the Wienerwald.

> The stench.
> Of all classes.
> The stench.
> Of all degrees.
> Islam's au revoir.
> The Poles have saved Paris.

LEOPOLD: Paris . . . ?

EMPRESS: Rome.

LEOPOLD: Rome . . . ?

EMPRESS: London. Copenhagen. Amsterdam. The Poles
have saved five million women, at this moment dreaming,
knitting, wiping the arses of their infants, sucking the cocks
of their husbands' friends, writing novels, hemming curtains,
get up now, the wind will change and here's a cloth soaked
in eau de Cologne, it has my monogram in lace which took
the embroiderer twenty-seven hours, that is a waste of life
some would argue, but no more fatuous than writing novels
or what passes now for freedom in progressive circles and at
least she has her bowels in, no Turkish dagger in her parts,
get up you dear and sensitive soul, I sometimes think the
barmy imaginings of the progressive rest on bayonets, do
you follow? I mean the very fatuous pattering in Paris is
predicated on the Poles, the spears of superstitious peasants
keep their words aloft, the Turks would soon shut down their
salons, in the harem with the bitches says the Seljuk, oh, you
are getting up, we have to make an entry to the city and give
thanks, God knocked Allah over this time . . . (*She sinks
down beside him.*) We have in one day an Empire back which
stretches from the Alps to the Baltic, I thought, I fully
thought, we would die in a seaside hotel, Leopold, kiss my
ugly mouth and I'll kiss yours —

LEOPOLD: They're looking — the staff are —

EMPRESS: I do not give a piss for them, kiss me in this
screaming sea, this swamp of horrid dead, we have Europe
back . . . (*He kisses her. The* OFFICERS *draw their swords.*)

OFFICERS: **The Hapsburg! The Hapsburg!**

Scene Two

A convent. A girl in a chair.

KATRIN: In my own words. (*Pause*)
           Words of my own. (*Pause*)
           The poor have neither words nor drawers. (*Pause*)
  Oh, for literacy, oh, for numeracy, oh, for any pack of lies!
(*Pause*)

          So the four soldiers said — (*Pause*)
          No.

  No. There may not have been four. And they may not have
been soldiers. But they did have weapons and the Turk does
not wear uniform so for the sake of. (*Pause*)
          Let's say four. (*Pause*)

  The four soldiers said lie down — well, they didn't say it,
no, they did not say the words they indicated by very simple
gestures this was expected of me, words were dispensed with,
words were superfluous though much language was expressed on either side, by me, by them, but words not really,
no. (*Pause*)

  Consequently I lay my face down in the relatively sympathetic grass. **Of course I am not in the least ashamed
description comes easily to me** but can I have a glass of
water? The dryness of my mouth suggests anxiety but I have
had a dry mouth since my throat was cut, some channel or
some duct was severed, something irreparable and anatomi-
cal. (*A* NUN *places a glass of water by the chair and
withdraws.*)
  It's you who are ashamed not me but I forgive in all
directions then one of them threw up my skirt excuse me —
(*She drinks.*)

  Or several of them, from now on I talk of them as plural,
as many-headed, as many-legged and a mass of mouths and
of course I had no drawers, to be precise — (*Pause*)

  I owned a pair but for special occasions. This was indeed
special but on rising in the morning I was not aware of it,
and I thought many things, but first I thought — no, I
exaggerate, I claim to know the order of my thoughts **what
a preposterous claim** — strike that out, no, among the
cascade of impressions — that's better — that's accurate —
cascade of impressions — came the idea at least **I did not**

have to kiss. (*Pause*) The lips being holy, the lips being sacred, the orifice from which I uttered my most perfect and religious thoughts only the grass would smear them but no. (*Pause*)

Can you keep up? Sometimes I find a flow and then the words go — torrent — cascade — cascade again, I used that word just now! I like that word now I have discovered it, I shall use it, probably ad nauseam, cascading! But you — (*Pause*)

And then they turned me over like a side of beef, the way the butcher flings the carcass, not without a certain familiarity, coarse-handling but with the very vaguest element of warmth, oh, no, the words are going, that isn't what I meant at all, precision is so — precision slips even as you reach for it, goes out of grasp and I was flung over and this **many mouthed thing** — (*She shudders as if taken by a fit, emitting an appalling cry and sending the water flying. The* NUN *supports her. She recovers.*)

Now I've spilled the water — don't say there's more where that came from — so it is with life — don't mop the floor, I can take it from the floor, so my mouth — (*Pause. The* NUN *withdraws.*)

My mouth which I had held to be the very shape and seat of intimacy they smothered with wet and fluid — I don't think you could call them kisses — **yes, yes, kisses, they were kisses** I try to hide behind the language, oh, the language I do twist like bars of brass to shelter in, no, they were **kisses** because a kiss can be made of hatred — kisses, yes, oh, yes . . . (*Pause*)

They soaked, they drenched, they swilled me with their kisses, and bruised my lips and bit my mouth and thrust these thousand tongues into my throat **and this was only the beginning only the beginning you with the book and pencil wait!** (*Pause. She controls her horror. A* PRIEST *appears from the darkness.*)

ORPHULS: I think, for today, we leave it there —
KATRIN: Why — —
ORPHULS: The tension of —
KATRIN: The tension, yes —
ORPHULS: Is making you —
KATRIN: Obviously —
ORPHULS: And us for that matter, we are also —
KATRIN: You also, yes, quite rightly, suffer as I —
ORPHULS: Greatly, and —

KATRIN: Greatly, yes, why shouldn't you — (*She sees the* NUN *leaving.*) **Don't go away!** (*The* NUN *continues her way. Pause.*) I'm mad, aren't I? I hate the word but technically it does seem suitable. Please call me mad I wish for it. I long for madness to be ascribed to me. I thirst for such a title.

ORPHULS: I don't believe you are at all insane, only —

KATRIN: **Oh, come on!** (*With a sudden inspiration.*) Listen, this is madness, this is proof! I dream, I passionately dream, of some pretty valley in the Danube where a Muslim girl is kneeling to the East. She bows to Mecca, she spreads her Turkish things, her Turkish mirror, her Turkish mat, and threads the Transylvanian flowers through her hair when down like wind swoop Christian troopers rancid with the saddle and **stake her to the ground with knives**, her naked haunches, her perfect breasts they slash into a running sieve of blood, all channels red, all drain of horror, what satisfaction could I have from dreaming only my Turks die? No, revenge must be upon the innocent. Now, am I mad?

ORPHULS: No . . . (*She laughs.*)

KATRIN: I have no breasts! I have no breasts! (*She laughs and sobs.* ORPHULS *holds her in his arms. A woman enters.*)

SUSANNAH: Is my sister there? (*The sobbing stops.*) Katrin?

ORPHULS: Yes.

SUSANNAH: It's so dark —

ORPHULS: It is dark. It must be dark.

SUSANNAH (*appearing in the shaft of light*): Yes . . . (*She extends a hand to* KATRIN.) Come home, now.

KATRIN: No.

SUSANNAH: Come home and —

KATRIN: **Home what's that**. (*Pause*) It's your peremptory tone I hate.

SUSANNAH: My tone's as kind as I can make it —

KATRIN: It's peremptory —

SUSANNAH: What a funny word, you do —

KATRIN: Love funny words, yes, give me a new word and I'll thank you, but home, stuff that, take home and bite it like a cold, raw egg, muck, ugh, spew, ugh, and sharp shell in the gums, no, you are peremptory and always were, beautiful, peremptory and unhappy, at least you are unhappy, thank God for that, I could like you, given time.

SUSANNAH: How much time? I carried you about, little sister.

KATRIN: I'm so cruel, aren't I? It comes of having a vocabulary and no breasts **don't touch**. (SUSANNAH *draws back*.) I can't bear to be touched now, even by those claiming pity.

SUSANNAH: I don't pity you, Katrin.

KATRIN: Why don't you? Everybody else does.

SUSANNAH: I think you are more cruel than any clot of raping mercenaries. (*Pause*) Now, you made me say that. You made me utter sentiments which in any case I do not feel. You do that to people. Let's go home.

KATRIN: I have finished with home, for which, all gratitude to Islam's infantry —

SUSANNAH: Silly —

KATRIN: **Don't call me silly in that way you do**. (*Pause*) I can't go home because — and do listen, this will be difficult for you, perhaps beyond your grasp — home is the instrument of reconciliation, the means through which all crime is rinsed in streams of sympathy and outrage doused, and blame is swallowed in upholstery, home is the suffocator of all temper, the place where the preposterous becomes the tolerable and hell itself is stacked on shelves, I wish to hold on to my agony, it's all I have. (*Pause*)

SUSANNAH: I had such a pleasant room prepared for you . . .

KATRIN: Use it to fuck in. (*She bursts out*.) Oh, I am unforgivable! I only said that because he is here! (*Pause*) But do, do use it for love, you drive men mad, you know you do. (*She looks at* ORPHULS.) She does. Their eyes go fixed. (*She turns to go*.)

SUSANNAH: Where will you go, then?

KATRIN: With the nuns, like any vagrant. (*She goes out. Pause*.)

ORPHULS: She is — she boils and fumes — she —

SUSANNAH: She always did. Her ordeal has made no difference. And of course, I hate her, too.

ORPHULS: Then why do you —

SUSANNAH: I don't know. We often choose to live with those we hate, so I observe. And those we think we love, we soon grow to hate. I exaggerate, of course, it is the effect of being with a priest in a dark room. There is no bread in the city. Have you any? I am starving. (*Pause. He looks at her*.) Turkish carpets and whole tents are being swopped for single cabbages, would you believe? (*She exposes her breast to him*.) Come on, the next thing will be an epidemic and we'll all be dead by Christmas.

ORPHULS (*turning away his face*): I should love nothing more than that, but I've no bread.

SUSANNAH: Chocolate, then?

ORPHULS: No . . . (*She covers her breast.*) What I would not give for a piece of chocolate now . . .

SUSANNAH: I know.

ORPHULS: All the chocolate one eats, and now —

SUSANNAH: It's the way, isn't it, of all things? But the Emperor's back and they don't appear without the kitchens, why are you interrogating my sister?

ORPHULS: We are recording all — God forgive me, I would die for a loaf now —

SUSANNAH: I understand, but —

ORPHULS: We are keeping testimony of the passage of Islam, I am commissioned by the See, Oh, God, give me a loaf, somebody, it is a sacred obligation to our people, anyway it is not an interrogation, she is under no compulsion, would you please leave now, you are subjecting me to terrible anxiety, how could I look at you again in times of plenty knowing I might have —

SUSANNAH: You may come to me and ask me, pay me the conventional attentions and if I am not otherwise engaged, who knows, I —

ORPHULS: Conventional attentions?

SUSANNAH: Yes, manners will be back as soon as the shops are open. (*She smiles.*) I am most dreadfully hungry. (*She pulls her clothing closer, goes to leave, stops.*) Obviously, you wouldn't have a loaf, would you? You would have given it away. (*Pause. They look at one another.*)

ORPHULS: Had I a single slice, I should pass by the dying and not show it. (*Pause. She turns, but at this moment, a small loaf is thrown from the darkness. It lands at OR-PHULS's feet. Both he and SUSANNAH go to grab it, but he is the swifter. Undoing her dress, she steps into the darkness. Pause, then he follows. After some moments, a hooded figure appears in the shaft of light. Pause. The sound of SUSANNAH's receding footsteps on the stone floor. OR-PHULS appears. He looks at the figure.*) Who the — who the fuck are — (*He tears off his hood. It is STARHEMBERG.*) Oh, fuck, it is the man who saved Vienna . . . (*He kneels at his feet.*) I am a most ambitious priest and love God, I assure you, in the heat of her sweltering . . .

STARHEMBERG: Excellent.

ORPHULS: But you . . . ?

STARHEMBERG: Me? I listen.

ORPHULS: And do you creep in many rooms? I only ask? I kiss your feet who saved a million souls, why do you listen to girls' miseries? Inform me, I am your servant and no matter what the sins I absolve you, I would be skewered on Islamic daggers but for you, make me your Confessor, I would be honoured not only to hear but share your pains. And thank you for the bun, I was in hell there. (*Pause.* STARHEMBERG *raises him, kisses him, and goes out.*)

Scene Three

A palace. courtiers. A chair. LEOPOLD *enters. He topples the chair and perches on the result. The courtiers shift uncomfortably.*

LEOPOLD: Sometimes, you will want to laugh. And you will feel, no, I must not laugh. Sometimes you will suffer, the embarrassment of one who feels exposed to an obnoxious privacy. You will feel, he should never have shown me that. And sometimes you will experience the terrible nausea that accompanies an idiocy performed by one for whom you felt respect. As if the world had lost its balance. I can only tell you, all these feelings I permit. So laugh when the urge seizes you, and then, be ashamed of the laugh. The Emperor only acts the insecurity of all order. Do you accept the truth of that? (*The courtiers shift uncomfortably.*) No one understands! Nihil comprehensa! Now, you may turn the chair up. (*The chair is put on its legs.* LEOPOLD *sprawls.*)

IPSTEIN: Morality.

LEOPOLD: Mm.

IPSTEIN: Has utterly collapsed.

LEOPOLD: It does in sieges. Like cakes left in the rain. And humour also, that deteriorates. The sort of joke you would not twitch a muscle for in peacetime sets crowds of starving rocking in a siege.

IPSTEIN: Humour I think, we can leave aside for —

LEOPOLD: **Why leave humour out!** (*Pause.* IPSTEIN *shrugs.*)

Do I bully you? Don't shudder, no one will hack your hand off, this is not Rome or Russia.

HARDENSTEIN: Women are selling themselves and the bourgeoises are the worst.

LEOPOLD: You should pity the privileged, how they suffer in adversity. See the best shops are stocked first. Next.

FALLENGOTT: The currency is unstable.

LEOPOLD: The currency is always unstable.

FALLENGOTT: Not like this.

LEOPOLD: I am sick of currency and its instability. I shrink to think a single life, a dog's or pigeon's even, should be warped by currency and its antics. Hang currency from trees.

FALLENGOTT: We might as well, it is that useless.

LEOPOLD: I sense the coinage has found a friend in you.

FALLENGOTT: Not a bit, but —

LEOPOLD: **Off your knees to coins**, it is a despicable sight. Are the bankers back yet?

HARDENSTEIN: The Jews never left.

LEOPOLD: The fall of shells is like a passing shower to them. Where is the Turkish treasure?

FALLENGOTT: Lying in ravines.

LEOPOLD: Then float the new economy on that. Enough, and thank you for your opinions, I weigh them all, I seem brusque, I seem shallow but in privacy I meditate profoundly, you must take that on trust, of course. (*They start to leave.* LEOPOLD *places his hand on the* PAINTER's *sleeve.*) Not you. (*The* COURTIERS *depart. Pause.*) I speak everything, like one variety of idiot. And you are silent, like the other. Draw me now. I pose. (*He kneels on the floor like a dog.*) I pose. And thus cheat your imagination.

PAINTER (*turning to a fresh page*): How?

LEOPOLD: Because the artist hopes his portrait shows a secret truth, and I show my secret. Call this 'He Comes Back to Vienna'.

PAINTER: Must I?

LEOPOLD: Yes. (*The* PAINTER *begins drawing.*)

PAINTER: I think, by discarding the formality of monarchy, you think you disrupt criticism, and by playing the fool, disarm any who would dare call you so, and thereby flatter your intelligence. I hope I am not offending you.

LEOPOLD: You were never this perceptive on the battlefield.

PAINTER: I was too cold.

LEOPOLD: **It is cold, this is Europe . . . !**

PAINTER: Yes . . . yes . . . so you said . . . at every foggy ditch and burial — (*He throws down the book.*) It's — really it's — impossible! You cannot — an artist cannot hope to paint an act! Find another — find a —

LEOPOLD (*abandoning his absurd pose, and sitting on the floor*): No, no, you are the one . . . you are . . . (*Pause. He is weeping.* STARHEMBERG *enters, looks at them.*) I'm crying again . . . Starhemberg . . . crying again . . . (STARHEMBERG *goes to him, cradles his head.*) Why? Why this weeping all the time? (*The* PAINTER *sketches this, furtively.*) Don't you weep? You don't, do you? **Why is it, then, it infuriates me** — (*The* PAINTER *goes to leave discreetly.*) Don't slip away with that! (*He stops.*) Show me the book. (*He offers the book.*) You see, he gets it down, the moment of despair, his fingers work like lightning to capture that, how well he seizes that — (*He tears out the page, gives the book back. The* PAINTER *leaves.*) Where do you go at nights? You are unobtainable.

STARHEMBERG: Am I not free? I have no titles which are not honorary now.

LEOPOLD: No, none, and at your own request. But half the time you are not in your premises, and the messengers say the state of the windows suggests the genius has quit. Four times I have left messages. You are a hero and yet you creep around in hats, we need our hero, we are afraid you will be discovered lying in some alley and then the word will go around Starhemberg is out of favour, there's gratitude for you, when nothing could be further from the truth!

STARHEMBERG: During the siege I had half the cannon turned to face in.

LEOPOLD: In? Why in?

STARHEMBERG: Every night a dozen citizens slipped out with handkerchiefs on which were written **we love Islam** in mis-shapen Arab script. I must tell you, at the lowest point I received a delegation who proposed the burning of all effigies of Christ, and as for the Imperial standard, I saw it stuffed inside a drain-pipe. Officers were tearing off their epaulets, and priests lurked in wigs. I forced freedom on them, and when they applaud me, their claps are drowning out the shame which roars inside their ears. I loathe the crowd. I love big hats.

LEOPOLD: They are only frail . . . they are only frail . . . I cannot criticize them . . . how can I, the arch-deserter, criticize? You must help us to restore ourselves. Be a mirror in which we dwarves may see the possibility of godlike self.

STARHEMBERG: No.

LEOPOLD: Restore us, Starhemberg, who has no flaws — (STARHEMBERG *turns to leave*.) **Who said yer can go!** (*He stops*.) I think you are a selfish and self-loving fantasist or you would have surrendered months ago. (*Pause*) No, no, listen, I owe you everything and don't despise me, I can have you made a saint, do you want to be a saint? It can be done, the long grey jaw and hooded eye, excellent, try that if you are tired of soldiering, but not this anonymity, or do you hate us? (*Pause*) You do . . . so that's your burden . . . you are thin with hate . . . Oh, Starhemberg, you are crueller than the worst Arab butcher, who stabs with childlike relish and then grows tired, and waking in the morning, plays with the infants he forgot to slay. Starhemberg, my maker, you are ill . . . (*He goes to him, holds him*.)

STARHEMBERG: The innocent are not innocent . . .

LEOPOLD: **I laugh! I laugh!**

EMPRESS (*entering*): Starhemberg! How rarely he! Oh, his unfamiliar! Kiss me, then! (*He kisses her hand*.) Cold mouth. Have you a mistress?

STARHEMBERG: I love a woman.

EMPRESS: But your mouth is cold!

LEOPOLD: He holds us all in spite.

EMPRESS: Not me.

LEOPOLD: Yes, you included! Someone is writing his biography, but he will give no evidence. And the city architect has sculpted him for Starhemberg Square, but without a face! It is ridiculous, when can he do the face?

STARHEMBERG: Let it have no face.

LEOPOLD: **I laugh. I laugh**.

EMPRESS: Are you loyal to the Hapsburgs?

STARHEMBERG: I can conceive of no improvement in the nature of the government.

LEOPOLD: You see! That is how he is!

EMPRESS (*looking at* STARHEMBERG): He thinks his boldness will win our admiration. He is very near offence, and thinks we will admire his subtlety. I do admire it, so there! Do sit, or won't you?

STARHEMBERG: No.

EMPRESS: Of course not! To sit would end his condescension, I do admire all your moves, I think you are a cold
and wonderfully imagined man, I mean, you are your own
invention, isn't that so?

LEOPOLD: My wife is so perceptive, her gaze melts
snow.

STARHEMBERG: Yes.

EMPRESS: There you are! And a reply of one syllable, for
more would only spoil the effect. I feel such attraction for
you, Starhemberg, I would run away with you to a pigman's
hut and fuck the rest of my existence out!

LEOPOLD: **I laugh!**

EMPRESS: You see, I can match all your gestures. No real
man is worth the effort, but one who invents, and re-invents
himself! He can keep us heated!

LEOPOLD: **I laugh!**

EMPRESS (*to* LEOPOLD): As you do, as you also do . . .
(*She kisses* LEOPOLD.) Starhemberg, we must invent the
European now, from broken bits. Glue head to womb and so
on. And fasten hair to cracked, mad craniums. And stop
being ashamed. Now, go, you excellent actor, do go . . . (*He
bows.*)

Scene Four

An Institute of Science. A semi-circle of physicians. KATRIN
naked to the waist. SUSANNAH *and* STARHEMBERG *in the
audience.*

GRUNDFELT: She is nineteen. She is from the agricultural
district of Thuringia. She is one of nine children. She is
literate. She suffered on the twenty-third of August. She was
without benefit of surgeons. She is pregnant and in the
fourth month of her term. She gave testimony to the Bishop's
Commission on Atrocity.

KATRIN: I volunteer my disfigurement.

GRUNDFELT: She comes of her own free will.

KATRIN: I needed no persuasion.

GRUNDFELT: She welcomes the scrutiny of the Institute.

KATRIN: I welcome it.

GRUNDFELT: We are grateful to this courageous and patriotic woman.

KATRIN: And I am grateful to you.

GRUNDFELT: Drawing is permitted. (*The audience rises and surrounds* KATRIN, *with books and pencils.*)

STARHEMBERG: They cluster her . . . How thick they are on her, and urgent . . .

SUSANNAH: Are you a surgeon? Hurry along with your pencil or you will miss the itemizing of the wounds.

STARHEMBERG: I shall see her . . .

SUSANNAH: Everyone will see her. She is determined her misery will go into print, and colour, too, you are staring at me in a way which at one time would have been thought offensive . . .

STARHEMBERG: Her absent breasts, and yours so very present . . .

SUSANNAH: It is peculiar, we would have thought at one time, to have such intellectual symposia among men who cannot muster a sandwich between them . . .

STARHEMBERG: Your succulence, and her aridity . . .

SUSANNAH: But we swiftly become used to anything, don't you find? All right, what have you got? I don't want pig fat, oh, God, you are Starhemberg —

STARHEMBERG: Introduce me to her.

SUSANNAH: Aren't you, you are Starhemberg, I am bathed in confusion —

STARHEMBERG: You honour me quite unnecessarily —

SUSANNAH: I bite my words —

STARHEMBERG: The world has dropped several rungs, and us with it, when will you speak to her?

SUSANNAH: Now, if you command it —

STARHEMBERG: I command nothing any more — (*She turns to go.*) Wait — I also love women —

SUSANNAH: What are you asking me?

STARHEMBERG: On the floor here, show me —

SUSANNAH: Show you?

STARHEMBERG: I have seen you fucked —

SUSANNAH: Impossible —

STARHEMBERG: No, it's so — go down and let me look at you — your hair — your crevices —

SUSANNAH: I prefer we —

STARHEMBERG: I only ask to gaze, there's no complica-
tion —

SUSANNAH: I must, since you saved Vienna. (*She lies down
among the benches, draws up her skirts. The voice of
GRUNDFELT drones. STARHEMBERG stares down at
her, and up occasionally.*)

STARHEMBERG: Up now, they're quitting — (*She rises
again, straightening her skirt.*) Introduce me, then wait in the
Ballgasse. (*She makes her way to the front.*)

GRUNDFELT: Our feelings of sympathy are not less profound for the objectivity we have attempted here in detailing
your condition —

OTHERS: Hear, hear —

KATRIN: Nor is my modesty less whole for the intensity of
your examination —

OTHERS: Hear, hear —

GRUNDFELT: We thank you both for this and for your
gracious manner.

KATRIN: I thank you equally, shall this be printed and in
colour? (*The physicians hesitate.*)

BRUSTEIN: At this moment we had only thought to record
your terrible misfortune for the archive of the Institute . . .

KATRIN: Oh, no, I understood there was a publication —

BRUSTEIN: In learned journals, some details might —

KATRIN: No, no, but in the shops, I mean —

BRUSTEIN: I — did we —

KATRIN: Oh, certainly!

GRUNDFELT: I have no recollection we —

KATRIN: Assuredly, some six thousand copies!

GRUNDFELT: I don't think any —

KATRIN: **Yes, six thousand**. I don't dream these figures.
They printed fifteen thousand of Duke Starhemberg, he
hangs in every pub, and eighteen thousand of the Emperor,
why not, there is a vast supply of cartridge in the city, and
ink's no problem, some have taken to drinking it —

SUSANNAH (*advancing with a shawl*): My sister is —

KATRIN: **Nothing**. My sister is. (*Pause*)

STARHEMBERG (*walking down*): Is there a drawing?

PAINTER: A preliminary sketch —

STARHEMBERG: Then tint it, and add her face.

SUSANNAH: My sister is —

KATRIN: Nothing. My sister is. Do arrange and hurry with
the proofs. If you have not my face, I'll sit here longer.

PAINTER: If the Duke commissions this, I —

KATRIN: What duke? It's me has all the copyright.

STARHEMBERG: Please, ask her to be covered . . . (*Pause. KATRIN allows SUSANNAH to draw a shawl over her naked shoulders. STARHEMBERG goes to the front.*) Arrange a sitting. She is staying in a convent.

KATRIN: And another, later, like this . . . ! (*She pretends to feed a child.*) I raise my infant, who is crying for his feed, but to the absent breasts, where no milk flows! His arms reach out, his tiny hands . . . ! Imagine my expression! Imagine his!

STARHEMBERG: Sketch as she says.

KATRIN: Ten thousand copies.

GRUNDFELT: I doubt this would achieve a sale of tens —

KATRIN: **You misjudge**. (*Pause*) And if they don't, then post them through the doors . . . (GRUNDFELT *bows, withdraws, with the physicians.*)

SUSANNAH: This is Duke Starhemberg. (KATRIN *looks at him.*)

KATRIN: The birth is for the seventeenth. I want it public in the square, and banks of seats. No awnings, even if it rains, and let actresses be midwives if nurses have their scruples. (*To STARHEMBERG.*) Why would you not look at me?

STARHEMBERG: I only look when I am certain I shall see.

KATRIN: You will see. (*She gets up, falls against SUSANNAH, who holds her. With an effort of will, KATRIN rids herself of SUSANNAH.*) Oh, you all so want me to be spoiled! Kiss me! (SUSANNAH *goes to kiss her. KATRIN removes her cheek.*) I don't trust kisses! Embrace me! (SUSANNAH *goes to hold her, she arches away.*) I suffocate! You only rub your grief against my flesh, as if it would come off, as a cow will back itself against the thorn and scrape its hide. That's how we kiss, that's how we hold! Where is my nun, I want to go now, Mother! (*She pulls on a gown.*) This was no endurance, do you know why? None would look me in the eye, and I have such lovely eyes. Are my eyes so dangerous? No Turk did either. (*The* NUN *enters.*) My eyes remain unravished, Mother, like unentered rooms . . . (*The* NUN *encloses her, leads her to the door.* ORPHULS *enters, bows to her.*)

STARHEMBERG: Let me father your child . . . (*Pause. KATRIN stops.*)

KATRIN: But it won't live! (*She goes out. Pause.*)

SUSANNAH: I think we live in Hell, but something makes Hell tolerable. What is it? Anger? I am so bad at anger.

ORPHULS: This is not Hell.

SUSANNAH: Not Hell? What's Hell, then?

ORPHULS: Absence.

SUSANNAH: I assure you, this is absence.

ORPHULS: Of God. (*Pause*)

SUSANNAH (*to* STARHEMBERG): Take me to the café. You said you would, for showing you God's absence . . . (*She goes out.*)

ORPHULS: The siege was simultaneously a moment of degeneracy and of the highest moral order. On the one hand, every fence to immorality was torn down, and on the other, peculiar sacrifices were made in the spirit of human love. Did you find this? (STARHEMBERG *does not reply.*) Every morning when we awoke, we felt the possibility of **utter transformation**, rising with the sun. Death, obviously, but worse, enslavement to all things foreign . . . the crying of the mullahs in their tents . . . shall we never hear again the crying of the mullahs in their tents? How tightly I did hold the woman's arse to me, her warmth, our miserable thin blanket and I kissed her hollowed neck with tears all down my face, **ring the bells I said, where are our bells today**? And then at last, the bells crashed back, drowning, waves of drowning, seas of booming iron, and she stirred slowly, some widow, some pale, inconsequential widow who held in her thin body all that was ours, all culture, all effigy in her broken lips. We pulled on our drawers under the dirty sheets, ice on the windows, and on the table, last night's greasy plate . . .

STARHEMBERG: Hearing you I know I could only love a corrupt priest . . .

ORPHULS: Don't betray me. I am ambitious.

STARHEMBERG: Never.

ORPHULS: Once you were seen in every street, on every barricade, I heard people swear you had been seen in seven quarters simultaneously, and though I never saw you, I imagined I did, and children pointed to your profile in the clouds and said 'I know that beak . . . !'

STARHEMBERG: I love the plumpness of your face. I know when you serve mass, you rarely think of Christ.

ORPHULS: I think of Him, but — (*Pause*) No, I hardly think of Christ, rather, I think — I am Him.

STARHEMBERG: Yes . . .

ORPHULS: I tell you this! I tell you, God knows why, why do I tell you? Don't betray me, I am so ambitious!

STARHEMBERG: I would rather take your blessing than a thousand cardinals stinking of celibacy shook their absolution over me. (*An old woman enters.*)

FIRST MOTHER: Is it him? Is it his voice crying love?

ORPHULS: No.

FIRST MOTHER: I find him everywhere!

STARHEMBERG: Yes, he is an itinerant priest. (*He goes out.*)

FIRST MOTHER: His long words, his lovely words, all his lovely education licks the ceiling and —

ORPHULS: I've no more bread. (*Pause*)

I mean —

I have a bit but —

I need that for —

Oh, fuck you, take it! (*He pulls some bread from under his cassock.*)

FIRST MOTHER (*taking it*): Don't swear so, you'll make enemies.

ORPHULS: I have only one enemy and that is you. I take that back.

FIRST MOTHER: You take everything back but only after you've said it.

ORPHULS: I hope you will not eat that here, it scalds my soul to think I might have fucked a woman for it and all it does is extend your burdensome life, I take that back, but you know what I mean.

FIRST MOTHER: I wouldn't burden you if your sisters were more like daughters.

ORPHULS: You have a miraculous appetite and thrive on bird shit. Most of the old collapsed and died in the first month of the siege. I looked in all their faces, but where were you? Take her swift, I prayed to God, but no, claw at the door before the morning guns . . .

FIRST MOTHER: You love me, that's what kept me whole.

ORPHULS: So you say.

FIRST MOTHER: You must do or you wouldn't tolerate me. You are kind and I am so demanding, you are busy and I pester you —

ORPHULS: Yes, well, I —

FIRST MOTHER: Oh, yes, but I shall be no trouble to you soon, my life's as good as chucked —

ORPHULS: So you keep on saying, but —

FIRST MOTHER: I live for you —

ORPHULS: For me, but —

FIRST MOTHER: My little one —

ORPHULS: Oh, God in Heaven —

FIRST MOTHER: His tiny arms went round me once, he hid his darling face in my poor skirt —

ORPHULS: **Please! Oh, please!** (*She is silent. She chews bread. Pause.*) I try, I do try, to eradicate you from my life, to erase you, every morning like a butcher rubbing down his bench . . .

FIRST MOTHER: Too deep a groove . . . (*He nods.*)

Too deep a stain . . . (*He turns his back. Pause.*)

Mind all these women.

ORPHULS: Yes. (*She starts to move away, stops.*)

FIRST MOTHER: I see you in that bishop's hat.

ORPHULS: You always did. Since I first joined the choir.

FIRST MOTHER: My son, almighty in his bishop's hat —

ORPHULS: **If I want to be a bishop I'll decide**.

FIRST MOTHER: Of course you will.

ORPHULS: I am not ambitious. It is you who is ambitious. Sickeningly so. I am happy as a pastor here. Happy and fulfilled.

FIRST MOTHER: Good. I won't keep you, then. You must have such a lot to do —

ORPHULS: Stay as long as you like, I — stay if you —

FIRST MOTHER: No, I must get on —

ORPHULS: Must you? Well, if you must, you —

FIRST MOTHER: Don't grieve for me.

ORPHULS: **You talk about dying all the time but do you!**

FIRST MOTHER (*with infinite patience*):   You will, of course. You will grieve for me.

ORPHULS: I hate the way you eat. Half the crumbs are on the floor.

FIRST MOTHER: Always ate this way.

ORPHULS: I know and it always horrified me.

FIRST MOTHER: I thought you liked the common people. We are common —

ORPHULS: **Sometimes I think I could murder you**.

FIRST MOTHER (*kneeling, brushing up the crumbs*):   I know. It's love.

ORPHULS: Stop that! Get up! (*She finishes, gets up.*) Go away, now.

FIRST MOTHER (*looking at him*): My own son. (*She goes out. Pause.*)

ORPHULS: I love you! I do love you! (*Pause*) If everything remains the same, why did we suffer? I buried thirty in a day and still I imitate! (*He examines himself.*) Other self. Other self unborn. Wrist inside my wrist. Lung inside my lung. (*Pause*) And in the hospitals they said — the young but not only the young — the injustice of my death so sours me, I have not been, I have not been yet what I might have been. But looking at them I thought, had you been, what would you have been? What magnificence? And I concluded, none. A gift of years they would have squandered in casual repetition and in servile acts. Clay, therefore. Complaining clay. (*He looks aside, sees* SUSANNAH, *who has returned, watching him.*)

SUSANNAH: Do you talk to yourself? Another madman of the siege? (*Pause*) You blush! Wonderful blush!

ORPHULS: I was — I was —

SUSANNAH: Praying?

ORPHULS: Not praying, no. (*Pause. He looks at her.*) I have no bread today.

SUSANNAH: I've eaten.

ORPHULS: Eaten? Oh . . . (*Pause. Then with immense will.*) Be my mistress, then. (*A prolonged pause.*)

SUSANNAH: Yes.

ORPHULS: Oh, my own bitch, yes . . . ! (*She goes towards him. He recoils.*) No.

SUSANNAH (*stopped*): No?

ORPHULS: You must not — simply —

SUSANNAH: No —

ORPHULS: Do you understand? Not simply, but —

SUSANNAH: Yes. (*Pause*)

ORPHULS: Suffer. (*Pause*)
                    It.

SUSANNAH *goes out.* ORPHULS *collapses to the floor, a ball of ecstasy.*

Scene Five

A cellar in Vienna. STARHEMBERG *among the out-casts.*

STARHEMBERG: In all calamity, the persistence of the destitute! In all catastrophe, the resilience of the poor! The tolerant, the semi-tolerant, **crushed to death!** The educated, the semi-educated, **trod to dust!** The cruel, the semi-cruel, **scorched to ashes**, but the carriers of neither hope nor property, **they shall inherit the earth!** That's you! (*He holds one tightly.*) Who are your true loves, those who drop small coins in your paw?

FIRST BEGGAR: No —

STARHEMBERG: No — those who come with leaflets preaching revolution?

FIRST BEGGAR: No —

STARHEMBERG: No — those who offer beds at Christmas, do you love those?

FIRST BEGGAR: No —

STARHEMBERG: No, the ones who drive their iron wheels over your splitting shins, they are your brothers!

FIRST BEGGAR: I don't see what —

STARHEMBERG: **Yes, the fraternity of bastardy!** (*He releases him.*) Yes, very few of you died, I notice, my dear friends, very few, oh, very few, and had Islam burst the gates they would not have stooped to hack your noses, those who have some gristle left, no, the beggar attracts so little violence, we must learn from him **don't stand behind me I hate that** do I lecture you, I don't mean to, I am in search of education, I clown, I misinform, I lick the oily effusion that trickles from your gut **don't come up behind me** —

SECOND BEGGAR: You are a mad and vicious fucker, Starhemberg —

STARHEMBERG: **Don't come up behind me I love to see your face in which is written survival of the fittest**, up you monarch! (*He hoists the* BEGGAR *onto his back, and parades with him.*) I am the horse to him! Spur me, you cannibal! Whip me, you angel!

SECOND BEGGAR: Put us down, yer cunt . . . !

STARHEMBERG: **I caught him with his gob in the corpse's belly!**

SECOND BEGGAR: Fuck off, you mouth and arsehole bastard —

STARHEMBERG: I did! And excellent! Withold respect? Not me! I canter, I perform my dressage, I am as perfect as the carriage horse, the hearse animal, oh, master, oh, genius in self-perpetuation, **I caught him with his gob in the entrails!**

SECOND BEGGAR: Who the fuck are —

STARHEMBERG: **Not you? Then it was your double!**

SECOND BEGGAR: Down or I'll kick the kidneys out yer arse —

STARHEMBERG: Down? To the humble soil? Tread pavements, you? Oh, no, not you, **Monarch!** (*He tips him brutally to the floor.*)

FIRST WOMAN BEGGAR: You should watch it, how you hurt the feelings of these gentlemen.

STARHEMBERG (*sitting*): Their sensitivity engulfs me.

FIRST WOMAN BEGGAR: They also breathe.

STARHEMBERG: Yes, I smell it.

FIRST WOMAN BEGGAR: They also suffer.

STARHEMBERG: What, the indigestion caused by human meat? No, I bow to such persistence, you know I do, I am your student, I am your novice, and my tongue hangs out to the dribble of your wit like the putti in the fountain, piss your life to me, I drink!

SECOND WOMAN BEGGAR: You are no fucking angel —

STARHEMBERG: No angel yet — but trying —

SECOND WOMAN BEGGAR: **Who fed you?**

STARHEMBERG: The army commissariat.

SECOND WOMAN BEGGAR: **I spit on that**.

STARHEMBERG: I feel your spit, a cool and perfect fluid . . .

FIRST WOMAN BEGGAR: Why do you come down here?

STARHEMBERG: To swim your gratitude! To bathe in your eternal thanks, why else? What's the gift of monarchy to your applause? The gratitude of wealth is pure selfishness, but those who only own the gutter, to be praised by them! (*He mockingly cups his ear.*)

> Deliverer, did you say?
> Redeemer, over there?
> No, didn't catch it, so deafening is the accolade —
> (*He fondles the* FIRST WOMAN BEGGAR.)

Fuck with me, I'll kiss your scabs, I'll be a Christ to you, an ageing Christ who slipped the crucifixion —

FIRST WOMAN BEGGAR: Oh, slag yerself, I done with rubbing —

STARHEMBERG: Rubbing, she calls love . . . !

SECOND BEGGAR (*threatening him closely*): Nothing fills me with more violence, mister, than a punctured snob who spunks from squalor —

STARHEMBERG: He identifies me —

SECOND BEGGAR: Lock yer gob, you shit picnic —

STARHEMBERG: How my lip swells from your compliments — (SECOND BEGGAR *goes to attack* STARHEMBERG, *but* STARHEMBERG *is the swifter and takes the* BEGGAR *in a terrible embrace.*) Oh, dance you terrible hater, dance, sick-with-life, **not dancing!** (*He jerks the* BEGGAR.) Oh, he shifts in some gavotte, some mockery of civil manners, teach me, I can't follow — (*He jerks him again.*) Oh, your movements, are these the **veiled messages of love** —

SECOND BEGGAR: You — hurt — you —

STARHEMBERG: Or symbols of the hierarchy? I can't imitate!

SECOND BEGGAR: Oh — fuck and —

STARHEMBERG (*lowering him in a hold*): Down now, piss-odour, to your loved level . . . (*He pushes the* BEGGAR's *mouth to the flagstones. A silence. He releases him, moves away, shuddering.*)

THIRD BEGGAR: You will end up eye-gouged, or nose-spiked, I dare suggest, the wretched harbour grievances, having little else to harbour . . . (STARHEMBERG *looks at him.*) I think it possible we are related . . .

STARHEMBERG: So's all humanity, if we could excavate the bedrooms.

THIRD BEGGAR: Touché, but I am an Esterhazy of the excluded line.

STARHEMBERG: I knew the nose.

THIRD BEGGAR: I am not after favours, have you seen my sister, I am not after favours, obviously, she was put in the asylum at Estragom —

STARHEMBERG: Go away, now —

THIRD BEGGAR: In a room, and chained, how could she write poetry in such a posture, the manacles were bolted to the ceiling, impossible I should have thought, she was committed for no other reason than her poetry, it did not rhyme, you see, I ask no favours, why have they dimmed, your eyes? (*He sits at* STARHEMBERG's *feet, silent.*)

FIRST WOMAN BEGGAR: You have hurt Larry's throat, you mad cat . . .

STARHEMBERG: Then he can shake his bowl for two defects instead of one.

FIRST WOMAN BEGGAR: You are a proper pig melt in this mood . . .

SECOND BEGGAR (*roaring at a distance*):   **I will blind 'is eyes!**

BEGGARS: Down, Larry, down, son . . .

SECOND BEGGAR: **Blind 'im, everyone!**

STARHEMBERG: You could not blind a pigeon if it sat trussed in your fingers . . .

SECOND BEGGAR: **Piss in yer mouth!**

BEGGARS: Steady, Larry . . .

SECOND WOMAN BEGGAR: 'ho asked you here in any case?

STARHEMBERG: Nobody asked, you once perfect, breath-stopping excellence — for whom I once would have crawled whole avenues of rotting butchery . . .

SECOND WOMAN BEGGAR: Piss in yer mouth.

STARHEMBERG: So you say.

FOURTH BEGGAR (*sitting by* STARHEMBERG):   You know, so tell me, shall there ever be a system with no poor?

STARHEMBERG: Never. Unless they gaol the poor in palaces. I don't rule that out.

FOURTH BEGGAR: And shall the poor men burn the rich men's houses?

STARHEMBERG: Yes, again, and again, or how else could the rich feel happy?

FOURTH BEGGAR: I follow nothing 'e says! Nothing!

SECOND BEGGAR: **Poke 'im in the eyeballs, then!**

FOURTH BEGGAR: **Shuddup!**

STARHEMBERG (*grabbing the* FOURTH BEGGAR *by the collar*):   Describe what hope you have, your hope, what is it?

FOURTH BEGGAR: Hope?

STARHEMBERG: Yes, you know the stuff, it came in with the mother's milk, had you no mother?

FOURTH BEGGAR: Yes —

STARHEMBERG: What, then? (*Pause*)

FOURTH BEGGAR: Dinner!

STARHEMBERG: **No, after dinner!** (*Pause*)

FOURTH BEGGAR: None, after dinner . . . (STARHEMBERG *gets up.*)

FIRST WOMAN BEGGAR: I don't think you should visit us. Let us be vicious, as we are, and you be vicious, as you are, and piss in all mouths, but no trespass. (*Pause.* STARHEMBERG *starts to go.*)

FOURTH BEGGAR: Take me...! (STARHEMBERG *stops, looks at the* FOURTH BEGGAR, *shakes his head, goes out. The* FOURTH BEGGAR *rushes after him.*)

Scene Six

A darkened room. An arid and dusty old woman in a chair. STARHEMBERG *enters.*

SECOND MOTHER: Why are you here?

STARHEMBERG: God knows.

SECOND MOTHER: Here again, and don't know why. Dux. Imperator. Have you aged?

STARHEMBERG: Yes.

SECOND MOTHER: Deliverer. Defender. One day you will enter and I shan't be here. A woman with a baby will be here, and the shutters open, all sunlight and diapers.

STARHEMBERG: Obviously.

SECOND MOTHER: I have nothing more to say and you keep coming here.

STARHEMBERG: Yes.

SECOND MOTHER: Do you love me so much?

STARHEMBERG: It would appear so.

SECOND MOTHER: It would. Tribune. Liberator.

STARHEMBERG: Once I saw you naked. But only once.

SECOND MOTHER: You want to talk of these things, but I have nothing to say.

STARHEMBERG: You have nothing to say but I have much to ask.

SECOND MOTHER: Speak your questions to my grave.

STARHEMBERG: I will do.

SECOND MOTHER: Why do I need to hear?

STARHEMBERG: I would have been your child. How I lay and wished I was your child. If I had been your child none of this would be necessary.

SECOND MOTHER: Generalissimus, you cannot know how tired I am.

STARHEMBERG: I also. And your breasts were like the breasts of a witch.

SECOND MOTHER: Is that the mid-day bell?

STARHEMBERG: The antithesis of sculpture.

SECOND MOTHER: It is. And now I wind my watch.

STARHEMBERG: The antithesis of abundance.

SECOND MOTHER: Thus is my day divided. Only at night do I open the shutter. On the eight o'clock bell. Thus is my day divided.

STARHEMBERG: I come as rarely as I can. Often I wish to come, and refuse myself.

SECOND MOTHER: Yes, rarely, Gloriosus Austriae.

STARHEMBERG: Naked, only once, and I believe you knew that I was there.

SECOND MOTHER: My teeth are falling.

STARHEMBERG: Mine also.

SECOND MOTHER: Sometimes I hear a tinkle as one strikes the tiles. I have been asleep and open-mouthed. The saliva stains my shoulder. My head goes always to the left.

STARHEMBERG: I came behind you and —

SECOND MOTHER: So the left collar of my dress is pale.

STARHEMBERG: **I must come here all the same**. (*He sits. A long silence. He rocks, head in hands.*)

SECOND MOTHER: Oh, my darling one, oh, my little son, my darling one . . . (*A long pause.*)

STARHEMBERG: Do they bring you food?

SECOND MOTHER: At one.

STARHEMBERG: Eat, then. Do eat.

SECOND MOTHER: Why? (*He shrugs.*)

STARHEMBERG: Cease eating, then. And my visits could cease, also.

SECOND MOTHER: Deus Imperator. My lip is thin as paper and it spontaneously bleeds . . . (*He rises to his feet.*)

        Deus . . .

        Deus . . . (*He goes to her. The interruption of a loud voice on the stairs.*)

EMPRESS: **Le sixième étage!** (*Footsteps on the boards.*)

        This is her room! (*The door opens.*)

   I enter! I burst in! A clumsy and unwelcome mound of governing flesh!

Lights!
Open the shutters! (*A* SERVANT *enters*.)
Is she here? I did not knock, I might surprise her straddling
the commode, but I am a woman of the world and more,
where are you, Mother of Deliverance? And why this hatred
of la clarté, das licht, are you afraid to witness your own
decay? (*The* SERVANT *throws back the shutters*.) I understand, I also have abolished mirrors and am half your age —
(*The light shows* STARHEMBERG *and the* SECOND
MOTHER. *The* EMPRESS *stops*.) Starhemberg. The filial
obligation. (*Pause. She bows to the* SECOND MOTHER.)
Madam, you have more magnetism for this man than all five
hundred rooms of the Kaiserhof. I think your son is a
remarkable swine.

SECOND MOTHER: He is not my son. I never suffered him,
nor any other infant.

EMPRESS: The light is cruel . . . does no one sweep in here?
My shoes crack biscuits and the skeletons of gorged mice . . .
it is a proper kaiserhof of rodents and merciless to the
nostrils, leave the door wide, je souffre, ich ersticke. (*To*
STARHEMBERG.) Why are you here, I am embarassed.

STARHEMBERG: I don't know.

EMPRESS: And why am I, you wonder, you cogitate behind
your level and perceptive gaze, I find he makes me stutter, as
if my head were suddenly a void! Does he do this to you,
unbrain you, my skull is like — well, what — an old
woman's room, does he do this to you?

SECOND MOTHER: Never —

EMPRESS: Well, you are lucky in all ways . . . (*Pause. No
sound but from the street below*.) Can you explain to me what
sexual preference is? (*Pause*)
            Its arbitrary — (*Pause*)
            Its pitiless arbitrariness — (*Pause*)
            Its — (*Pause*)
            Well, I longed to see you. I had to see you. And
            I have!
Tell the coach, get lost, I walk home unattended and may
take hours. (*The* SERVANT *leaves. To* STARHEMBERG.)
You must talk more. You force the most undigested vomit
of dissonance and trash from those surrounding you, which
is a gambit on your part, like everything, I believe nothing
you do is not calculated in utter coldness, and you let your
mother stink. (*She turns, stops*.) They want to name a

regiment The Starhemberg but someone must present the colours. Do it. In the knowledge they will splash their flesh against some wall in Hungary. (*He bows.*) The Turks chop off their genitals, why is that? And the noses, why is that?

STARHEMBERG: They are afraid to love.

EMPRESS: Aren't we? (*To* SECOND MOTHER.) I was so curious to meet you. And of course, it all makes sense. (*She turns to leave.*)

SECOND MOTHER: He came up behind me, on a hill.

EMPRESS: Who did?

SECOND MOTHER: And he — so wanted to touch me — such suffering — it marked me — like a disfigurement — I could not turn but felt his awful stare — I felt my entire body flush with blood — the kidneys gush — the whole length of my bowel — hot rush of blood . . .

EMPRESS: That is a poem — (*Pause. She looks at* STAR-HEMBERG.) She did not think that. It is a poem. By Ady. **Absurd!** I know the poem by heart. (*She goes out.*)

Scene Seven

A park in Vienna. KATRIN *sits for the* PAINTER. SUSANNAH *watches.*

SUSANNAH: My throbbing priest. My cogent and distended priest **I love him terribly and all he does is write me notes**. (*Pause*) He is addicted to these little notes which are surely — which are half-hearted penetrations, surely? I don't understand a word of them, I hold them this way up, and that way up, I read them diagonally, I cut them up with scissors, scatter them and pick them up again **I have struck him twice across the jaw** and do you blame me? And oh, he was white! White with pride and reticence and then forgave me. He wanted to hit me but he didn't, he forgave me instead. What is all this **didn't** with him? I want a child. God knows why. What do I want a child for?

KATRIN (*maintaining her pose*): It is not a matter of you wanting a child. It is the child wanting. I know. I never wanted a child. But the child wanted. All this 'I never asked to be born' etcetera, piss and nonsense! I know. The unborn, the unconceived, force the act upon the parents **Get her on the ground it says. Get him in your body it says**. I know. I do know all this. You must get knowledge, Susannah, from anywhere, but get it.

SUSANNAH: Knowledge?

KATRIN: Yes, and make yourself again! There, now I've given you all this time, and all the time I've given you is time lost for myself, what am I, a charity? (*She holds her belly.*) It moves, my master . . . (*Pause*) Do feel him . . . he is every bit as violent as his fathers . . . (SUSANNAH *touches her belly.*) He is perfectly loathesome the way he shoves. He longs to be out and about and intent on damage! **He rampages!** (SU-SANNAH *withdraws.*) Pity the land when he is out. Do you think I will be proud of him, and secretly gloat at every little crime he does? Mums do, they worship their terrors, their stabbings they collect like exam certificates. I know. I dread the criminality of motherhood. It is a criminal relation.

PAINTER: From here on a good day you can see to Transyl-vania . . . (*He peers, holding his brush.*)

KATRIN (*inspired*): Imagine a room, crowded, locked and barred, in which a poison cloud has drifted . . . ! Imagine the mother of the infant trampling the occupants, her heels, her spikes, go into eyes and cheeks as she climbs the dying mound for the last cubic inch of oxygen, the infant stretched aloft, **spare mine!** Oh, I have blinded you with my heel, oh, I have punctured your face, **spare mine!** (*She smiles.*) Accurate. Oh, so accurate . . . (*She closes her eyes.*)

SUSANNAH (*to* PAINTER): You're a man. You're a man, aren't you? Why should a man not wish to make love?

PAINTER (*staring, off*): Europe, how it shines! As if a grimy sheet were lifted off, and sunlight fell on all its fields and forests!

KATRIN: And its graves. Its wonderful acres of graves!

SUSANNAH: Is it to torture me? As for fidelity, he asks for none, which makes it worse. **I want to be forced to be faithful**.

PAINTER: The war, how tedious it was! I ached to paint women.

KATRIN: Women are in wars. Where were you?

SUSANNAH: And his thing is hard against me. A branch of maleness. So it is not impotence, surely?

PAINTER: I do so adore the company of women . . . !

SUSANNAH: He had me once, of course. But that was prostitution. That was opportunism. That was not love, or if it was love, love of a different — (*She stops, following his distracted gaze.*) What are you looking at? I am short-sighted, what?

PAINTER (*putting aside his brush, taking up his sketchbook as if by habit*): They are executing a man . . . (*He drifts away, drawn inexorably to the scene.*)

KATRIN: Who? Who! (*She prepares to follow him.*) I must watch.

SUSANNAH: Why?

KATRIN: I must, that's all. (*She drifts a little way.*) It's a park. This is a park, and they — (*She goes out. SUSANNAH, alone, goes to the canvas. Slowly. Her body is convulsed by shuddering. She grasps the easel for support, embracing it. The front of her dress is smothered in paint. She recovers. KATRIN returns.*)

KATRIN: The head fell . . . no . . . it did not fall . . . it spun . . . it whirled away like a top . . . and the blood was four fountains . . . four geysers . . . but . . . obviously, he could still see . . . the head could see as it flew and he knew . . . he both knew himself to be decapitated and also registered the crazy nature of his flight . . . his confusion . . . and his . . . clarity . . . ! (*She sees SUSANNAH's dress.*) You have ruined your dress . . . (*The PAINTER appears with a head.*)

PAINTER: The consciousness is draining out of him . . . (SUSANNAH *turns away.*)

KATRIN: He can still see . . .

PAINTER: Yes . . . he sees us . . . as through a telescope reversed . . .

KATRIN: Down tunnels which are darkening . . .

PAINTER: Our hostile stares are —

KATRIN: Not hostile —

PAINTER: Our curious stares . . .

KATRIN: Peer down from daylight, as if into a darkening cell . . . (*The PAINTER puts the head on the grass and begins sketching.*)

PAINTER: Unfortunately he lopped his tartar hair, the better to conceal himself —

KATRIN: Absurd!

PAINTER: Absurd, with eyes like those —

KATRIN: Which proclaim his distant origins . . . (*He sketches feverishly.*)

PAINTER: He was captured in an alley.

KATRIN (*plucking flowers*): The alley is the European thing the silly horseman could not hope to navigate. Oh, silly horseman, I do feel such contempt for him . . . ! (*She drapes the flowers round the head.*)

SUSANNAH: Do stop it . . .

KATRIN: Stop it, why?

SUSANNAH: **Stop it, I said**. (*The* PAINTER *looks up, sees her dress, then the canvas.*)

PAINTER: Oh, bloody God, you've — (*He throws down his pencil as two executioners enter, one with a sword, the other lumbering a crucifix.*)

SHYBAL: I can't let you keep the head.

KATRIN: That's all right, we don't want the head.

SHYBAL: Which is peculiar, when the country is so head-choked . . .

KATRIN (*handing it to him*): Oh, but rules are rules . . .

McNOY (*popping the head in a sack*): He was not bad, Johnny the Turk . . .

KATRIN: Oh, really, wasn't he?

McNOY: The women liked him.

KATRIN: Did they? Peculiar, the female nature. Deep as a pool. Or shallow as a puddle, arguably. What do you say?

McNOY: We're country boys.

KATRIN: No, female nature, though?

McNOY: Yokels, I say . . .

KATRIN: **Don't say yokels** why did they like him **yokels my arse** do say what it is with women that they do so swiftly turn themselves upside down for strangers —

SUSANNAH: Katrin —

KATRIN: **Country boys** no, they do so lurk inside their ignorance, they do so skulk inside their illiteracy as if it were a cave **like Turks why did they like them say**. (*Pause.* SHYBAL *stares at her.*)

SHYBAL: I found it in a Turkish trench, this crucifix. They had chopped bits off it, and it bled.

McNOY: And wept. It does at times, still bleed and weep . . . (KATRIN *looks at it.*)

KATRIN: Yes, I can see it does . . .

SHYBAL: And now we carry it, down all the lines, gun on left shoulder, Christ on right!

KATRIN: Yes . . . good . . . **Love Christ and wreck His enemies!**

SHYBAL (*looking into her*): I think you were one of them.

KATRIN: What?

SHYBAL: Turks' woman . . . (*They go off, passing* STAR-HEMBERG. KATRIN *turns to him, sudden and brittle.*)

KATRIN: We only meet in public places! Is that because you follow me? Or do you feel you can be more familiar in a park? Why not? What's a park, in any case, a rather dirty place **blood on the grass**. (*Pause*) Starhemberg, I am frightened of everyone, especially you, and I would not be otherwise, I am so alive with fear, I am skinless, I am flayed and the nerves tremble on the slightest passage of a man like leaves on birches flutter at the poorest breeze . . .

STARHEMBERG: I feel them.

KATRIN: Good. To fear is to be alive. Of course I shan't live to be old, the body cannot take the strain.

STARHEMBERG: I dog you.

KATRIN: Yes, you do, and I find your face terrible. You know you have a terrible face **don't touch me** I would shudder if you touched me and some cry would issue from the very bottom of my gut like afterbirth sings in the grate or a green log screams, no, I wish to marry a young man of no character whose good looks charm my mother and whose manners are immaculate, a lover of families who will spend all Christmas round the fire, perhaps a teacher at the university when they open it again, and so ambitious, **so very ambitious!** He will know how to demolish any argument, his humour will be infectious and —

STARHEMBERG: You have no mother.

KATRIN: So what —

STARHEMBERG: Your mother perished the same day as you.

KATRIN: I did not perish —

STARHEMBERG: Yes.

KATRIN: You see, he must know everything, **how did I perish I was made**. (*Pause*) Let us leave the park — Susannah — (*She extends a hand to her.*) The park fills me with despair — Susannah — hardly have the howitzers ceased and the prams are out — look, they are pulling a gun out of its pit and the nanny rushes in to spread the picnic cloth, **the speed of oblivion!** (*She shudders, her hand still stretched.*) All right, kiss me if it helps you, press your thin mouth to my thin mouth, all cracked with wind . . . (STARHEMBERG *does*

not move. SUSANNAH *gets up, takes her hand.*) How well
am I known? Is it selling, my print? (*They start to go.*)
STARHEMBERG: Help me, or I think we'll die alone . . .
KATRIN: Why not? Why not die alone? How would you die?
To the sound of violins, with your children clinging to your
feet as if your soul could be pulled back through the ceiling?
Help you how. (*Pause, she looks at him, laughs, then the
women go out.* . . STARHEMBERG *is left alone on a darkening stage, which fills with members of the Academy, clapping
the entrance of* LEOPOLD.)

Scene Eight

A circle of critics at The Imperial Academy of Art. LEOPOLD
enters to polite applause.

LEOPOLD: Not the room as we would want it. Not the salon
we would choose, the swags being somewhat chipped and the
putti lacking gilt, but in such pock-marked landscapes imagination might erupt, I call upon you to elucidate the
principles of a new art, because the stir of Europe from its
sleep commands a terrible and unrelenting movement of the
soul. I only have half an hour. What shall the art be like
now, you say! (*He sits. Pause.*) Yes, you say. (*Pause*)
ARST: A People's Art.
LEOPOLD: No. Anybody else? (ARST *sits. Another rises.*)
FELIKS: An art of celebration.
LEOPOLD: What do you want to celebrate?
FELIKS: Us, of course!
LEOPOLD: You? What is there to celebrate in you? The fact
you are alive and not a stinking thing among the pine trees?
Well, you go and celebrate that, but don't ask us to join you.
STENSH: A celebration of the heroism of the —
LEOPOLD: No, no, leave out the heroism, please, the hero-
ism was not conspicuous, in my own case barely perceptible,
and much as we have reason to be grateful to the Polish
cavalry I think an art based on lancers is likely to become
repetitive, debased, mechanical, and pleading muslims just as

bad, we must move on, **celebrate what exactly**, Bomberg, you speak, your dark face is full of irritation, which is inspiration, surely? (*Pause.* BOMBERG *does not rise.*)

BOMBERG: Shame. An art of shame.

LEOPOLD: Elucidate.

BOMBERG: That's all.

ARST: What is there to be ashamed of? (BOMBERG *shakes his head.*) No, don't just shake your head, that is appalling arrogance . . . (*He shakes it again.*) I think that gesture is typical of Professor Bomberg, who is needless to say, not among the most popular of teachers —

LEOPOLD: **Who cares if he is popular?** (*Pause.* ARST *concedes with a movement of the shoulders.*)

ARST: The fact is the students are unwilling even to attend his lectures which —

LEOPOLD: **Who cares about the studens?**

ARST: Well —

LEOPOLD: **Everything you say is meaningless.** (*Pause*) All that matters is whether he is right. (*Pause*) On the other hand, Bomberg, do speak. (*Pause*)

BOMBERG: First, we must know who we are. And to know who we are, we must know who we were. I do not think at this moment, we know who we were, and consequently —

FELIKS: You will depress the people with your introspection.

ARST: He knows nothing of the people, go into the street and see the people, you talk to nobody —

FELIKS: Listen to the people —

BOMBERG: The people have a million mouths —

ARST: You see, you are a pessimist —

BOMBERG: **You want to claim the people. You want to own the people. None of you trusts the people**.

ARST: This is why his lectures are so ill-attended —

BOMBERG: **You suffocate the people** —

LEOPOLD: Bomberg —

BOMBERG: **You invent the people** —

LEOPOLD: Bomberg —

BOMBERG: **Shut up about the people!** (*Pause*)

ARST: The people clamour for solidarity —

BOMBERG: No, they ache for truth —

FELIKS: Happiness, surely —

BOMBERG: Fuck happiness —

FELIKS: You see? What's wrong with happiness?

LEOPOLD: **Bring in a happy painter! You!** (*He points out the*
PAINTER.) Stand up. Don't be intimidated by men with
words, you can pick words out of the gutter.

ARST: It is where the best words are.

LEOPOLD: Rubbish. Rubbish and condescension. (ARST
shrugs bitterly.) Shh! (*To the* PAINTER.) Are you a happy
person?

ARST: This is not exactly what we had in mind —

LEOPOLD: Shh! You want to dominate everything! These
also are the people. These are the ones whom we must trust.
(ARST *shrugs again*.) **I wish you would not shrug like that**.
(*To the* PAINTER.) Are you happy?

PAINTER: I — (*Pause*) No.

LEOPOLD: Why not?

PAINTER: I — perhaps a defect in my character —

BOMBERG: **It's not a defect it's a quality**.

LEOPOLD: Shh! If only — may I say this and then forget it
— how I wish you gentlemen had shown such viciousness
when Islam thrust its bayonets between the city gates — if
only — now forget it! (*To the* PAINTER.) Can you paint
happy pictures? And if not, why not?

PAINTER: It is not a happy time.

ARST: Then why not make it so?

FELIKS: I think that's asking a great deal of —

ARST: Is it? Why? He is a craftsman, isn't he, he has a duty
to the people — (BOMBERG *lets out a long and terrible cry*.)
Yes — yes — a duty to — God lent him the skill and — what
he does with it is — yes —

LEOPOLD: Who do you love?

PAINTER: Who do I love?

LEOPOLD: Not woman. Artist. Which?

PAINTER: Giovanni Carpeta.

FELIKS: Be serious.

PAINTER: Giovanni Carpeta.

ARST: Miserable, satanic, gloom-sodden egoist of idiotically
unreal landscapes which —

PAINTER: I don't agree —

ARST: Which induce suicidal thoughts in those already suicidal —

PAINTER: Nevertheless —

ARST: And sends you lurching for the sunlight — one looks
at Carpeta and sees at once why the young are turning in
their droves to the Spanish and Chinese Schools —

BOMBERG: So what —

ARST: What does Carpeta say, what does Carpeta lend to people already crippled with despair —

PAINTER: He speaks to me —

ARST: I don't think a single canvas of the man would last two minutes in the market square —

PAINTER: **I revere him! I revere him!**

ARST: It would be torn from its stretcher and the crowd would say —

PAINTER: **I revere him**!

ARST: You insult us with your pessimism — (*The* PAINTER *lets out a long moan.*) Yes, your human loathing — end of speech! (*He shows empty hands. The* PAINTER *sobs.*)

LEOPOLD (*to* the PAINTER): You have to — I'm afraid — defend your soul against the bullies of the mind . . .

ARST: I must say I am extremely weary with souls, which as far as I can see are merely pretexts for self-adulation.

PAINTER (*to* ARST): I must tell you . . . if I meet you again, I'll kill you . . .

ARST: **Now who's the bully**! (*He laughs. The* PAINTER *leaves.*) Soul, I assume? The passing of soul? (*Pause, then to* ART's *horror,* BOMBERG *grips him from behind about the throat.* LEOPOLD *bursts out laughing.* FELIKS *tries to unlock* BOMBERG's *manic grip. The* EMPRESS *appears.*)

LEOPOLD: **I laugh! I laugh!**

ARST (*as* BOMBERG *releases him, falling back into his chair*): Mad — man . . . !

LEOPOLD: Bomberg, I think you must join the church . . . (BOMBERG *shakes his head, weeping into his hands.*) Yes, he must take Orders, mustn't he?

FELIKS: This has been a foolish meeting —

STARHEMBERG: It is a very foolish time. The snake cut into seven pieces writhes absurdly as it tries to join itself, but in what order! How could it be otherwise . . . ?

LEOPOLD: You speak. You've said nothing yet.

STARHEMBERG: Nothing I say will be true.

EMPRESS: We don't ask for miracles.

STARHEMBERG: Everything I say I will later retract.

LEOPOLD: We are familiar with this tendency.

STARHEMBERG: The apparent logic of my position is only the dressing of flagrant incompatibilities.

EMPRESS: Obviously, And that is why we trust you, Starhemberg. (*Pause*)

STARHEMBERG: What I need. And what there will be. I need an art which will recall pain. The art that will be will be all flourishes and celebration. I need an art that will plummet through the floor of consciousness and free the unborn self. The art that will be will be extravagant and dazzling. I need an art that will shatter the mirror in which we pose. The art that will be will be all mirrors. I want to make a new man and new woman but only from the pieces of the old. The new man and new woman will insist on their utter novelty. I ask a lot. The new art will ask nothing. And now I am going to bed . . .

EMPRESS: I do not think, Starhemberg, you have quite grasped the temper of the times, has he? I think what Europe needs is rococo and a little jazz! (STARHEMBERG *gets up, bows, is about to leave, but stops.*)

STARHEMBERG: During the war, while the ground rose under the shellfire and the sky was black with rising and falling and rising clods, and rising and falling flesh, and everything was racing from itself, the eye from the socket and the arm from the joint, you heard in the fractional silences a singing record going round, deep in a cellar, and the lips of the soon-to-be-dead were mouthing sentiments of banal happiness . . .

EMPRESS: And why not . . . ? (*He bows, goes out.*) **Why not**. (*The sound of a popular march played by a band, rising to a crescendo.*)

ACT TWO

Scene One

A bed in a public square, overlooked by benches. STARHEM-
BERG *watches an old woman dragging a sheet over the stage.*
She flings it on the bed.

STARHEMBERG: Have you given birth?
MIDWIFE: To a proper bastard.
STARHEMBERG: Tell me then, what to expect.
MIDWIFE: Abuse, ducks.
STARHEMBERG: Abuse? Why abuse? It's supposed to be a
  miracle.
MIDWIFE: So was the saving of Vienna, but all I heard was
  blasphemy.
STARHEMBERG: Birth's a thing of beauty, surely?
MIDWIFE: It's a thing of pain.
STARHEMBERG: Yes, but pain's divisible.
MIDWIFE: It divided me. I thought I'd never come together
  again.
STARHEMBERG (*turning away*): Oh, choke on your wit,
  I'm sorry I bothered you. (ORPHULS *appears*.) **Humour!**
  Humour! They creep among jokes like the lonely sentry in
  fortifications! I say pain's divisible. There's pain for some-
  thing and pain for nothing, so birth's tolerable and torture's
  sheer disintegration, surely? (*He looks at him.*) I am thinner
  than yesterday, and you are even fatter.
ORPHULS: No, I am —
STARHEMBERG: Yes, you swell with gratification —
ORPHULS: On the contrary, I am deprived —
STARHEMBERG: Then you swell on that. Everything
  agrees with you. (*He goes close to* ORPHULS.) I think all

teeth rotted in the siege but yours. **That's her bed**. Where are you sitting? (*He goes to the woman.*) Mother, how much are the benches?

MIDWIFE: I do the bed.

STARHEMBERG: Oh, she is bed specialist. (*He calls off.*) **Bench Man!**

ORPHULS: Is she — has her labour begun?

MIDWIFE: There's been some show, so I get on.

STARHEMBERG: **Bench Man!**

ORPHULS: I think this is — I know you are full of admiration for her but —

STARHEMBERG: The benchman is elsewhere, making humour from his cataracts —

ORPHULS: What is the virtue in it?

STARHEMBERG: Or showing his stumps and making fun of the absent legs —

ORPHULS: I ask you, what —

STARHEMBERG: **No virtue in it. None**. (LEOPOLD *enters.* ORPHULS *sits disconsolately on a bench.*)

LEOPOLD: It's cold, I shan't stay for all of it. And what's her game, in any case? I told Elizabeth this had to be illegal. No, she said, not yet! (*The audience is drifting in.* LEOPOLD *spots the* PAINTER.) Here is the vantage point! (*He propels the* PAINTER *to the front.*) This also is a battle! And now it rains! She gets all he asks for! (*He pulls up his collar. Umbrellas go up.* KATRIN *appears, supported by the* MID-WIFE. *Silence descends. She looks into the crowd. Pause.*)

KATRIN: Not as many as I'd hoped. Don't they like a spectacle? Not the numbers I'd predicted, but — (*A spasm of pain doubles her. The* MIDWIFE *goes to assist her.* KATRIN *pushes her away.*) **Nobody help me birth the child**. (*Pause. She steadies herself.*) Can everybody see all right? Some people — over there — the view's restricted, surely? (*Pause. She stares into the audience.*)

> I bring you hope.
>
> I bring you History. (*She is doubled again. The* MIDWIFE *goes to assist but is repelled.*)
>
> **What are you** —

MIDWIFE: Only helping, lady —

KATRIN: No, that isn't it —

MIDWIFE: Helping —

KATRIN: **That's not what it is**. (*Pause. The* MIDWIFE *looks to* LEOPOLD, *to* ORPHULS.)

MIDWIFE: This is how we get in labour — all abusive, but we don't mean anything —

KATRIN: **I do mean something**.

MIDWIFE: I know darling, but — (*A further spasm.* KATRIN *staggers.*)

LEOPOLD: I can't watch this! (*He half-turns away.*) I can't watch this! Do something, somebody! (ORPHULS *goes to move, with the* MIDWIFE, *but* STARHEMBERG *blocks them, drawing a knife.*)

STARHEMBERG: I'll burst the spleen of anyone who nears her bed. (*A pause.*)

ORPHULS: She is delirious.

STARHEMBERG: She is lucid.

ORPHULS: She is in agony!

STARHEMBERG: Her pain she needs. Her suffering she requires. **No thieving by the compassionate!** (*Pause.* KATRIN *struggles on the bed.*)

LEOPOLD: Starhemberg, if she dies, you are responsible. (*Pause*)

MIDWIFE: You are in such a bad position, lady . . . !

KATRIN: Good! Let it find daylight through my arse!

MIDWIFE: You see, that's 'ow they go, let me —

STARHEMBERG (*threatening*):   Move and you die.

MIDWIFE: **I'm a woman, aren't I?**

ORPHULS: Starhemberg, you are under some awful curse . . . (*A cry from* KATRIN. *She clutches her belly.*)

LEOPOLD: **End this! I can't watch this!** (*Men, and the* MID-WIFE, *rush forward, overwhelming* STARHEMBERG, *who is disarmed and held.* KATRIN *is covered with umbrellas.* NUNS *drape the scene of birth. The* EMPRESS *appears.*)

EMPRESS (*going to* STARHEMBERG, *where he is still held*):   Starhemberg, was that real love? (*He looks at the ground.*) Not if love's caring, but maybe caring's base?

STARHEMBERG: They pretend to pity her, but they steal her pain. Don't chain her in some madhouse.

EMPRESS: It's you they wish to chain . . . (*She indicates with a move of her head that* STARHEMBERG *be released. A cry of joy and applause from the birth place.*)

LEOPOLD: It's over, and alive! (*A baby is handed to* LEO-POLD. *He holds it high.*) What History spoiled, let History mend. I christen her — Concilia! (*Applause. The baby is handed to a* SERVANT. LEOPOLD *and the* EMPRESS *depart.*)

ORPHULS (*to* STARHEMBERG): Come to Christ, now . . .

STARHEMBERG: I do. I come to you at all hours. I raise you from your bed and beg you reasons why I should love men.

ORPHULS: Christ also suffered the intensest hate, or He could never have found charity. The good have little purchase on the memory. Who would follow the innocent? No, you follow him who triumphs over himself, who boils within and in whose eyes all struggle rages. Him you follow to the water's edge, and no other . . . (*He kisses* STARHEMBERG's *hand.*)

KATRIN (*from the bed*): Starhemberg! (STARHEMBERG *turns to go to her.* ORPHULS *clings to his hand.*)

ORPHULS: I must become a bishop.

STARHEMBERG: You must, it's obvious. (*He goes to her.*)

KATRIN: It's perfect, isn't it? Quite perfect?

STARHEMBERG: No loving husband could have made a better child in sheets of wedded honour.

KATRIN: They cheated me . . .

STARHEMBERG: Yes.

KATRIN: And made of my horrors reconciliation.

STARHEMBERG: Yes.

KATRIN: **History they made of me**.

STARHEMBERG: Yes, but we will deny them yet . . .

KATRIN (*with a wail*): How . . . ? How . . . ? (*Pause, then* STARHEMBERG *walks away. The* MIDWIFE *accosts him.*)

MIDWIFE: You have some pain, mister . . .

STARHEMBERG: Pain? Me?

MIDWIFE: I think you will find death difficult.

STARHEMBERG: Yes. I won't have it near me.

MIDWIFE: You tease me, but I'd give you good advice if you would let me.

STARHEMBERG: Do! I like the fact your hands are caked in blood. So were mine until recently. (*The* MIDWIFE *goes close to him, intimately.*)

MIDWIFE: Hang yourself. (*Pause.* STARHEMBERG *nods, as if in appreciation. The* MIDWIFE *squeals with laughter. He seizes her hand. She senses danger.*)

STARHEMBERG: It's you that must hang.

MIDWIFE: Only a joke!

STARHEMBERG: Yes, but I have no sense of humour. (*The* EMPRESS *appears. The* MIDWIFE *hurries away, off.*)

EMPRESS: Starhemberg . . .

STARHEMBERG: She is a witch, the midwife. She must hang. (*Pause*)

EMPRESS: If you say so.

STARHEMBERG (*calling*): **Don't let her escape, there!**

EMPRESS: Starhemberg, your mother's dead ... (*He looks at her.*)

STARHEMBERG: Once they are in the slums, it takes a regiment to find them ... (*Pause.* ORPHULS *goes to* STAR-HEMBERG *and embraces him swiftly.*) Dead? But I hadn't finished with her yet ...

ORPHULS: We shall bury her ...

STARHEMBERG: I shall have to see her naked, shan't I? I shall have to wash her and she was not clean ...

ORPHULS: We'll bury your mother ...

STARHEMBERG: Together ...

ORPHULS: Yes ...

STARHEMBERG: And then, perhaps ... kill yours ... (*Pause. He departs.* ORPHULS *is left alone as night falls.*)

Scene Two

A plot in the city. ORPHULS *alone.* SUSANNAH *enters.*

SUSANNAH: I would lick you all over if you'd let me. I would take your testicles in my mouth and roll them gently as if they were blown eggs of such rarity, of such fragility. I would take your arse in my hands if you'd let me and raise it like a sacrifice, oh, listen, I must tell you I will marry somewhere else if you don't give me your flesh to love. An officer with four cows has made me a proposal. (*He turns to look at her.*)

ORPHULS: Marry him. (*Pause*)

SUSANNAH: I will. I will marry him.

ORPHULS (*turning away*): And lie awake whole wretched nights with your brain bursting. I will crouch in your imagination like a bear in a crate. I will pace there all your hours.

SUSANNAH: I will have children, whose wailing will drown out your memory.

ORPHULS: It's a tempting prospect, I can see, red-armed on the acre and a basketful of screamers. Is he drunk, this officer? Drunk and poxed? As he climbs on you to satisfy some savagery the cows will bellow in the downstairs room, what perfection! And how far from the city? They say there is rough pasture eighty miles outside Vienna where the old troopers are settling, though the bodies of the Janissaries must be cleared from it, **you cataclysmic bitch**, all you have will disintegrate in a single winter! (*He turns to others offstage.*) **Here!** (*He points to the earth. Cloaked figures enter with shovels.*) And not deep. (*They begin to excavate the spot.*)

SUSANNAH: What have you done . . . ?

WORKMAN: **Here!** (*They dig faster.*)

SUSANNAH: What have you done . . . !

ORPHULS: I shall inhabit you. I shall swim your veins and smile like a gargoyle from the walls of your womb . . .

SUSANNAH (*as LEOPOLD and others enter*):   What has he done! (ORPHULS *laughs as* SUSANNAH *runs off.*)

LEOPOLD: Not funny! Where?

WORKMAN: Here! (*The* EMPRESS *goes to look at the excavation.*)

LEOPOLD: Don't look! (*She persists.*) Hideous! Don't look! (*She ignores him.*) All right, look if you must. (LEOPOLD *goes to* ORPHULS.) Are you mad? **Cover the grave!** What is to become of Vienna? You want to be a bishop and you kill your mother, are you mad? **Cover it entirely!** We are building a new Europe and you do this, you are in love with Starhemberg, he eats your soul, you horrify me! (*The* EMPRESS *joins them.*) We must arrest him and declare him mad. What else do you suggest?

ORPHULS: I am not mad. I am perfectly normal, only more so.

LEOPOLD: **In what sense!**

ORPHULS: I was never more fitted for my task.

LEOPOLD: **What task!** (*He turns to the* EMPRESS.) He looks the perfect cleric, he exudes authority, who would not confess to him the most lurid sin and yet — (*He turns to* ORPHULS.) Do you want to be tried, is that what you want? Do you want to be hanged, is that what you want?

ORPHULS: Perhaps.

LEOPOLD: Perhaps? You require it, obviously!

ORPHULS: I require unhappiness, that's obvious.

EMPRESS: And this is such a happy age! There never was such happiness! All this happiness, and you go and bash your mother with a rock. Was it a rock?

ORPHULS: A plank.

EMPRESS: A plank. (LEOPOLD *groans*.)

ORPHULS: She placed no value on her life. It was a burden to her. Whereas her death meant much to me. So all things pointed to her extinction.

LEOPOLD: Especially Starhemberg! His finger, especially. I might have wished to kill my mother. What if I had, what should I have been!

ORPHULS: Excessively alive. (*He holds* LEOPOLD.) It is a second birth, and like the first, induces such a rush of air to unopened lungs, I struggled on the ground red as an infant, my unused limbs thrashing the air, and he carried me, he bore me home like the maternal nurse! There! (*He points*.) There is the site of my nativity! (*Pause*)

LEOPOLD: A new morality we asked for. And we get this.

ORPHULS: Feel me! I'm **new.**

LEOPOLD: Take your claw off me! You should shrivel in a furnace, and the skull, as it popped, should invite spontaneous applause!

EMPRESS: Oh, do be quiet —

LEOPOLD: **You say be quiet and —**

EMPRESS: Think. Think.

LEOPOLD: When I think of my mother —

EMPRESS: That is not thinking, is it? Stop generalising and think. (*She looks at* ORPHULS, *who smiles*.) What have you learned?

ORPHULS: Learned . . . ?

EMPRESS: Learned, yes, for neither you nor Starhemberg do things except for learning. Deliver us your sermon. Not on murder, but what came of it. Quick, now! And you! (*She calls to the workmen*.) Yes! Down your tools and gather, cluster the Bishop, who will speak, cluster him, he knows things you do not. (*She turns away, waiting. The men reluctantly form a circle.* ORPHULS *prepares, and then with the force of inspiration, turns to deliver his oration*.

ORPHULS: All that occurs, does it not occur that I should be its beneficiary, nourished on it, be it filth or excellence? Even the death of love is food to the soul and therefore what is evil? Is there evil except not to do? I do not blaspheme when I say the gift of life is paltry and our best service to

God is not to thank Him, endless thanking, no, but to
enhance His offer, and yet you do not, I think if I were God
I would declare with some weariness or even vehemence, how
little they do with the breath I gave them, they exhale
repetitions, they applaud the lie, they sleep even in their
waking hours, why did I make them thus, I erred in some
respect, they fill me with disgust, have you no notion of
God's horror? I am thinking of the God in us whose
profound groan is the background to our clatter — (*He
identifies one of the uncomprehending workmen.*) You shake
your head in silence, is that freedom? If silence was freedom
it is so no longer, the word is volatile, am I too difficult for
you? **Liar! You hide behind the so-called simplicity of Christ,
but is that not a blasphemy?** (*Pause*) If I had not done evil,
how could I address you who have perhaps thought evil
only? If I did not know cruelty could I know pity, they are
the twin towers of the soul? Do not hold hands in false
gestures as if by crowding you could exclude the groan of
God, no, you must hear the sound of His despair, and we
must learn from Judas whose Gospel is not written, we must
learn from him who stood alone, for Judas did not sell Christ
nor was he corrupt, but Judas was cruel for knowledge, and
without Judas there could be no resurrection, Beauty,
Cruelty, and Knowledge, these are the triple order of the
Groaning God, I speak as your adviser in whose pain you
may see beauty, I praise my beauty and you must praise
yours! (*Pause*) I end here, in a proper and terrible exhaustion. I have laid myself before you, which is the duty of a
priest. (*Pause*)

EMPRESS: How wonderful you are . . . I shall not forget one
word you said. How wonderful you are, I could truly love
you. But we can't know that, and you must die . . . mustn't
he? (*She looks at* LEOPOLD. *The bell of a great church.*)

Scene Three

A room in Vienna, shuttered. The bell ceases. Into the obscurity,
STARHEMBERG *walks slowly. He removes his clothing, item*

by item. He goes to a chair, and sits. KATRIN *is discovered, already naked, in a chair distantly opposite his own. They gaze, unfalteringly.*

KATRIN: I show myself to you. I show myself, and it is an act of love. Stay in your place!

STARHEMBERG: I was not moving. Only looking.

KATRIN: You were not moving, no . . . (*Pause*) I am in such a torment it would be an act of pity to approach me, pure pity, but you will not, will you? I know because you are not kind, thank God, you spare us kindness, and your body is quite grey, it is so far from perfect, spare us perfection also! You are a beautiful man, so beautiful my breath is stiff as mud to breathe, don't come near me.

STARHEMBERG: You shudder . . .

KATRIN: Yes, may I call you my love, whether or not you love me I must call you my love, **don't get up!**

STARHEMBERG: I shan't get up . . .

KATRIN: I am in the most beautiful Hell. Praise me a little, mutter me a bit, describe, describe for Christ in Heaven's sake, I could gnaw your knees to blood, and you mine, I know you could —

STARHEMBERG: Yes . . .

KATRIN: I would rather take one look from you than pulp a night in hopeless effort, there, I'm better now, much better . . . (*Pause*) It's odd, but though I have done all that suggested itself to me, I never looked at any man but you, I think. Looked, I mean. I never knew to look was love. (*Pause*)

        What do you see?

        What do you see? (SUSANNAH *enters, opening the shutters one by one.*)

SUSANNAH: My priest is dead. (*Pause. Light floods in.*)
        With all Vienna watching. (STARHEMBERG *and* KATRIN *are still.*)
        My priest is dead, and I am marrying a farmer. (*She freezes.*)
        Not difficult if you try. (*Pause, then* STARHEMBERG *rises, pulls a long coat over himself. A child's cries distantly.*)

STARHEMBERG: We are going to Wallachia.

SUSANNAH: Wallachia? Why?

STARHEMBERG: To inspect the forts.

SUSANNAH: What forts?

STARHEMBERG: Within whose compass New Europe is to
breathe. Under whose benign regard the vines may ripen
undisturbed, and marriages be blessed with endlessness . . .
(*He leans his head on* SUSANNAH's *shoulder.*)

KATRIN: Yes! Show me the frontier! I will study the trajectory of shells, and arcs, dead grounds and fields of fire, I have
Holbein, Durer, Montecucculi in my library! What don't I
know of wars! (*She pulls a gown over herself as a nurse enters
holding* CONCILIA, *crying and swaddled.* STARHEMBERG
goes to the nurse and takes the child in his arms.)

STARHEMBERG: And Concilia! Concilia, obviously! (*He
lifts her in the air. A fortress wall descends. The sound of
knocking on a door.*)

Scene Four

The fort in Wallachia. STARHEMBERG *alone, half-dressed.*

STARHEMBERG: Come in! (*An* OFFICER *enters.*)

OFFICER: There is a Turkish regiment two miles off.

STARHEMBERG: Whose?

OFFICER: Jemal Pasha's Lancers.

STARHEMBERG: Show Jemal my standard.

OFFICER: That's done already. We think it most unlikely
they will attack a fort.

STARHEMBERG: That's my opinion also. (*The* OFFICER
bows, goes to leave.) Tell Jemal I have a gift for him.
Hostages, safe conduct and the rest of it. (*The* OFFICER
bows and is about to leave when STARHEMBERG *grabs him
violently.*) Talk to me! Talk!

OFFICER: Talk . . . ?

STARHEMBERG: Yes, yes, my gorgeous one, lie down and
tell me your life.

OFFICER: Lie down?

STARHEMBERG: (*propelling him towards a chair*): There
— yes —

OFFICER: But that's your —

STARHEMBERG: My cot, yes, but you have it, you spread, you luxuriate, and off with lovely tunics —

OFFICER: I'm rather cold —

STARHEMBERG (*unbuttoning him*):   Forget the cold, and I will come to you as a child to a long-lost relative, I will place my head just — there — forget the cold, the cold is not our enemy —

OFFICER: No, I suppose —

STARHEMBERG: Not in the least our enemy, and tell me in a child-like way, for my infant ears, the beauty of your life . . . (*He lays his head in the* OFFICER's *lap, and draws his hand to his head.*)

OFFICER: Beauty of it . . .

STARHEMBERG: Yes, do —

OFFICER: I don't know that it's —

STARHEMBERG: Mmm . . .

OFFICER: That it's very —

STARHEMBERG: Mmm . . .

OFFICER: Beautiful — I wouldn't —

STARHEMBERG: No, no, make me adore you —

OFFICER: Well, I —

STARHEMBERG: Go on —

OFFICER: I er — I er —

STARHEMBERG: Mmm . . .

OFFICER: I was —

STARHEMBERG: Mmmm . . . ?

OFFICER: One of — seven children —

STARHEMBERG: Seven! Really? Seven?

OFFICER: And er — was born in Lombardy —

STARHEMBERG: Lombardy?

OFFICER: Yes — land of — er — many poplars there and — I can't remember much of it but —

STARHEMBERG: No, no, paint it! Paint it! Make me love you.

OFFICER: Poplars and — and —

STARHEMBERG: Say, do say . . . (*The* OFFICER *dries, holds his head in despair.*) Must. Must. (*The* OFFICER *is in agony.*) Must.

OFFICER (*with sudden invention*):   I got up one morning — before anybody else — I don't know why — got up and crept downstairs — the sun was brilliant and —

STARHEMBERG: Mmm . . .

OFFICER: Walked down the street — it's not true, this —
the streets were full of — were full of — horses!

STARHEMBERG: Mmmm . . .

OFFICER: A cavalry brigade were tethered there and — I
took one and unbridled it — and rode it — clattering across
a bridge — the water was all — chopped and sparkling with
sunlight — I rode and rode — up four hills and down four
valleys — and when the horse stopped, so did I and I — slid
off and —

STARHEMBERG: Yes —

OFFICER: And —

STARHEMBERG: Don't stop! Don't stop!

OFFICER: I saw — a — beautiful girl —

STARHEMBERG: Make it an old man.

OFFICER: What?

STARHEMBERG: An old man. Make it an old man, please.

OFFICER: This old man, and he —

STARHEMBERG: Yes —

OFFICER: He — er — (KATRIN *enters, silently. He observes her. She perches, silently, on a chair.*) He — er — had a
long beard — and —

STARHEMBERG: How long?

OFFICER: **Ridiculously long!**

STARHEMBERG: Are you sure?

OFFICER: Yes!

STARHEMBERG: Go on . . .

OFFICER: Which reached to the ground — and he took my
hand — and his hand was — bleeding —

STARHEMBERG: Why?

OFFICER: I don't know why — it was anyway and — I put
my little hand in his wet hand —

STARHEMBERG: Why though?

OFFICER: **Don't interrupt!** And led me — willingly — I did
not protest to a — a — (*His eyes meet* KATRIN's. *He
perseveres.*) well — which when I looked was —

STARHEMBERG: What was in the well?

OFFICER: I'm coming to that —

STARHEMBERG: Forgive me, I —

OFFICER: Was — absolutely —

STARHEMBERG: Yes? Yes?

OFFICER: **Full of bricks!**

STARHEMBERG: Bricks?

OFFICER: Full of bricks, why not bricks!

STARHEMBERG: No reason, I —

OFFICER: Bricks, yes —

STARHEMBERG: That was why his hands were bleeding!

OFFICER: Obviously!

STARHEMBERG: I do like you! I like you very much!

OFFICER: And these bricks were so deep and so jumbled —
so chaotic and so — arid —

STARHEMBERG: Yes —

OFFICER: They had caused the death of many animals . . .
(*Pause*) whose bodies . . . lay littered round the rim . . .

STARHEMBERG: They couldn't reach the —

OFFICER: Not a drip . . . (*Pause. He holds* STARHEM-
BERG's *hand*.)

STARHEMBERG: Go on . . .

OFFICER: And the old man begged me — No, he didn't beg
me, actually, he — insisted — most cruelly insisted that I —
unblock the well . . . And I was only ten . . .

STARHEMBERG: Ten . . .

OFFICER: And the sun beat down, and the smell of decom-
posing sheep was . . .

STARHEMBERG: Poor boy . . .

OFFICER: **Vile** and — I thought — climbing in all that
rubble thought — shifting the bricks, thought . . .

STARHEMBERG: What?

OFFICER: Many things, but — he was so severe — his ugly
face over the rim was going — **Faster! Faster!**

STARHEMBERG: Vile man —

OFFICER: Vile man, yes —

STARHEMBERG: Thirsty, too!

OFFICER: Yes, that must have been — partly the explanation for his vileness, but — I felt — his beard hung over —
hideous beard hanging right over — and I —

STARHEMBERG: Yes —

OFFICER: Instead of just throwing the bricks out I —

STARHEMBERG: **You didn't** —

OFFICER: Yes —

STARHEMBERG: **You hit him with the brick**. (*Long pause*.)
A terrible, terrible, story . . . (*Pause. The* OFFICER *gets up,
does up his tunic*.)

OFFICER: If I am to reach Jemal, I ought to . . . was that all
right?

STARHEMBERG: So you never drank?

OFFICER: What?

STARHEMBERG: You never drank . . .

OFFICER: I . . . no, I suppose not . . . no . . . (*He goes out.* STARHEMBERG *dresses in fresh clothes.*)

STARHEMBERG: Bring Concilia . . . Bring the child of impeccable origins . . .

KATRIN: It's late.

STARHEMBERG: Yes. Bring her from her little bed.

KATRIN (*puzzled*): Why . . . ?

STARHEMBERG: Concilia, whose forehead is a little swamp of Imperial kisses, and whose ears are tiny basins of kind sentiment . . . bring her here . . .

KATRIN: Why, Starhemberg?

STARHEMBERG (*finishing his dress*): Because we must love each other, now. (KATRIN *looks at him.*) I don't think she has ever seen the stars! (KATRIN *goes out. A cry is heard on the fortifications, which is repeated nearer.*)

THE WATCH: One bo — dy! One bo — dy! (*Pause, then a Turkish officer enters and stands.*)

STARHEMBERG: Why have your attacks all fallen off? You are good at rushing things but bad at standing under fire. Is that the personality of Turks, or the poor quality of officers? (*Pause*) And always you maim. Coolly, maim. This sickened me for some years, because I thought a cruel act done in temper has its own excuse, but this slow hacking has not even the decent motive of a butcher.

JEMAL: The ceaseless propoganda of the Christian church has stirred up subject races, some of whom we have convincing proof are cutting off parts of their bodies to discredit the Ottoman authorities.

STARHEMBERG: I think it is to do with fear of love. I think in the very moment of the cruellest torture, the perpitrator suffocates the possibility of freedom in himself. And thus it becomes habitual, a narcotic.

JEMAL: You persist in identifying me with all atrocity which is —

STARHEMBERG: No, no, I was merely being philosophical . . . (KATRIN *enters, holding the child in a shawl. She stops, horrified.* STARHEMBERG *looks at her.*) Oh, the great chaos of this continent. The beating of lives in the bowl of obscure quarrels, the batter of perpetual and necessary horror. Who would not be a European if he could? I have a present for Jemal. (*Pause*)

KATRIN: Starhemberg . . . (*Pause*)

STARHEMBERG: Yes. (*Pause*)

KATRIN: She wants to stay in Austria! (JEMAL *looks at* STARHEMBERG, *confused.*)

STARHEMBERG: Yes, but what has that to do with anything?

KATRIN: She loves us and —

SUSANNAH (*entering*): Shh . . . (KATRIN *looks with bewilderment, first at* SUSANNAH, *then at* STARHEMBERG.)

KATRIN: **I refuse whatever you are** —

SUSANNAH: Shh . . . (*Pause, then suddenly* KATRIN *attempts to leave with the child, but* STARHEMBERG *blocks her, holding her firmly. She is still.*)

KATRIN: Love? Did I say love?

JEMAL: This is a most unpleasant thing to witness in a State called civilized and I —

STARHEMBERG: The child's a Turk. (*Pause*)

JEMAL: A Turk?

STARHEMBERG: Of Turkish fathers whose untimely executions left her stranded in this foreign territory . . . (KATRIN *shudders.* STARHEMBERG *holds her closer.*) How do we escape from History? We reproduce its mayhem in our lives . . .

JEMAL: I refuse your gift!

STARHEMBERG: Refuse and you die. And my hostage officer, him too. (STARHEMBERG *takes the child from* KATRIN, *who is as if petrified. Suddenly she is seized by a physical delirium.* SUSANNAH *embraces her, overcomes her, stills her. She emerges, smiling, from the ordeal.*)

KATRIN: In any case, she might so easily have been seized in a raid.

STARHEMBERG (*giving the child to* JEMAL, *who hesitates*): It happens all the time . . . (*He holds the baby out.*) You will convert her to the true faith, obviously . . .

KATRIN: And who knows what might have befallen her if she stayed in Vienna? Smallpox? Carriage accidents? Anything! (JEMAL *takes the child.*) And in a year, it will be as if I never knew her! (*She looks at* JEMAL. *He returns her look, then turns on his heel and goes out. The cry of the sentries is heard.*)

THE WATCH: One bo — dy and a child! One bo — dy and a child!

KATRIN (*to* STARHEMBERG):   Look at me. What do you
see? (*He gazes at her. Suddenly, an eruption of fireworks,
explosions and coloured lights, cheering from the entire fort.
The* EMPRESS *enters with the court, in riding cloaks.*)

EMPRESS: Starhemberg, who never answers the Imperial
Despatch! Starhemberg, obscure in Wallachia! But we will
not be deprived! (*She embraces him.* LEOPOLD *enters.*)

LEOPOLD (*greeting* KATRIN):   The Mother! And the Child!
Where is the Child? (*He looks from* KATRIN *to* SUSAN-
NAH.) Concilia, where's she? (*A burst of fireworks.*)

SUSANNAH: She's been returned.

LEOPOLD: Returned?

KATRIN: To her creators. She's with them. (*The* EMPRESS
looks from KATRIN *to* STARHEMBERG.)

EMPRESS: Starhemberg —

KATRIN: He —

EMPRESS: Starhemberg . . . ?

KATRIN: Wait! (*A firework trickles down the sky.*) Let me
finish it. (*She speaks with infinite calculation.*) He has —
made — restitution — of — their property — (*Pause*) for
which — I — merely was — (*Pause. She grins.*) Curator . . .
(*She grips* LEOPOLD *by the arm. He is horrified.*) Congratulate me!

LEOPOLD: Concilia . . . !

KATRIN: Congratulate me, then!

LEOPOLD: **Con — cil — ia!**
Con — cil — ia! (*Lights rise and fall.* KATRIN
walks unsteadily to STARHEMBERG. *They
embrace. They kiss.*)
I laugh!
I laugh!

WOMEN BEWARE WOMEN

CHARACTERS

LEANTIO	A Factor
BIANCA	His Wife
THE WIDOW	His Mother
GUARDIANO	Uncle to the Ward
FABRITIO	Father to Isabella
LIVIA	His Sister
ISABELLA	His Daughter
HIPPOLITO	Her Uncle
WARD	A Rich Young Heir
SORDIDO	His Man
DUKE OF FLORENCE	
LORD CARDINAL	His Brother
MESSENGER	
MAN	A Passer-by

PART ONE

Scene One

LEANTIO *with* BIANCA *and the* WIDOW.

WIDOW: Thy sight was never yet more precious to me! Welcome, with all the affection of a mother, that comfort can express from natural love! Since thy birth joy, thou wast not more dear to me than this hour presents thee to my heart!

LEANTIO: Alas, poor affectionate soul, how her joys speak to me! I have observed it often, and I know it is the fortune commonly of knavish children to have the loving'st mothers.

WIDOW: What's this gentlewoman?

LEANTIO: Oh, you have named the most undervalued'st purchase, that youth of man had ever knowledge of! As often as I look upon that treasure, and know it to be mine, it joys me that I ever was ordained to have a being, and to live amongst men! I must confess I am guilty of one sin, mother, more than I brought into the world with me; but that I glory in; 'tis theft, but noble as ever greatness yet shot up withal.

WIDOW: How's that?

LEANTIO: Never to be repented, mother, though sin be death! Do you now behold her! Look on her well, she's mine: look on her better! Now, say, if it be not the best piece of theft that ever was committed. And I have my pardon for it. 'Tis sealed from Heaven by marriage.

WIDOW: Married to her!

LEANTIO: You must keep council, mother, I am undone else. If it be known, I have lost her. From Venice her consent and I have brought her, from parents great in wealth, more now in rage; but let storms spend their furies. Now we have got a shelter over our quiet innocent loves, we are contented.

Little money she has brought me, view but her face, you may see all her dowry, save that which lies locked up in hidden virtues, like jewels kept in cabinets.

WIDOW: You know not what you have done. What ableness have you to do her right, in maintenance fitting her birth and virtues, which every woman of necessity looks for, and most to go above it, not confined by their conditions, bloods or births, but flowing to affections, wills and humours?

LEANTIO: Speak low, sweet mother; you are able to spoil as many as come within the hearing. I pray do not you teach her to rebel, when she's in a good way to obedience. I'll prove an excellent husband — here's my hand — lay in provision, follow my business roundly, and make you a grandmother in forty weeks! Go, pray salute her, bid her welcome cheerfully.

WIDOW: Gentlewoman, thus much is a debt of courtesy. (*She kisses* BIANCA.) And now, salute you by the name of daughter, which may challenge more than ordinary respect. (*She kisses her again.*)

BIANCA: Well, this is well now, and I think few mothers of three score will mend it.

WIDOW: What I can bid you welcome to is mean; but make it all you own. We are full of wants and cannot welcome worth.

LEANTIO: Now this is scurvy! These old folks talk of nothing but defects, because they grow so full of them themselves!

BIANCA: Kind mother, there is nothing can be wanting to her that does enjoy all her desires. I have forsook friends, fortunes, and my country, and hourly I rejoice in it. I'll call this place the place of my birth now — and rightly, too, for here my love was born, and that's the birthday of a woman's joy. (*To* LEANTIO.) You have not bid me welcome since I came . . .

LEANTIO: That I did, questionless.

BIANCA: No sure, how was it? I have quite forgot it.

LEANTIO: Thus. (*He kisses her.*)

BIANCA: Oh, sir, 'tis true, now I remember well; I have done thee wrong, pray take it again, sir. (*She kisses him.*)

LEANTIO: How many of these wrongs could I put up with in an hour? and turn up the glass for twice as many more!

BIANCA: Thanks, sweet mother; the voice of her that bore me is not more pleasing. (*They go in.*)

LEANTIO: Though my own care and my rich master's trust lay their commands both on my factorship, this day and night I'll know no other business but her and her dear welcome. It is a bitterness to think upon tomorrow, that I must leave her still to the sweet hopes of the week's end. Oh, melancholy Florence! Dist thou but know what a most matchless jewel thou art now mistress of, a pride would take thee able to shoot destruction through the bonds of all thy youthful sons! But 'tis great policy to keep choice treasures in obscurest places; should we show thieves our wealth 'twould make them bolder. The jewel is cased up from all men's eyes; who could imagine now a gem were kept, of that great value, under this plain roof? Old mothers know the world, and such as these, when sons lock chests, are good to look to keys.

Scene Two

GUARDIANO, FABRITIO, LIVIA.

GUARDIANO: Has your daughter seen him yet?

FABRITIO: No matter, she shall love him.

GUARDIANO: Nay, let's have fair play! He has been now my ward some fifteen year, and it is my purpose, as time calls upon me, to tender him a wife. Now, sir, this wife I'd fain elect out of a daughter of yours. You see, my meaning's fair. If now this daughter, so tendered, should offer to refuse him —

FABRITIO: I still say she shall love him.

GUARDIANO: Yet again? And shall she have no reason for this love?

FABRITIO: Why, do you think that women love with reason? I had a wife. She ran mad for me. She had no reason for it aught I could perceive. What do you think, lady sister? You're an experienced widow.

LIVIA: I must offend you, then, if truth will do it, and take my niece's part, and call it injustice to force her to love one she never saw. Maids should both see and like — all little enough. If they love truly after that, 'tis well. She takes one man till death, that's a hard task, I tell you.

FABRITIO: Why, is not man tied to the same observance, lady sister, and in one woman?

LIVIA: 'Tis enough for him. Besides, he tastes of many dishes that we poor wretches never lay our lips to — as obedience, subjection, duty and such kickshaws, all of our making, but served into them; and if we lick a finger then, sometimes, we are not to blame. Your best cooks use it.

FABRITIO: Thou art a sweet lady, sister, and a witty.

LIVIA: A witty! Oh, the bud of commendation, fit for a girl of sixteen! I am blown, man! I should be wise by this time. I have buried my two husbands in good fashion, and never mean more to marry.

GUARDIANO: No, why so, lady?

LIVIA: Because the third shall never bury me. I think I am more than witty. How think you, sir?

FABRITIO: I have often paid fees to a counsellor had a weaker brain.

LIVIA: Then I must tell you, your money was soon parted. Where is my niece? If you have any hope 'twill prove a wedding, 'tis fit she should have one sight of him.

FABRITIO: Look out her uncle, and you are sure of her. Those two are never asunder. They've been heard in argument at midnight, moonshine nights are noondays with them, they walk out their sleeps. They're like a chain, draw but one link, all follows. (HIPPOLITO, ISABELLA *enter*.)

GUARDIANO: Oh affinity, what piece of excellent workmanship art thou? It's work clean wrought, for there's no lust but love in it, and that abundantly, when in stranger things, there is no love at all but what lust brings . . .

FABRITIO (*to* ISABELLA): On with your mask, for it's your part to see now, and not be seen. See what you mean to like — nay, and I charge you — like what you see. Do you hear me? There's no dallying. The gentleman's almost twenty, and it's time he was getting lawful heirs, and you abreeding on 'em.

ISABELLA: Good father!

FABRITIO: Tell me not of tongues and rumours! You'll say the gentleman is somewhat simple — the better for a hus-

band, were you wise, for those that marry fools live ladies'
lives. On with the mask, I'll hear no more. He's rich, the
fool's hid under bushels.

LIVIA: Not so hid, neither, but here's a great foul piece
of him, methinks, what will he be when he comes altogether?
(*Enter* WARD *and* SORDIDO, *with trapsticks.*)

WARD: Beat him? I beat him out the field with his own
catstick, yet gave him the first hand!

SORDIDO: Oh, strange . . . !

WARD: I did it, then he set jacks on me.

SORDIDO: What, my lady's tailor?

WARD: Ay and I beat him, too!

SORDIDO: Nay, that's no wonder, he's used to beating . . .

WARD: I tickled him when I came once to my tippings!

SORDIDO: Now you talk on 'em, there was a poulterer's
wife made a great complaint of you last night to your
guardiner, that you struck a bump in her child's head as big
as an egg!

WARD: An egg may prove a chicken, then in time the
poulterer's wife will get by it. When I am in game I am
furious; came my mother's eyes in my way I would not
lose a fair end! No, were she alive with but one tooth in
her head, I should venture the striking out of that!
Coads me, my guardiner! Prithee lay up my cat and catstick
safe!

GUARDIANO: Ward!

WARD: I feel myself after any exercise horribly prone . . . let
me but ride, I'm lusty — a cock-horse straight, in faith!

GUARDIANO: Ward! I must new school you!

WARD: School me? I scorn that now, I am past schooling. I
am not so base to learn to read and write, I was born to
better fortunes in my cradle. (GUARDIANO, SORDIDO,
WARD *go out.*)

FABRITIO: How do you like him, girl? This is your husband.

LIVIA: Oh, soft there, brother! Though you be a justice, your
warrant cannot be served out of your territory. You may
compel, out of the power of a father, things merely harsh to
a maid's flesh and blood, but when you come to love, there
the soil alters.

FABRITIO: Marry him she shall then; let her agree upon
love afterwards. (*He goes out.* LIVIA *kisses* HIPPOLITO *on
the cheek.*)

LIVIA: Prithee, cheer up thy niece with special counsel ...
(*She goes out.*)

HIPPOLITO: I would 'twere fit to speak to her what I would,
but 'twas not a thing ordained, Heaven has forbid it. Feed
inward, you my sorrows, make no noise; consume me silent,
let me be stark dead ere the world know I'm sick ...

ISABELLA: Marry a fool! Oh, the heartbreakings of miserable maids, where love's enforced! The best condition is but
bad enough — when women have their choices, commonly
they do but buy their thraldoms, and bring great portions to
men to keep 'em in subjection. Men buy their slaves, but
women buy their masters. What, are you sad too, uncle?
'Faith, then there's a whole household down together; where
shall I seek my comfort now, when my best friend's dis-
tressed? What is it afflicts you sir?

HIPPOLITO: 'Faith, nothing but one grief that will not leave
me.

ISABELLA: Oh, be cheered, sweet uncle, how long has it
been upon you? I never spied it! How long, I pray, sir?

HIPPOLITO: Since I first saw you, niece, and left Bologna.

ISABELLA: And could you deal so unkindly with my heart,
to keep it up so long hid from my pity?

HIPPOLITO: You of all creatures, niece, must never hear on
it. 'Tis not a thing ordained for you to know.

ISABELLA: Not I, sir! All my joys that word cuts off! You
made profession once you loved me best — 'twas but profession!

HIPPOLITO: Yes, I do it truly, and fear I shall be chid for
it. Know the worst, then. I love thee dearlier than an uncle
can.

ISABELLA: Why, so you ever said, and I believed it!

HIPPOLITO: So simple is the goodness of her thoughts they
understand not yet the unhallowed language of a sinner. I
must be forced to come nearer. As a man loves his wife, so I
love thee.

ISABELLA: What's that? Methought I heard ill news come
towards me, which commonly we hear too soon. It shall
never come so near mine ear again. Farewell all friendly
solaces and discourses, I'll learn to live without ye, for your
dangers are greater than your comforts! (*She goes out.*)

Scene Three

LEANTIO.

LEANTIO: Methinks I'm even as dull now at departure as
men observe great gallants the next day after a revels; you
shall see 'em look much of my fashion, if you mark 'em well.
'Tis even a second hell to part from pleasure when man has
got a smack of it. (BIANCA *and the* WIDOW *enter, above.*)
I have no power to go now and I should be hanged. Farewell
all business! I desire no more than I see yonder. Let the
goods at quay look to themselves, why should I toil my
youth out? Oh, fie, what a religion have I leaped into! Get
out again, for shame! The man loves best when his care's
most — that show his zeal to love. Good to make sport when
the chest's full and the long warehouse cracks.

BIANCA: I perceive, sir, you are not gone yet. I have good
hope you'll stay now.

LEANTIO: Farewell, I must not.

BIANCA: Come, come pray return. Tomorrow, adding but a
little care more, will despatch all as well — believe me, it will, sir.

LEANTIO: I could well wish myself where you would have
me; but love that's wanton must be ruled awhile by love
that's careful, or all goes to ruin.

BIANCA: But this one night, I prithee . . .

LEANTIO: Alas, I'm in for twenty if I stay. Again, farewell
to thee . . .

BIANCA: Since it must, farewell, too . . . (LEANTO *goes
out.*)

WIDOW: 'Faith, daughter, you are to blame. You take the
course to make him an ill husband, troth you do, and that
disease is catching, I can tell you. What cause have you to
weep? Would that I had no more, that have lived threescore
years! His absence cannot last five days at utmost. (*Enter
applauding crowd.*)

BIANCA (*recovering*): What's the meaning of this hurry, can
you tell, mother?

WIDOW: What a memory I have! I see by that years come
upon me. Why 'tis a yearly custom and solemnity, religiously
observed by the duke and state to St Mark's Temple, the
fifteenth of April. See if my dull brains had not quite forgot
it! I would not be ten years younger again that you had lost

the sight. Now you shall see our duke, a goodly gentleman of his years.

BIANCA: Is he old, then?

WIDOW: About fifty-five.

BIANCA: That's no great age in a man. He's then at best for wisdom and for judgement.

WIDOW: You shall behold all our chief states of Florence. Take this stool. (DUKE *enters, with* CARDINAL *and* HIPPOLITO.)

DUKE (*to* CARDINAL):   Brother, what is it commands your eye so powerfully? Speak, you seem lost!

CARDINAL: The thing I look on seems so. To my eyes lost forever.

DUKE: You look on me.

CARDINAL: What grief it is to a religious feeling to think a man should have a friend so goodly, so wise, so noble, nay, a duke, a brother, and all this certainly damned!

DUKE (*seeing,* BIANCA, *stops, stares up*). How?

CARDINAL: 'Tis no wonder, if your great sin can do it. Dare you sleep, for fear of never waking but to death? And dedicate upon a strumpet's love the strength of your affections, zeal, and health? I shall show you how more unfortunate you stand in sin than the low private man. All his offences, like enclosed grounds, keep but about himself and seldom stretch his own soul's bounds, but great man, every sin thou commit'st shows like a flame upon a mountain, 'tis seen far about, and with a big wind made of popular breath, the sparkles fly through cities!

DUKE (*still gazing up*):   If you have done, I have. No more, sweet brother . . .

CARDINAL: I know time spent in goodness is too tedious. How dare you venture on eternal pain that cannot bear a minute's reprehension? Oh, my brother, what were you, if you were taken now! Think upon it, brother! Can you come so near it for a fair strumpet's love, and fall into a torment that knows neither end nor bottom?

DUKE (*tearing his eyes away, looking to* CARDINAL):   Brother of spotless honour, let me weep the first of my repentance on thy bosom, and show the blest fruits of a thankful spirit. And if I ever keep a woman more unlawfully, may I want penitence at my greatest need . . . (*The* CARDINAL *smiles with joy, kisses his hand. With a parting glance at* BIANCA, THE DUKE *moves on.*)

WIDOW: How like you, daughter?
BIANCA: Methinks my soul could dwell upon the reverence
  of such a solemn and most worthy custom. Did not the duke
  look up? Methought he saw us.
WIDOW: That's everyone's conceit that sees a duke!
BIANCA: Most likely so.
WIDOW: Come, come, we'll end this argument below!

Scene Four

HIPPOLITO, LIVIA.

LIVIA: A strange affection, brother, when I think on't! I
  wonder how thou camest by it.
HIPPOLITO: Even as easily as man comes by destruction,
  which oft-times he wears in his own bosom.
LIVIA: Is the world so populous in women, and creation so
  progidal in beauty and so various, yet does love turn thy
  point to thine own blood? 'Tis somewhat too unkindly. Must
  thy eye dwell evily on the fairness of thy kindred, and seek
  not where it should?
HIPPOLITO: Never was man's misery so soon sewed up.
LIVIA: Nay, I love you so, that I shall venture much to keep
  a change from you so fearful as this grief will bring upon
  you. Let not passion waste the goodness of thy time and of
  thy fortune. I can bring forth as pleasant fruits as sensuality
  wishes in all her teeming longings. This I can do.
HIPPOLITO: Oh, nothing that can make my wishes perfect . . .
LIVIA: Sir, I could give as shrewd a lift to chastity as any she
  that wears a tongue in Florence. She'd need to be a good
  horsewoman and sit fast whom my strong argument could
  not fling at last.
HIPPOLITO: I am past hope.
LIVIA: You are not the first, brother, has attempted things
  more forbidden than this seems to be. Thou shalt see me do
  a strange cure as ever was wrought on a disease so mortal
  and near akin to shame. When shall you see her?

HIPPOLITO: Never in comfort more.

LIVIA: You're so impatient, too.

HIPPOLITO: Will you believe — 'death, she has forsworn my company, and sealed it with a blush.

LIVIA: So, I perceive, all lies upon my hands, then. The more glory when the work's finished. (*She kisses him.*) Your absence, gentle brother. I must bestir my wits for you.

HIPPOLITO: Ay, to great purpose. (*He goes out.*)

LIVIA: I take a course to pity him so much now, that I have none left for modesty and myself. This 'tis to grow so liberal — you have few sisters that love their brother's ease above their own honesties. (*Enter* ISABELLA.) Niece, your love's welcome. Alas, what draws that paleness to thy cheeks? This enforced marriage?

ISABELLA: It helps, good aunt, amongst some other griefs.

LIVIA: Indeed, the ward is simple.

ISABELLA: Simple! That were well! Why, one might make good shift with such a husband. But he's a fool entailed, he halts downright in it.

LIVIA: And knowing this, I hope 'tis at your choice to take or refuse, niece.

ISABELLA: You see it is not. I loathe him more than beauty can hate death.

LIVIA: Let it appear, then.

ISABELLA: How can I, being born with that obedience that must submit unto a father's will?

LIVIA: Be not offended, prithee, if I set by the name of niece awhile, and bring in pity in a stranger fashion. It lies here in this breast, would cross this match.

ISABELLA: How, cross it, aunt?

LIVIA: Ay, and give thee more liberty than thou hast reason yet to apprehend.

ISABELLA: Sweet aunt, in goodness keep not hid from me what may befriend my life.

LIVIA: Yes, yes, I must when I return to reputation, and think upon the solemn vow I made to your dead mother, my most loving sister . . . 'twas a secret I have took special care of, delivered by your mother on her deathbed — that's nine years now, and I'll not part from it yet, though never was fitter time nor greater cause for it!

ISABELLA: As you desire the praise of a virgin!

LIVIA: Good sorrow! I would do thee any kindess! (*Pause, she seems to suffer.*) Let it suffice, you may refuse this fool, or you may take him as you see occasion. You cannot be enforced.

ISABELLA: Sweet aunt, deal plainer.

LIVIA: Say I should trust you now upon an oath, and give you in a secret that would start you. How am I sure of you, in faith and silence?

ISABELLA: Equal assurance may I find in mercy, as you for that in me.

LIVIA: It shall suffice. Then know, however custom has made good, for reputation's sake, the names of niece and aunt 'twixt you and I, we are nothing less.

ISABELLA: How's that?

LIVIA: I told you I should start your blood. You are no more allied to any of us than the merest stranger is, or one begot at Naples when the husband lies at Rome. Did never the report of that famed Spaniard, Marquess of Coria, since your time was ripe for understanding, fill your ear with wonder?

ISABELLA: Yes, what of him? I have heard his deeds of honour often related when we lived in Naples.

LIVIA: You heard the praises of your father, then.

ISABELLA: My father!

LIVIA: That was he. But all the business so carefully and so discreetly carried that fame received no spot by it, not a blemish. How weak his commands now, whom you call father? How vain all his enforcements, your obedience? And what a largeness in your will and liberty to take or reject, or to do both? For fools will serve to father wise men's children — all this you have time to think on. Oh, my wench, nothing overthrows our sex but indiscretion! But keep your thoughts to yourself, from all the world, kindred or dearest friend — nay, I entreat you, from him that all this while you have called uncle; and though you love him dearly, as I know his deserts claim as much even from a stranger, yet let not him know this, I prithee do not.

ISABELLA: Believe my oath, I will not.

LIVIA: Why, well said . . . (*She turns to go.*) Who shows more craft to undo a maidenhead, I'll resign my part to her. (HIPPOLITO *comes in.*) She's thine own, go. (LIVIA *goes out.*)

ISABELLA: Have I passed so much time in ignorance, and never had the means to know myself till this blest hour! Thanks to her virtuous pity that brought it now to light —

would I had known it but one day sooner, he had then received in favours what, poor gentleman, he took in bitter words! (*She turns to* HIPPOLITO.) Prithee, forgive me. I did but chide in jest; the best loves use it sometimes, it sets an edge upon affection. When we invite our best friends to a feast, 'tis not all sweet meats that we set before them, there's somewhat sharp and salt both to what the appetite and make 'em taste their wine well. So, methinks, after a friendly, sharp and savoury chiding, a kiss tastes wondrous well and full of the grape — (*She kisses him.*) How thinks't thou, does't not?

HIPPOLITO: 'Tis so excellent, I know not how to praise it, what to say to it!

ISABELLA: The marriage shall go forward.

HIPPOLITO: With the ward? Are you in earnest?

ISABELLA: Should my father provide a worse fool yet I'd have him either. The worse the better. So discretion love me, desert and judgement, I have content sufficient. Pray make your love no stranger, sir, that's all. (*She goes out.*)

HIPPOLITO: Never came joys so unexpectedly to meet desires in man. How came she thus? But I'm thankful for it. This marriage now must of necessity go forward, it is the only veil wit can devise to keep our acts hid from sin-piercing eyes.

Scene Five

GUARDIANO *and* LIVIA.

LIVIA: How, sir, a gentlewoman so young, so fair, as you set forth, spied from the widow's window?

GUARDIANO: She!

LIVIA: Our Sunday-dinner woman?

GUARDIANO: And Thursday-supper woman, the same still. I know not how she came by her, but I'll swear she's the prime gallant for a face in Florence, and no doubt other parts follow their leader. The duke himself first spied her at the window, then in a rapture, as if admiration were poor when it were single, beckoned me, and pointed to the wonder warily. I never knew him so infinitely taken with a woman, nor can I blame his appetite, she's a creature able to draw a state from serious business. What course shall we devise? He has spoken twice now.

LIVIA: Twice? I long myself to see this absolute creature that wins the heart of love and praise so much.

GUARDIANO: Shall you entreat her company? I would 'twere done, the duke waits the good hour, and I wait the good fortune that may spring from it. (FABRITIO *comes in.*) Signor Fabritio!

FABRITIO: Oh, sir, I bring an alteration in my mouth now! My daughter loves him.

GUARDIANO: What, does she, sir?

FABRITIO: No talk but of the ward, she would have him to choose 'above all men she ever saw.

GUARDIANO: Why, then sir, if you'll have me speak my thoughts, I smell 'twill be a match.

FABRITIO: Ay, and a sweet young couple if I have any judgement.

GUARDIANO: Let her be sent tomorrow before noon, and handsomely tricked up.

FABRITIO: I warrant you for handsome. I will see her things laid ready, every one in order, and have some part of her tricked up tonight. 'Twas a use her mother had when invited to an early wedding; she'ld dress her head o'ernight, sponge up herself, and give her neck three lathers.

GUARDIANO: Ne'er a halter?

FABRITIO: On with her chain of pearl, her ruby bracelets, lay ready all her tricks and jiggambobs.

GUARDIANO: So must her daughter. (FABRITIO *goes out.*)

LIVIA: How he sweats in the foolish zeal of fatherhood ... and here comes his sweet son-in-law that shall be. They're both allied in wit before the marriage, what will they be hereafter, when they are nearer? (*She goes out.*)

The WARD *and* SORDIDO *enter, with shuttlecocks and battledores.*

GUARDIANO: Now, young heir!

WARD: What's the next business after shuttlecock?

GUARDIANO: Tomorrow you shall see the gentlewoman must be your wife.

WARD: There's even another thing too must be kept up with a pair of battledores. My wife! What can she do?

GUARDIANO: Nay, that's a question you should ask yourself, ward, when you're alone together.

WARD: That's as I list! A wife's to be asked anywhere, I hope. I'll ask her in a congregation, if I have a mind to it, and so save a licence.

SORDIDO: Let me be at the choosing of your beloved, if you desire a woman of good parts.

WARD: Thou shalt, sweet Sordido!

SORDIDO: I have a plaguey guess. Let me alone to see what she is. If I but look upon her — 'way, I know all the faults to a hair you may refuse her for.

WARD: Dost thou? I prithee let me hear 'em, Sordido.

SORDIDO: Well, mark 'em then. I have 'em all in rhyme.

> The wife your gardener ought to tender
> Should be pretty, straight and slender;
> Her hair not short, her foot not long,
> Her hand not huge, not too loud her tongue;
> No pearl in eye nor ruby in her nose,
> No burn or cut but what the catalogue shows.
> She must have teeth, and that no black ones,
> And kiss most sweet when she does smack once;
> Her skin must be both white and plumpt,
> Her body straight, not hopper rumped,
> Or wriggle sideways like a crab.
> She must be neither slut nor drab,
> Nor go too splay-foot with her shoes
> To make her smock lick up the dews.
> And two things more which I forgot to tell ye;
> She neither must have bump in back nor belly.

These are the faults which will not make her pass.

WARD: And if I spy not these am I a rank ass!

SORDIDO: You should see her naked, for that's the ancient order.

WARD: See her naked? That were good sport, in faith, but stay! How if she should desire to see me so too? I were in a sweet case, then; such a foul skin!

SORDIDO: But you have a clean shirt, sir, and that makes amends.

WARD: 'Faith, choosing of a wench in a huge farthingale is like buying of ware under a great penthouse; what with the deceit of one, and the false light of the other, mark my speeches, he may have a diseased wench in his bed, and rotten stuff in his breeches! (*They whoop with laughter, go out.*)

LIVIA (*entering with the* WIDOW): Widow, come, come! I have a great quarrel to you, 'faith, I must chide you, that you must be sent for! You cannot be more welcome to any house in Florence.

WIDOW: My thanks must needs acknowledge so much, madam.

LIVIA: I sit here sometimes whole days without company! I know you are alone, too, why should we not we, like two kind neighbours, then, supply the wants of one another, having tongue-discourse, experience in the world, and such kind helps to laugh down time, and meet age merrily?

WIDOW: Age, madam! You speak mirth. 'Tis at my door, but long journey from your ladyship yet.

LIVIA: My faith, I'm nine and thirty, every stroke, wench, and 'tis a general observation, wives or widows, we account ourselves then old, when young men's eyes leave looking at us. Come, now, I have thy company I'll not part with it till after supper.

WIDOW: Yes, I must crave pardon, madam —

LIVIA: I swear you shall stay supper.

WIDOW: Some other time I will make bold —

GUARDIANO: No, pray stay, widow.

LIVIA: Faith, she shall not go. Do you think I'll be forsworn? (*She brings table and chess.*)

WIDOW: 'Tis a great while till supper time. I'll take my leave then now, madam, and come again in the evening —

LIVIA: In the evening! By my troth, wench, you have great business, sure, to sit alone at home! I wonder strangely what pleasure you take in it! Come, we'll to chess or draughts; there are an hundred tricks to drive out time till supper, never fear.

WIDOW: I'll make but one step home and return straight, madam.

LIVIA: I'll not trust you, you use more excuses to your kind friends than ever I knew any! What business can you have, if you be sure you have locked the door?

WIDOW: As good as tell her now, then, for she will know. I have always found her a most friendly lady. (*She turns to* LIVIA.) To tell you truth. I left a gentlewoman sitting all alone, which is uncomfortable, especially to young bloods.

LIVIA: What gentlewoman? Pish! Another excuse!

WIDOW: Wife to my son indeed, but not known, madam, to any but yourself.

LIVIA: Now I beshrew you! Could you be so unkind to her and me, to come and not bring her?

WIDOW: I feared to be too bold. And she's a stranger, madam.

LIVIA: The more should be her welcome. Make some amends, and fetch her, go.

WIDOW (*rising to go*): It must be carried wondrous privately from my son's knowledge; he'll break out in storms else.

LIVIA: Now comes in the heat of your part.

GUARDIANO: True, I know it, lady, and if I be out, may the duke banish me from all employments, wanton or serious. (BIANCA *comes in, curtsies.*)

LIVIA: Gentlewoman, you are most welcome, trust me, you are, as courtesy can make one, or respect due to the presence of you.

BIANCA: I give you thanks, lady.

LIVIA: I heard you were alone, and it had appeared an ill condition in me to have kept your company from you and left you all solitary. (*To the* WIDOW.) Come widow — look you, lady, here's our business. Are we not well employed, think you? An old quarrel between us, that will never be at an end. I pray, sit down forsooth, if you have the patience to look upon two weak and tedious gamesters . . .

GUARDIANO: 'Faith, madam, set these by till evening. The gentlewoman, being a stranger, would take more delight to see your rooms and pictures.

LIVIA: Marry, good sir, and well remembered! I beseech you show 'em her, that will beguile time well. Here, take these keys, show her the monument too — and that's a thing everyone sees not, you can witness that, widow!

MOTHER: And that's a worth sight indeed, madam.

BIANCA: Kind lady, I fear I came to be a trouble to you, and to this courteous gentleman that wears a kindess in his breast so noble and bounteous.

GUARDIANO: If you but give acceptance to my service, you do the greatest grace and honour to me that courtesy can merit.

BIANCA: I pray you lead, sir.

LIVIA: After a game or two, we are for you, gentlefolks . . . (BIANCA *and* GUARDIANO *go out.* LIVIA *plays chess.*) Alas, poor widow, I shall be too hard for thee.

WIDOW: You're cunning at the game, I'll be sworn, madam
. . .

LIVIA: It will be found so, ere I give you over . . . She that
can place her man well . . .

WIDOW: As you do, madam . . .

LIVIA: As I shall, wench, can never lose her game. Nay, nay,
the black king's mine.

WIDOW: Cry you mercy, madam.

LIVIA: And this my queen.

WIDOW: I see it now.

LIVIA: Here's a duke will strike a sure stroke for the game
anon; your pawn cannot come back to relieve itself.

WIDOW: I know that, madam.

LIVIA: You play well the whilst. How she belies her skill. I
give you check and mate to your white king, simplicity itself.

WIDOW: Well, ere now, lady, I have seen the fall of subtlety.
Jest on! What remedy but patience! (GUARDIANO *and*
BIANCA, *above*.)

BIANCA: Trust me, sir, mine eye never met with fairer
ornaments.

GUARDIANO: Nay, livelier, I'm persuaded, neither
Florence nor Venice can produce.

BIANCA: Sir, my opinion takes your part highly.

GUARDIANO: There's a better piece yet, than all these . . .
(*Enter unseen the* DUKE.)

BIANCA: Not possible, sir!

GUARDIANO: Believe it. You'll say so when you see it.
Turn but your eye now. (*He goes out.*)

BIANCA: Oh, sir!

DUKE: He's gone, beauty! Pish, not look after him, he's but
a vapour that when the sun appears is seen no more.

BIANCA: Oh, treachery to honour!

DUKE: Prithee, tremble not. I feel thy breast shake like a
turtle panting under a loving hand that makes much on't.
Why art so fearful? As I'm friend to brightness, there's
nothing but respect and honour near thee. You know me,
you have seen me; here's a heart can witness I've seen thee.

BIANCA: The more's my danger.

DUKE: The more's my happiness. Pish, strive not, sweet!
This strength were excellent employed in love, now, but here
'tis spent amiss. Strive not to seek thy liberty and keep me
still in prison.

BIANCA: Oh, my lord!

DUKE: Take warning, I beseech thee. Thou seem'st to me a
creature so composed of gentleness I should be sorry the
least force should lay an unkind touch upon thee.

BIANCA: Oh, my extremity! My Lord, what seek you?

DUKE: Love.

BIANCA: 'Tis gone already, I have a husband.

DUKE: That's a single comfort. Take a friend to him.

BIANCA: That's a double mischief, or else there's no religion.

DUKE: Do not tremble at fears of thine own making.

BIANCA: Nor great lord, make me not bold with death and
deeds of ruin because they fear not you.

DUKE: Sure, I think thou know'st the way to please me. I
affect a passionate pleading above an easy yielding — but
never pitied any. They deserve none that will not pity me. I
can command. Think upon that.

BIANCA: Why should you seek, sir, to take away that you
can never give?

DUKE: But I give better in exchange! Wealth, honour! She
that is fortunate in a duke's favour lights on a tree that bears
all women's wishes. If your own mother saw you pluck fruit
there, she would commend your wit and praise the time of
your nativity. Take hold of glory. Do not I know you have
cast away your life upon necessities, means merely doubtful
to keep you in indifferent health and fashion — a thing I
heard too lately and soon pitied . . .? And can you be so
much your beauty's enemy to kiss away a month or two in
wedlock, and weep whole years in wants for ever after?
Come, play the wise wench and provide for ever . . . (*They go
out.*)

LIVIA: Did I not say my duke would fetch you over, widow?

WIDOW: I think you spoke in earnest when you said it,
madam . . .

LIVIA: And my black king makes all the haste he can, too, I
have given thee blind mate twice . . . !

WIDOW: You may see, madam, my eyes begin to fail . . .

LIVIA: I'll swear they do . . .

GUARDIANO (*entering*): I can but smile as often as I think
on it! How prettily the poor fool was beguiled, how unexpectedly! It is a witty age, never were finer snares for women's
honesties than are devised in these days. Yet to prepare her
stomach by degrees to Cupid's feast, I showed her naked
pictures by the way — a bit to stay the appetite . . .

LIVIA: The game's even at the best now. You may see
widow, how all things draw to an end. Has not my duke
bestirred himself?

WIDOW: Yes, 'faith, madam, he has done all the mischief in
this game . . .

BIANCA (*entering*): Now bless me from a blasting! I saw that
now fearful for any woman's eye to look on. Infectious mists
and mildews hang at his eyes, the weather of a doomsday
dwells upon him. Yet, since mine honour's leprous, why
should I preserve that fair that caused the leprosy? Come
poison all at once! Thou in whose baseness the bane of virtue
broods, I'm bound in soul eternally to curse thy smooth-
browed treachery that wore the fair veil of a friendly welcome! And I a stranger, think upon it! Murders piled up
upon a guilty spirit at his last breath will not lie heavier than
this betraying act upon thy conscience. I'm made bold now,
I thank thy treachery. Sin and I'm acquainted, no couple
greater.

GUARDIANO: Well, so the duke loves me I fare not much
amiss, then. Two great feasts do seldom come together in one
day.

BIANCA: What, still at it, mother?

WIDOW: You see we sit by it. Are you so soon returned?
You have not seen all, since, surely?

BIANCA: That have I, mother, the monument and all!
'Faith, I have seen that I little thought to see in the morning
when I rose . . .

WIDOW: Nay, so I told you before you saw it, it would
prove worth your sight. I give you great thanks for my
daughter, sir, and all your kindness towards her.

GUARDIANO: Oh, good widow! Much good may it do
her — forty weeks hence, in faith . . . !

LIVIA (*rising*): We'll walk to supper. (*To* BIANCA.) Will it
please you, gentlewoman?

BIANCA: Thanks, virtuous lady — you are a damned bawd!
I'll follow you, forsooth. Pray take my mother in, this
gentleman and I vow not to part . . . (*She and* GUARDIA-
NO *go out. The* WIDOW *leads the way*.)

LIVIA: Are you so bitter? 'Tis but want of use, her tender
modesty is sea-sick a little, being not accustomed to the
breaking billow of woman's wavering faith, blown with
temptations. Sin tastes at the first draught like wormwood
bitter, but drunk again, 'tis nectar even after.

Scene Six

The WIDOW

WIDOW: I would my son would either keep at home or I
were in my grave! She was not but one day abroad but ever
since she's grown so cutted, there's no speaking to her.
Whether the sight of great cheer at my lady's, and such mean
fare at home, work discontent in her, I know not, but I'm
sure she's strangely altered. I'll never keep daughter-in-law in
the house with me again if I had a hundred.

BIANCA (*entering*): This is the strangest house for all defects
as ever gentlewoman made shift withal to pass away her love
in! Why is there not a cushion cloth of drawn work, or some
fair cut-work pinned up in my bed-chamber, a silver and gilt
casting bottle hung by it?

WIDOW: She talks of great things here my whole state's not
worth . . .

BIANCA: Never a green silk quilt is there in the house,
mother, to cast upon my bed?

WIDOW: No, by troth is there! Nor orange-tawny, neither.

BIANCA: Here's a house for a young gentlewoman to be got
with child in!

WIDOW: What, cannot children be begot, think you, without
gilt casting-bottles? 'Tis an old saying, 'one may keep good
cheer in a mean house'.

BIANCA: Troth, you speak wondrous well for your old
house here, 'twill shortly fall down at your feet to thank you.
Must I live in want because my fortune matched me with
your son? I ask less now than what I had at home when I
was a maid, kept short of that which a wife knows she must
have, nay, and will! Will, mother, if she be not a fool born.
And report went of me that I could wrangle for what I
wanted when I was two hours old . . . ! (*She goes out.*)

WIDOW: When she first lighted here, I told her then how
mean she should find things — she was pleased forsooth!
None better! I laid open all defects to her, she was contented
still! But the devil's in her. What course shall I think on? She
frets me so . . . (*She goes out.*)

LEANTIO (*entering*): How near I am now to happiness that
earth exceeds not. Not another like it! I scent the air of
blessings when I come but near the house! Honest wedlock is

like a banqueting house built in a garden, when base lust
with all her powders, paintings and best pride is but a fair
house built by a ditch side. Now for a welcome able to draw
men's envies upon man! After a five days' fast she'll be so
greedy now, and cling about me, I take care how I shall be
rid of her! And here it begins! (BIANCA *and the* WIDOW
enter.)

BIANCA: Oh, sir, you are welcome home.

LEANTIO: Is that all? Why this? Sure you are not well,
Bianca. How dost, prithee?

BIANCA: I have been better than I am.

LEANTIO: Alas, I thought so.

BIANCA: Nay, I have been worse, too, that now you see me,
sir.

LEANTIO: I'm glad thou mend's yet. I feel my heart mend,
too. How came it to thee? Has anything disliked thee in my
absence?

BIANCA: No, certain . . . I have had the best content that
Florence can afford . . .

LEANTIO: Thou mak'st the best of it. Speak, mother, what's
the cause? You must needs know.

WIDOW: Troth, I know none, son. Let her speak herself.

BIANCA: Methinks this house stands nothing to my mind,
I'ld have some pleasant lodging in the high street, sir. Or if
it were near the court, that were much better — 'tis a sweet
recreation for a gentlewoman to stand in a bay window and
see gallants.

LEANTIO: Now, I have another temper, a mere stranger to that
of yours, it seems. I should delight to see none but yourself.

BIANCA: I praise not that. Too fond is as unseemly as too
churlish. I would not have a husband of that proneness to
kiss me before company, for a world! Beside, 'tis tedious to
see one thing still, sir, be it the best that ever heart affected.
You are learned sir, and, know I speak not ill. 'Tis full as
virtuous for a woman's eye to look on several men as for her
heart, sir, to be fixed on one . . .

LEANTIO: Now thou com'st home to me! A kiss for that
word!

BIANCA: No matter for a kiss, sir, let it pass. Let's talk of
other business and forget it. What news now of the pirates?
Any stirring?

WIDOW: I'm glad he's here yet to see her tricks himself. I
had lied monstrously if I had told 'em first.

LEANTIO: Speak, what's the humour, sweet, you make your
lip so strange? This is not wont.

BIANCA: Is there no kindness betwixt man and wife unless
they make a pigeon-house of friendship and be still billing?
Alas, sir, think of the world, how we shall live, grow serious.
We have been married a whole fortnight now.

LEANTIO: How, a whole fortnight! Is that long? (*A knock.*)
Who's there, now? Withdraw you, Bianca, thou art a gem no
stranger's eye must see, however thou please now to look
dull on me. (*She goes out. A* MESSENGER *enters.*) You're
welcome, sir. To whom your business, pray?

MESSENGER: To one I see not here, now.

LEANTIO: Who should that be?

MESSENGER: A young gentlewoman I was sent to.

LEANTIO: A young gentlewoman?

MESSENGER: Ay, sir, about sixteen. Why look you so wildly?

LEANTIO: At your strange error. You have mistook the
house, there's none such here, I assure you.

MESSENGER: I assure you, too. The man sent me cannot be
mistook.

LEANTIO: Why, who is it sent you, sir?

MESSENGER: The duke.

LEANTIO: The duke! Troth, shall I tell you, sir, it is the most
erroneous business that e'er your honest pains were abused
with. His grace has been most wondrous ill-informed. Pray
so return it, sir. What should her name be?

MESSENGER: Then I shall tell you straight, too. Bianca
Capello.

LEANTIO: How, sir, Bianca? What do you call the other?

MESSENGER: Capello. Sir, it seems you know no such,
then?

LEANTIO: I never heard of the name.

MESSENGER: Then 'tis a sure mistake. I will return and
seek no further. (*He goes.*)

LEANTIO: Come forth, Bianca. Thou art betrayed, I fear
me.

BIANCA (*appearing*): Betrayed? How, sir?

LEANTIO: The duke knows thee.

BIANCA: How should the duke know me? Can you guess,
mother?

WIDOW: Not I with all my wits. Sure, we kept house close.

LEANTIO: Kept close! Not all the locks in Italy can keep
you women so! You have been gadding, and ventured out at

twilight to the court-green yonder, without your masks. I'll
be hanged else! Thou hast been seen, Bianca, by some
stranger. Never excuse it.

BIANCA: I'll not seek the way, sir. Do you think you have
married me to mew me up not to be seen? What would you
make of me?

LEANTIO: A good wife, nothing else.

BIANCA: Why, so are some that are seen every day, else the
devil take 'em.

LEANTIO: No more, then. I believe all virtuous in thee
without an argument. 'Twas but thy hard chance to be seen
somewhere . . .

WIDOW: Now I can tell you son, the time and place!

LEANTIO: When? Where?

WIDOW: What wits have I! When you last took your leave,
if you remember, you left us both at window. And not the
third part of an hour after the duke passed by in great
solemnity. He looked up twice to the window.

LEANTIO: Looked he up twice! And could you take no
warning?

WIDOW: Why, once may do as much harm, so, as a thousand, do you not know one spark has fired an house as well
as a whole furnace?

LEANTIO: My heart flames for it! Yet let's be wise and keep
all smothered closely. I have bethought a means. Is the door
fast?

WIDOW: I locked it myself after him.

LEANTIO: You know, mother, at the end of the dark parlour there's a place so artificially contrived no search could
ever find it. There will I lock my life's best treasure up.
Bianca!

BIANCA: Would you keep me closer yet? Have you the
conscience?

LEANTIO: Why, are you so insensible of your danger to ask
that now? The duke himself has sent for you!

BIANCA: Has he so! And you the man would never yet
vouchsafe to tell me of it till now. You show your loyalty
and honesty at once, and so, farewell, sir.

LEANTIO: Bianca, whither now?

BIANCA: Why, to the duke, sir, you say he sent for me.

LEANTIO: But thou dost not mean to go, I hope?

BIANCA: No? I shall prove unmannerly, rude and uncivil,
mad, and imitate you? Come, mother, come, follow his

humour no longer. We shall all be executed for treason shortly.

WIDOW:　Not I, in faith. I'll first obey the duke, and taste of a good banquet. I'm of thy mind.

BIANCA:　Why, here's an old wench would trot into bawd now for a piece of fruit or marzipan! (*They go out.*)

LEANTIO:　Oh, thou the ripe of time of man's misery, wedlock, when all his thoughts, like over-laden trees, crack with the fruits they bear, in cares and jealousies. What a peace he has he that never marries! If he knew the benefit he enjoyed, or had the fortune to come and speak with me, he should know then the infinite wealth he had, and discern rightly the greatness of his treasure by my loss. Nay, what a quietness he has above mine, that wears his youth out in a strumpet's arms and never spends more care upon a woman than at the time of lust, but walks away, and if he finds her dead at his return, his pity is soon done. But all the fears, shames, jealousies, costs and troubles, and still renewed cares of a marriage bed live in the issue when the wife is dead . . .

MESSENGER (*entering*):　Though you were pleased just now to pin an error on me, you must not shift another in your stead too. The duke has sent for you.

LEANTIO:　How, for me? I see then, 'tis my theft. Well, I'm not the first has stolen away a maid! (*They hurry out.*)

Scene Seven

A banquet.

GUARDIANO:　Take you especial note of such a gentlewoman, she's here on purpose. I have invited her, her father and her uncle to this banquet.

WARD:　'Faith, I should know her now, among a thousand women. A little pretty, deft and tidy thing, you say?

GUARDIANO:　Right.

WARD:　With a lusty, sprouting sprig in her hair?

GUARDIANO:　Thou goest the right way still. Take one mark more. Thou shalt never find her hand out of her uncle's. The love of kindred never yet stuck closer than theirs to one another. He that weds her marries her uncle's heart, too.

WARD: Say you so, sir! Then I'll be asked in the church to both of 'em!

GUARDIANO: Fall back, here comes the duke!

WARD: He brings a gentlewoman, I should fall forward, rather!

DUKE: Come Bianca, of purpose sent into the world to show perfection once in woman. I'll believe henceforward they have every one a soul, too, against all the uncourteous opinions that man's uncivil rudeness ever held of 'em. Glory of Florence, light into mine arms. (LEANTIO *enters.*)

BIANCA: Yon comes a grudging man will chide you, sir. The storm is now in his heart, and would get nearer and fall here if it durst — it pours down yonder.

DUKE: If that be he, the weather shall soon clear. Listen, and I'll tell thee how. (*Whispers to her.*)

LEANTIO: A kissing, too? I see 'tis plain lust now, adultery boldened. What will it prove anon, when 'tis stuffed full of wine and sweetmeats, being so impudent fasting?

DUKE: We have heard of your good parts, sir, which we honour with our embrace and love. Is not the captainship of Rouens' citadel, since the late deceased, supplied by any yet?

GUARDIANO: By none, my lord.

DUKE: Take it, the place is yours, then. (LEANTIO *kneels.*) And as faithfulness and desert grows, our favour shall grow with it. Rise now, the captain of our fort at Rouens!

LEANTIO: The service of whole life give your grace thanks. (*Aside*) This is some good yet, and more than ever I looked for — a fine bit to stay a cukold's stomach! All preferment that springs from sin and lust, it shoots up quickly, as gardeners' crops do in the rottenest grounds.

LIVIA: Is that your son, widow?

WIDOW: Yes, did your ladyship never know that till now?

LIVIA: No, trust me, did I. Nor ever truly felt the power of love and pity to a man, till now I knew him. I have enough to buy me my desires, and yet to spare, that's one good comfort. Hark you? Pray let me speak with you, sir, before you go . . .

DUKE: Here's a health now, gallants, to the best beauty at this day in Florence!

BIANCA: Whoe'r she be, she shall not go unpledged, sir . . .

DUKE: Here's to thy health, Bianca . . .

BIANCA: Nothing comes more welcome to that name than your grace . . .

LEANTIO: So, so! Here stands the poor thief now that stole the treasure, and he's not thought on.

DUKE: Methinks there is no spirit amongst us, gallants, but what divinely sparkles from the eyes of bright Bianca — we sat all in darkness but for that splendour. Who was it told us lately of a match-making rite, a marriage-tender?

GUARDIANO: 'Twas I, my lord.

DUKE: 'Twas you indeed. Where is she?

GUARDIANO: This is the gentlewoman.

FABRITIO: My lord, my daughter.

WARD: The ape's so little, I shall scarce feel her. I have seen almost as tall as she sold in the fair for tenpence . . .

FABRITIO: She has the full qualities of a gentlewoman, I have brought her up to music, dancing and whatnot, that may commend her sex and stir her husband . . .

WARD: See how she simpers — as if marmalade would not melt in her mouth . . .

DUKE: And which is he?

GUARDIANO: This young heir, my lord.

DUKE: What is he brought up to?

WARD: To cat and trap.

GUARDIANO: My lord, he's a great ward, wealthy but simple. His parts consist in acres.

DUKE: Oh, wise acres!

GUARDIANO: Y'have spoke him in a word, sir!

BIANCA: 'Las, poor gentlewoman, she's ill bestead, unless she's dealt the wiselier and laid in more provision for her youth. Fools will not keep in summer.

LEANTIO: No, nor such wives from whores in winter.

DUKE (*to* FABRITIO): Yea, the voice too, sir?

FABRITIO: Ay, and a sweet breast too, my lord, I hope, or I have cast away my money wisely — she took her pricksong earlier, my lord, that any of her kindred ever did.

DUKE: Let's turn to a better banquet, then. For music bids the soul of man to feast! (*Music*)

LEANTIO: True, and damnation has taught you that wisdom. You can take gifts, too! Oh, that music mocks me!

LIVIA: I am as dumb to any language now but love's, as one that never learned to speak! I am not yet so old, but he

may think of me. My own fault — I have been idle a long
time.

ISABELLA (*singing*): What harder chance can fall to woman,
Who was born to cleave to some man,
Than to bestow her time, youth, beauty,
Life's observance, honour, duty,
On a thing for no use good
But to make physic work, or blood
Force fresh in an old lady's cheek?
So that would be
Mother of fools, let her compound with
me . . .

WARD: Here's a tune indeed! Pish! I would rather hear one
ballad sung in the nose now, of the lamentable drowning of
fat sheep and oxen, than all these simpering tunes played
upon cat-guts and sung by little kitlings.

FABRITIO (*to* GUARDIANO):   Will it please you now, sir,
to entreat your ward to take her by the hand and lead her in
a dance before the duke?

WARD: Dance with her! Not I, sweet guardiner, do not urge
my heart to it, 'tis clean against my blood. Dance with a
stranger!

GUARDIANO: Why, who shall take her, then?

WARD: Look, there's her uncle! Perhaps he knows the manner of her dancing, too?

GUARDIANO: Thou'lt be an ass, still.

WARD: Ay. All that 'uncle' shall not fool me out . . .

GUARDIANO (*to* HIPPOLITO):   I must entreat you, sir, to
take your niece and dance with her. My ward's a little wilful,
he would have you show him the way.

HIPPOLITO: Me, sir! He shall command it at all hours, pray
tell him so.

GUARDIANO: I thank you for him. He has not wit himself, sir.

The Dance. Enter, surreptitiously, SORDIDO.

GUARDIANO (*to* WARD):   Do it when I bid you, sir . . .

WARD: I'll venture but a hornpipe with her, guardiner, or
some such married man's dance . . .

WARD: Well, venture something sir! (*Turns.* SORDIDO
comes to the WARD's *side.*)

WARD: Here she's come again. Mark her now, Sordido . . .
(*He declares half publicly.*)

Plain men dance the measures, the cinquepence the gray;
Cuckolds dance the hornpipe, and farmers dance the hay;
Your soldiers dance the round, and maidens that grow big,
Your drunkards the canaries, your whore and bawd, the jig.
Here's your eight kind of dancers — he that find the ninth,
Let him pay the minstrels. (*He goes to dance.*)

DUKE: Oh, here he appears once in his own person! I thought he would have married her by attorney, and lain with her so, too. (*The* WARD *ridiculously imitates* HIPPOLITO.)

BIANCA: Methinks, if he would take some voyage when he's married, dangerous or long enough, and scarce be seen once in nine year together, a wife them might make indifferent shift to be content with him . . . (*The* WARD *and* ISABELLA *dance.*)

ISABELLA: And how do you like me, now, sir?

WARD: 'Faith, so well I never mean to part with thee, sweetheart, under some sixteen children.

GUARDIANO: How now, ward and nephew, speak, is it so, or not?

WARD: 'Tis so, we are both agreed, sir. (GUARDIANO *bows to The* DUKE.)

DUKE: My thanks to all your loves! Come, fair Bianca, we have took special care of you, and provided your lodging near us now.

BIANCA: Once more, our thanks to all.

ALL: All blest honours guard you!

LEANTIO: Oh, hast thou left me then, Bianca, utterly! Bianca, now I miss thee — oh, return, and save the faith of woman. I never felt the loss of thee till now, 'tis an affliction of greater weight than youth was made to bear!

LIVIA: Sweet sir!

LEANTIO: As long as mine eye saw thee, I half enjoyed thee . . .

LIVIA: Sir?

LEANTIO: Can'st thou forget the dear pains my love took, how it has watched whole nights together in all weathers for thee, yet stood in heart more merry than the tempests that sung about mine ears, and then received thee from thy father's window into these arms at midnight, when we embraced as if we had been statues only made for it, to show art's life, so silent were our comforts . . .

LIVIA: This makes me madder to enjoy him now. Sir!

LEANTIO: Cry mercy, lady! What would you say to me? My sorrow makes me so unmannerly, I had quite forgot you.

LIVIA: Nothing, but even in pity to that passion, would give your grief good counsel.

LEANTIO: Marry, and welcome, lady, it never could come better.

LIVIA: You missed your fortunes when you met with her, sir. Young gentlemen that only love for beauty, they love not wisely; such a marriage rather proves the destruction of affection. It brings on want, and want's the key of whoredom. I think you had small means with her?

LEANTIO: Oh, not any, lady.

LIVIA: Alas, poor gentleman! What mean'st thou, sir, quite to undo thyself with thine own kind heart? Thou art too good and pitiful to woman. Thank thy lucky stars for this blest fortune that rids the summer of thy youth so well from many beggars that had lain a-sunning in thy beams only else till thou hadst wasted the whole days of thy life in heat and labour. What would you say now to a creature found as pitiful to you as it were even sent on purpose from the whole sex general to requite all that kindness you have shown to it?

LEANTIO: What's that, madam?

LIVIA: Couldn'st thou love such a one that, blow all fortunes, would never see thee want? Nay, more, maintain thee to thine enemy's envy? And shalt not spend a care for it, stir a thought, nor break a sleep — unless love's music waked thee, no storm of fortune should. Look upon me, and know that woman.

LEANTIO: Oh, my life's wealth, Bianca!

LIVIA: He's vexed in mind. I came too soon to him. Where's my discretion now, my skill, my judgement? I'm cunning in all arts but my own love. (*She goes out.*)

LEANTIO: Is she my wife till death, yet no more mine? Methinks by right I should not now be living, and then 'twere all well! She's gone forever — utterly! There is as much redemption as a soul from hell as a fair woman's body from his palace! Why should my love last longer than her truth? What is there good in woman to be loved when only that which makes her so has left her? My safest course, for health of mind and body is to turn my heart and hate her, most extremely hate!

LIVIA (*returning*): I have tried all ways I can, and have not
power to keep from sight of him. How are you now, sir?

LEANTIO: I feel a better ease, madam . . .

LIVIA: You never saw the beauty of my house yet, nor how
abundantly fortune has blessed me. I have enough, sir, to
make my friend a rich man in my life, a great man at my
death. If you want anything and spare to speak, troth, I'll
condemn you for a wilful man, sir.

LEANTIO: Why sure, this can be but the flattery of some
dream . . .

LIVIA: Now, by this kiss, my love, my soul, my riches, 'tis
all true substance. Take what you list, the gallanter you go,
the more you please me, but to me only sir, wear your
heart of constant stuff. Do but you love enough, I'll give
enough.

Scene Eight

The Palace. CARDINAL, DUKE *and* BIANCA.

CARDINAL: You vowed never to keep a strumpet more, and
are you now so swift in your desires to knit your honours
and your life fast to her? Must marriage, that immaculate
robe of honour, be now made the garment of leprosy and
foulness? Is this penitence, to sanctify hot lust?

DUKE: The path now I tread, is honest. I vowed no more to
keep a sensual woman — 'tis done. I mean to make a lawful
wife of her.

CARDINAL: Do not grow too cunning for your soul, good
brother! Is it enough to use adulterous thefts, and then take
sanctuary in marriage?

BIANCA: Sir, I have read you over all this while in silence,
and I find great knowledge in you, and severe learning;
yet 'mongst all your virtues I see not charity written, which
some call the first born of religion, and I wonder I cannot see
it . . .

DUKE: I kiss thee for that spirit! Thou hast praised thy wit
a modest way! (*He turns back to* CARDINAL.) Here y'are

bitter without cause, brother. What I vow, I keep safe as you
your conscience. All this needs not. I taste more wrath in it
than I do religion, and envy more than goodness . . .
(CARDINAL *goes out*.)

BIANCA: How strangely woman's fortune comes about! This
was the farthest way to come to me that knew me born in
Venice and there with many jealous eyes brought up. 'Tis not
good, in sadness, to keep a maid so strict in her young days.
Restraint breeds wandering thoughts. I'll never use any girl
of mine so strictly — however they're kept, their fortunes
find 'em out.

LEANTIO (*entering beneath* BIANCA's *window*): I long to
see how my despiser looks now she's come here to court,
these are her lodgings! I took her out of no such window,
I remember, first. That was a great deal lower, and less
carved . . .

BIANCA: How now, what silkworm's this, in the name of
pride! What, is it he? Methinks you are wondrous brave, sir!

LEANTIO: A sumptuous lodging!

BIANCA: You have an excellent suit, there.

LEANTIO: A chair of velvet!

BIANCA: Is your coat lined through, sir? Who's your
shoemaker? He has made you a neat boot.

LEANTIO: Will you have a pair? The duke will lend you
spurs.

BIANCA: Yes, when I ride.

LEANTIO: 'Tis a brave life you lead.

BIANCA: I could never see you in such good clothes in my
time.

LEANTIO: In your time?

BIANCA: Sure, I think, sir, we both thrive best asunder.

LEANTIO: Y'are a whore.

BIANCA: Oh, sir, you give me thanks for your captainship.
I thought you had forgot all your good manners.

LEANTIO: And to spite thee as much, look there, there read!
Vex! Gnaw! Thou shalt find there I am not pitiless but there
was ever still more charity found out than at one proud
fool's door.

BIANCA: Y'are simply happy, sir, yet I'll not envy you.

LEANTIO: No, court-saint, not thou! You keep some friend
of a new fashion. There's no harm in your devil, he's a
suckling, but he will breed teeth shortly, will he not?

BIANCA: Take heed you play not then too long with him.

LEANTIO: Why, here's sin made and never a conscience put
it it! Why do I talk to thee of sense or virtue that art as dark
as death? To an ignorance darker than thy womb I leave thy
perjured soul. A plague will come!

PART TWO

Scene One

LEANTIO, *undressed.*

LEANTIO: We fuck the day to death. And suffocate the
night with tossing. Time stands still, she says so. Rolls back,
even. As for the bed, it's our whole territory, the footboard
and the headboard are the horizons of our estate, rank with
the flood of flesh. Oh, beautiful odour of the utter fuck! And
come? No, never come, for that's to end it. Clerks come, and
butchers prior to a good night's kipping, farmers with their
eight strokes, who's not heard their mechanistic butting? I
know, was I not a clerk myself, and salesman? Oh, the bars
and barmaids of the provinces, dead minds spewing the dead
opinion, dead eyes on the dying bra strap slipping **fuck all
that watery desire** no woman under forty is worth entering!
(*LIVIA enters.*) Did I hurt you? For one moment I thought
I have killed her. We do strive in one another, all bruises and
dragged hair . . .
LIVIA: You hurt me, and I welcome the hurt. I thought once,
I am dying, and I did not mind. I have no indignation left,
surprise, or petty reservation. No thing I won't yield up, nor
thought ashamed to utter. May I tell you, I have never
wanted to be free of you. All other men I thought, enough,
roll off and leave my premises. The ecstasy of being left,
silence and the reclamation of myself. Not you, though. It's
five days since we stepped outside. Are there still streets, and
what colour are the buses? (*She looks out the window.*) Oh,
people look the same! Two legs and heads down, the shuffle
and the stagger, **repetition of the mundane life!** (*She selects
among the crowd.*) She'll lend a little of her hip, he'll tamper

with a giggle, that one might yield her place to satisfy
persistence, and him mutter as he shudders but **transformation . . . !** (*She turns back to* LEANTIO.) **Yes I am arrogant**.
Do you complain about my arrogance? You made me so,
and I might have died unknowing . . .

LEANTIO (*at the window*): There has been change here!
Look, they paint the lamp posts for the royal wedding!

LIVIA: All this bunting clinging to a dirty world! And look,
Bianca in silver paint staring in our bedroom! I heard no
workmen hammering!

LEANTIO: The bitch reviles me! Close the shutter!

LIVIA: Even in paint, her ambitious lip . . .

LEANTIO: And they applaud her, call her innocence!

LIVIA: You never touched her womb, Leantio. Had you
done so she could not revile you without wanting you as
well. Revile and clamour, clamour and revile. Tell me you
don't feel her still, she could give you nothing but shallow
prodding, you could not thrust against her heart like you do
mine, I promise you.

LEANTIO (*going to her*):   I am slave and master to you alone.
Above me I struggle with a girl, beneath I submit to the hag
who lurks inside your creases, who has not possessed you!
Tell me your fuck history, you used and used again whore —

LIVIA: He abuses me . . .

LEANTIO: Yes! And by abuse I praise you, lavish bitch,
hunted and devoured female —

LIVIA: Are we insane? I think it possible we are insane!

LEANTIO: Yes, and good riddance to their sense, their swop
of stale banalities!

LIVIA: I would not be a girl again —

LEANTIO: So every woman of your ripeness should say, who
finds her match at last! (*He kneels to her.*) Recite to me,
who lay in you before me, scratch your memory! (*He kisses
her belly.*) I suffer on you, you are my cross, the pain,
you know the pain do you, you are a rack also to stretch me
on . . .

LIVIA: Yes, all you know, I do too . . .

LEANTIO (*stops*):   But I do hate Bianca. I wish I could be
happy to despise, but no, I hate . . .

LIVIA: Good! Hate!

LEANTIO: Must I?

LIVIA: Those whose love runs deep dispense no charity. You
are no bridegroom whose handshake is free to all, and I no

bride all teeth. Through pain of longing we have trod down sickening conviviality. Shudder, shudder at behaviour I tinkled over once. I tinkled then, I did not laugh, and now I find, laughter! Real laughter! Don't suffer shame for proper hates . .

LEANTIO: Your brother wants me dead.

LIVIA: My brother! Whose tender honour bruises so! Oh, my honour, my sister is a bint for fucking with the factor! The man's a snob, and coarse for all his culture! Listen — (*She draws him to her.*) The world hates passion. Fornication's all its taste, what's good for telling over dinner, how the empty girl was taken, and she smiles, she smiles in willing collaboration, the used smiling at her usage! (*She releases him, turning away.*) And I tried to tell him! **Absurd undertaking!** (*She laughs.*) Such was his contempt I feared he'd chain me as a lunatic! They think of love as discharge, something in the groin to be delivered, I know them, I do know, did I not giggle over their thin and sour longings? **Hunger!** What do they know of that? Touch me and I know I live! (*He caresses her.*) Beloved man, if you perished tonight in some backstreet stabbing, I would say even this little was enough, this was light and transformation. It made me hate my life. All hate your lives and change the world!

Scene Two

The DUKE, *the* CARDINAL, *observing.*

DUKE: She is so old . . .

CARDINAL: Gone forty, yes . . .

DUKE: I think our officers, however lowly, ought not to scandalize us with weird appetites. Can't he speak to girls?

CARDINAL: I couldn't say.

DUKE: Bianca was a torment to him.

CARDINAL: Really?

DUKE: She tells me he was done before she started.

CARDINAL: Is that so . . .

DUKE: Mind you, they all say that, I won't tell you the cuckolds I've heard denigrated . . .

CARDINAL (*aside*):   Stop your philandering, I said. Stop this
endless fingering of flesh. I said the public do not like to see
this in their governor, but they do! I was wrong there.
Profoundly wrong. Who rips the sheets with him, and who
was grappled half way down the stairs is all public speculation, keeps the masses warm with itching. It's the entertainment of the modern state and the proper function of an
aristocracy! No, carry on, I was wrong to reprimand him!
There, church dignitary bows to insatiable appetite of prince
. . . (*He bows.*) There is another sex, however . . .

DUKE: I have never touched a woman over thirty! Not
knowingly. Fifteen is best. They gasp in wonder, don't dare
speak, eyes all big, half terror and half vanity!

CARDINAL: I think there is another sex, however . . .

DUKE: What? I've done it all. (*He turns to the* CARDINAL.)
Is there some posture I've not tried? Some practice of the
Arabs you in your dusty library have uncovered? **Banned
books!** (*He laughs.*) I assure you this is something I also have
researched. Look at me, brother, fifty-five, and no part of a
girl's anatomy I'm not versed in. Can place my finger
blindfold and make them shudder at a licking.

CARDINAL: Yes, I do not doubt it, though this I think is
not to do with posture or with bringing off, but something
else.

DUKE: What, then?

CARDINAL: Something which unlocks the discipline of the
civil state.

DUKE: Go on.

CARDINAL: Let all the population copulate, seduce daughters, bring out the waywardness of wives, whelps and growls
from upper storeys all night long, good, satisfaction and
quiescence everywhere, but this might lever up whole pavements and turn the fountains red. (*He walks a little, stops.*)
You see, it does not lead to childbirth, which by responsibility, might modulate its strength . . .

DUKE: Oh, come on, stuff your theological euphemisms,
what is it, sodomy?

CARDINAL: I don't know yet . . .

DUKE: Whatever it may be, I've done it.

CARDINAL: Perhaps, I am celibate, and imagine union
more immaculate than actually it is. That two might lock,
and in locking, undo whole cliffs of discipline seems to me
possible . . .

DUKE: The fevered fantasy of the deprived. Dear brother, you stick to politics.

CARDINAL: **But it is, you see. It is politics.** (*The* DUKE *looks at him, with contempt. Then returns to his observations.*)

DUKE: He dotes upon her, licks the experience out of her wrinkles. And there are girls tight in their skin on every pavement!

Scene Three

The WARD's *garden.*

WARD: I do love to be in a garden! To poke my head among the flowers and make my hair a roost for doves! I do! I do! Sing me a song, there's a good bitch. (*He sits.*) Am I nice and tame? I have not been out three weeks for cricket, hunting or the like, have not tumbled headlong off the horse and staggered home all shit and brandy, have I? I am the model husband. Sing him a song, he is an idiot. Do you love your idiot?

ISABELLA: You are not advised to call yourself an idiot or —

WARD: I shall be taken for one! Horror! Stack me in the summerhouse, prop me like a deckchair stiff against the wall, or do you have a better use for it? The summerhouse? By the way your breath smells. And only three weeks on the nuptials! Don't neglect yourself or I may lose my fascination with you.

ISABELLA: What fascination? You mean pinching my arse? Your fascination consists entirely in pulling up my skirt and whooping.

WARD: Yes, it does and all! I am an idiot! Lock me in the summerhouse! Or do you have another use for it? I do miss Sordido! I love the doves, I love the clematis, but Sordido was good to sit with in a storm and watch the lightning. I do think sitting with your legs apart is not the way to charm me. I mention it in passing.

ISABELLA: Oh, he cares for my legs, how they face the world!

WARD: I'm not the world, beloved . . .

ISABELLA: I don't require you stay by me. Please, to your clubs and bars by all means.

WARD: No, no! A man who marries must enjoy the woman not only in the night but in all the glitter of her personality! Is it tedious to be married to an idiot?

ISABELLA (*darkly*): I am not married to one.

WARD (*dark in turn*): No, indeed, but the wife of . . . ? (*He stares at* ISABELLA, *and suddenly, clowns.*) Catstick! Catstick! (*He stops again.*) I think it is a dirty world, where we are stuck together by some senile whim which thinks our youth will match their sentiments, and our fucking lubricate their arid transactions. (*She looks at him, amazed.*) **Catstick! Catstick!** (*He shudders.*) I do not like you, you are full of grimy sweetness, like a toffee left in pockets . . .

ISABELLA: You do not need to be the child to me. The fat boy. Do you? You do not . . .

WARD: Show us yer bum, do! (ISABELLA *turns, goes out.*) I find my only comfort in the mocking of their shallow ardours. I could no more dance attention on these frills and bustles than shove my hand straight to the wet mouth of their hips, **I do like women with a terrible liking but they are not actual, are they?** (*He pretends to recall.*) Went down to the river with Sordido once, out of the city in the summer and saw a woman on the bank who looked — in simple cloth dress — looked at me, and I hung there, hung back until she wound me in with her desire like something on a hook, closer and closer I went, wordless to her lips, by the washing basket and the scrubbing brush, she found me straight and I found her, no diversion, up to her heart I reached while Sordido lit a pipe beneath the tree and at the finish she went shh, finger to the lips as if words or gratitude would spoil it, as if to speak would bring sin to its purity . . . (*Pause*) True story . . . (*Pause*) **True like fuck it is**. (*He roars with contemptuous laugher.* SORDIDO *bounds in.*)

SORDIDO: She hurries to her uncle, why?

WARD: Her uncle, why?

SORDIDO: I can't think why!

WARD/SORDIDO: **Oh, why, oh, why!** (*They jerk their pelvises in a ritual.*)

WARD (*embracing him*): I have missed you! I can say in utter honesty, in prefect truth, in sworn and honourable veracity so help me God I longed for your foul observations, did I not!

SORDIDO: Truth? Truth? A perfect truth, what's that?

WARD (*pointing to the floor*):   **Saw one!**

SORDIDO: Truth, oi!

WARD (*diving*):   Caught it! Down you bugger!

SORDIDO: Net! Net!

WARD: Slippery . . . slippery . . .

SORDIDO (*pretending to grapple with invisibility*):   Says — says —

WARD (*cupping his ear*):   What?

SORDIDO: Squeaks . . . **Nice — place — you — got.** (*He releases it.*)

WARD: She brought money. She brought flesh. With one tit in my paw I glance across the garden which is designed according to my whim, shape of the dollar enclosing female lip, the box tree is the dollar and the geraniums the lip, and I think where is my mate, his squalid den? And lo, he bounds into my presence. I hate all, and the more I have, the more I hate, old men especially, them I would kill. Women less, they are farcical merely. The duke prods bossy virgins and they think, bliss, oh, bliss, **what is bliss exactly?** I thought of hanging myself with a tennis net, to carry my act to the end, my funeral would be the gladdest event in the social calendar . . . (SORDIDO *puts his arm around him.*) Shall we do a murder? Shall we strangle Isabella, or the uncle, in some shuddering copulation up against the summerhouse? That appeals to me, but no, it would be taken as a vengeance, as if I cared who shagged her place! I have not entered her, but laid beside her, irritatingly. Have you yet?

SORDIDO: What?

WARD: Been with a woman?

SORDIDO: Never, as you know.

WARD: Explains their hunger of you, as if by restraint some unknown power's gathered in your parts. It's cruelty! You being rather dirty and rather handsome, two things they stir for in collaboration, they almost whimper as you pass **what is bliss** it's murder, surely?

SORDIDO: Here comes all we loathe, and all we loathe in its company . . .

FABRITIO: Good news! Good news!

WARD: **'o says yer can waddle in my garden!** (GUARDIANO *and* FABRITIO *enter. The* WARD *bows a mocking greeting.*) Hatred of age . . . Hatred of age . . .

FABRITIO: Good news!

WARD: You don't have a key, do you? Walking in on us, I might be in your daughter's frills and then what? Tact! Tact! Under the meandering bees, sticky fingered and arse-rampant! Tact! Tact!

FABRITIO (*wounded*): You were less coarse-spoken prior to the matrimonial . . .

WARD: I was less used. I find stacks of vocabulary in my humiliation. Well, humiliation they call it who know me not, among them I count you, beloved guardian, who spent my loot and in cruel boarding houses got me off your back, and you believed my school report I was the dunce!

GUARDIANO: You were! It said so! And you behaved it well enough!

WARD: A proper love would see through a malicious schoolboy's pain.

GUARDIANO: I had such business to attend to I —

WARD: **Catstick!**

GUARDIANO: The responsibilities of the estate —

WARD: **Cat — stick!** (*Pause.* GUARDIANO *concedes.*) My dead parent who enabled me this prettiness the Turks strung across a rigging, tongue out, guts out, genitalia ripped up by the roots, most appropriate, Christian trader, Christian money-hunter, would have swopped his bowel for a dollar, but must admire them, the spirit of adventure, **spirit of adventure it was avarice,** for coming home and buying cunt in furs, this man knows adventure — (*he indicates* SORDIDO) — this is the great adverturer, who never strays from Florence and her gutters, this is the great explorer, the immaculate cartographer of human vice, stuff your funny tribes and exotic animals, your zoos and exhibitions, **all beasts live in Florence, I know, they clamber on my back.** (*He nudges* SORDIDO.) Describe our fauna, you know them best.

SORDIDO (*examining* FABRITIO *and* GUARDIANO): Here, for your inspection, two common specimens, adult and mature, in plumage of the mating season —

GUARDIANO: I do not see why we —

WARD: **Respect his genius.**

GUARDIANO: Should be subjected to —

WARD: **His genius. His wit.** (*Pause.* GUARDIANO *acts patience.*)

SORDIDO: The mating season which is not a season but is permanent, stamping their webbed feet on the ground as signal of peculiar distress make calls thus, 'My dignity! My dignity!', a somewhat ugly cry and beaks a-quiver with olfactory obsession with tail feathers of the female. Relation to the European magpie, pica pica, has huge appetite for silver, with which it lines its rather squalid nest, and flocks about midday to the exchange, making the repeated call of 'cash, cash, cash!' until with the onset of the feeding hour, which occupies all afternoon, it makes its graceless flight to overstocked barns leaking dung —

GUARDIANO: All right, all right —

SORDIDO: Most unedifying spectacle, the life cycle of this parasitic bird —

GUARDIANO: Childish —

FABRITIO: Infantile —

GUARDIANO: Repetition of stale ideology . . . (*He walks a little way, then pointedly.*) What a beautiful garden . . .

WARD (*embracing* SORDIDO):   He knows everything, and has not strolled beyond the river . . . what brings you here? And what's bliss, I long to know . . .

FABRITIO: You have bliss in your bedroom if I know it.

WARD: What, my wife? He calls bliss a body? They know nothing, this ornithology!

FABRITIO: I'll rescue her, she'll not stay with a fiend like you who tricked us playing idiot — (THE WARD *feints to butt him.*) Hit me! Dare you? Hit me?

WARD: No, I shan't crack your eggshell, vain old sparrow, shan't give you the satisfaction, though to strike old men is not offensive to my values . . .

GUARDIANO: We'll end our visit here, and tell you plain and dry what should have been cause for celebration. The Duchess of Florence, soon to be, has chosen your abused young wife as maid at her wedding. Now, you see, a great honour we thought to bring with love you've wrecked with spite and barracking.

FABRITIO (*in angry tears*):   Yes, knife-mouth! And she'll not lie with you if I'm her father!

SORDIDO: He don't in any case, except to pinch her bum when she is sleeping. Now, buzz! (*He swings a kick at* FABRITIO, *and follows them off menacingly.* ISABELLA *appears from cover, staring after them.*)

ISABELLA: Peculiar parenthood, that gladly sells me to an idiot, but finding he has mind, is all a-scuttle to rescue me . . . (*She turns to the* WARD.) Talk to me . . .

WARD: Never.

ISABELLA: Lie with me, then. Now, in the sunshine, throw the window open and turn back the sheet. Tell. Do tell.

Scene Four

The Palace. The WIDOW *and* BIANCA

WIDOW: I was a widow, having been the good wife to a man not very passionate. Loyal, though not without temptation. For forty years bred children and cleaned shirts. Pride in polish. Honour in starch. And now, on the rim of the grave I see — **the riot of lost possibilities!** (*She weeps.*) Oh, roll back the hours, toss off the years! Give me back my luscious breasts, I was robbed . . .

BIANCA: You have your compensations, surely? Though I can't lay words to them.

WIDOW: Oh shut up, you well-fucked thing. All I can draw to me are scabby, legless soldiers and they would dare to call me hag . . .

BIANCA: Tell you what! On your grave I'll have inscribed the one word **Honesty**. How's that?

WIDOW: Arrogant bitch.

BIANCA: No! I'll have the mason chip **She cooked for five**. How's that?

WIDOW: Mock on, juvenile, your eyes won't pull forever . . .

BIANCA: Or better still, **Here lay the cleanest carpet in all Florence**.

WIDOW: Piss.

BIANCA: I wound you only to endorse myself. The little conscience lurked, did most certainly, until your son abused me. Then I saw, under his charm lay hatred. Undo the rope of love just once and like a sack of dead and rancid cats all stench pours over your knees and feet. I think men do not like us, though they sweat with wanting, or if they like us, can't fuck except with jogging fondness. No love without hate. That's my discovery to date. Correct me if I'm wrong. Does that accord with your experience?

WIDOW: How would I know . . . Rather a punch in a sodden bedroom than what I got.

DUKE (*entering*): Oh, your best friend weeping!

BIANCA: Yes, for all the phantoms she would not embrace.

DUKE: I'm not a phantom, embrace me!

WIDOW: I dare not, for some smothered feeling might uncoil . . .

DUKE: God forbid!

WIDOW (*to* BIANCA): Kiss him, do, I bow down to your ambition . . . my idiot boy would have worked all hours to get you half a knicker you now toss to the servants from a single wearing . . . fondle her, she is perfect, she is ruthless, more so than you . . .

DUKE: And she cannot get enough of me!

WIDOW: Today . . .

BIANCA: Yes, I am mad for him, and it's not to do with dresses, nor with dinners neither —

WIDOW: No, no . . . !

BIANCA: It's not! He draws me, look at him. He is a manly man, who makes a woman proud, and after, weak. Strong to be loved by him, and a puddle for his desires . . .

WIDOW: Excellent. And yet he's ugly! Begging your indulgence. By all we thought in my day. But so what? He's ugly.

DUKE: I am not ugly. I am the Duke.

WIDOW: He is the Duke.

DUKE: No duke is ugly. I could go like the lice-infested tramp, all fingers in the arm pits, and assure you, all the blades would call it fashion and go scratching likewise, and all women would say, how well he scratches, he is the essence of manhood!

BIANCA (*crossly*): It is not so!

DUKE (*placatory*): No, no, indeed . . .

BIANCA: You humble your fineness, you — (HIPPOLITO *enters. She turns to him, bewildered.*) It is not so, surely, that — he is worth five mundane husbands, surely?

HIPPOLITO: Ten, if yours is fit to go by.

WIDOW: How does he go, my old discarded boy? Often at his castle? He don't invite me ever.

HIPPOLITO: My sister is a fool for him. They carry their joint lechery into the street when they snatch time from the bedroom.

DUKE (*mocking*) In the street! That you would never do! No, sir, discretion is your prime quality.

HIPPOLITO: I do my best.

DUKE: Who would know, to look at him, his neck had travelled through his niece's skirts? Not me, sir!

HIPPOLITO: I'm sorry you find something comical in caution. I shall enjoy my treasure without taking her against the alley wall.

DUKE: Wall-fucking! And the woman is forty!

HIPPOLITO: I think we understand, notionally at least, the power of the oligarchy rests on respect —

DUKE: Respect, is it?

HIPPOLITO: Respect, yes, which is not wall-fucking, is it?

BIANCA: They are in love . . .

HIPPOLITO: Me, too. But if all love to be believed must entail straddling in public —

DUKE: **Respect? Respect?** Nay, stuff respect. It's violence. Pageantry and violence.

HIPPOLITO: You phrase it nakedly.

DUKE: Why not? I tell you how we govern. Tinsel to the nostrils and a spike at the arse. (HIPPOLITO *bows*.) He looks affronted! Oh, the tasteful man, and he reads books! Hippolito is chock with wisdom, and when he dies, will do it quietly, as he fucks, secure in the knowledge all he did was done with taste and judgement, never coarse and never loud . . . (*He entertains*.) It is not fair! Is it? Not fair! Some men succeed at everything! I have a mind to glance at Isabella. Where does he keep his clandestine wife?

BIANCA: You dare go sniffing at her skirt —

DUKE: A mind, I said, I have a mind —

BIANCA: Great bastard, I would hack thy organ — (*She advances on him*.)

WIDOW: I think, seeing the way they go on here, it was a simple crew down at the tavern, and I thought them gross when they swore fuck . . . no, they had no evil such as yours.

DUKE: Drivel, they merely lacked the leisure to refine their lust. Hippolito, you be best man at my marriage.

HIPPOLITO: I thank you, that great honour.

DUKE: And help pay for it!

HIPPOLITO: I thank you for that honour also.

DUKE: He thanks me all the time. All this gratitude, first sign of treason.

HIPPOLITO: Never. I'm of your party.

DUKE: Of it? Squire, you made it! We were shit but one decade ago, forever in the courts of bankruptcy! Now kiss me, and don't get murdered by the opposition. (HIPPOLITO *kisses his cheek*.) My popularity was never higher, and she dangles from me, flashing like some encrusted gem, blinding discontent and dazzling the cynic. Duchess of Florence! How does the title please you?

BIANCA: It enhances my beauty.

DUKE: It does so, and your enhanced beauty in turn enhances me. It would not have troubled me were you a laundress with eight bastards, I would have carried you here. I must have beauty.

WIDOW: Yes, but what is it, this thing beauty?

DUKE: What it is I couldn't tell you. What it is not I know when I look at you.

WIDOW: She has a straight nose, and last year curved noses were in . . .

DUKE (*stung*): Stuff your wisdom. I'll tell you what beauty is, it is what all men collude in desiring, and what all men desire I must have, and fuck it, so there, silence your curiosity with that. (BIANCA *looks at him reproachfully*.) She forces crudity out of me, and now I am embarrassed, why do you keep her here? (*He turns to the* WIDOW.) You will see, old mother, that the dossers will applaud my wedding and go home warmer than they would be from a meal, there is great nourishment in pageantry. Later, the royal birth will have them gasping who cannot conceive themselves, and those that can will name their stinking brats after ours immaculate . . . (*He goes to* BIANCA.) Why has she not conceived already, she might grow a belly from a kiss so sweet is her saliva and so fecund her red mouth . . . (*They gaze at one another*.)

HIPPOLITO: I'll come back later for the details of the wedding . . .

WIDOW: Be off and leave us . . . I could watch for hours, like staring at a living picture book . . . (*The* CARDINAL *enters, and watches*.)

CARDINAL: It is comprehensible, I do insist!

BIANCA (*detaching herself*): You would have scientists put microscopes to women's breasts and weigh them in the scales and come out only with the circumference or gravity, not one smatter wiser why it drives a prince to melancholic death he cannot touch them. Mystery! Adore it! There is little enough and it eases my journey through this puddle of dead dreams to know a man might murder for me, just as when I grow loose on my skeleton like her, to know no man will spare me half a glance will help me say, so, time I quit, and make death easy.

DUKE: Hooray! She owns all the words, and all the juices, marvel at her, moist and brilliant bitch, she cuts the air with phrases, then seduces it!

CARDINAL: She is most philosophical for seventeen . . .

BIANCA: No, I only repeat what clergy tell me, that we all swill in sin. I have trod by beggars and thought, not, oh, charity, oh, alms, but oh, fragility of consciousness, give me a man who finds me in all this horror — divine!

Scene Five

The street. LIVIA.

LIVIA (*gazing about her*): This hogheap. This ratpile. This dosserdom. The hand goes from mouth, to genital, to arse. Fill, rub, and wipe. The geometry of servile continuation. And yet — in all of them I think the possibility of ridiculing the meanness of God's gift, of yelling to his paucity, I chuck off the three points of my loneliness, I will not be animal but ecstasy!

HIPPOLITO (*entering, taking her roughly by the arm*): There you are, come off the alley —

LIVIA: Don't handle me, I am lecturing the universe —

HIPPOLITO: You expose the madness in yourself, you were better plotting liaisons in the parlour.

LIVIA: Well, I fixed you up, how is your fingering? I will not flatter it by a better title — **you hurt**.

HIPPOLITO: What are you to criticize? You know nothing of our passage.

LIVIA: I do. I see you are the man you were. Therefore your love is drivel.

HIPPOLITO: I loathe your arrogance — your breast is out!

LIVIA: It is . . . ! Don't dare replace it, or cover the adored and worshipped thing. It fills him with wonder, for all its papery and worn contour, see, it reads you its history, it is no girl's balloon.

HIPPOLITO: Madness! You have come apart somewhere —

LIVIA: Well, yes, all over!

HIPPOLITO: I need but a pair of signatures and you can be transported to a high and ventilated room where nuns will rope you to a bed. I need but two doctors' signatures.

LIVIA: A doctor's signature! I think there is nothing cheaper, or more willingly lent to the state. Look, there goes a doctor, hey! This woman has found a proper use for her — down here, sir — write on a paper she has caught some terrible employment for her — down here, sir — **don't say the word** — it's a thing for making soldiers for the state — (*To* HIPPOLITO.) **If you had known desire you would not look at me like that.** (*Pause*) Dear brother, I think you are utterly corrupt, as I was once, and if I'm mad, it's only health to be so. I fling off all the junk of sitting rooms that eased me slowly to a sickening retirement. I am utterly alive, and flow where once I rattled dry as straw on saltmarsh, truly . . .

HIPPOLITO: I do not know you, sister, and wish I did. Those afternoons bathed in the fountain of your wit, you teased all of society, and every hit was centre . . .

LIVIA: Teased it, yes, but altered it? I would not go to my grave with such an epitaph as this — she had her salon, she had her wit, she had her teacups and her gin. No, I loathe wit, the rattle of dry words and poets licking one another's sisters. I think we lived an elegant and disgusting life.

HIPPOLITO: We? We? I smell him on your clothes!

LIVIA: Yes!

HIPPOLITO (*seizing her again*): I cannot witness this! This rotting of a woman! (*They struggle.* SORDIDO *appears.*)

SORDIDO: Oi! You gents make too much noise. Get gone. (HIPPOLITO *looks at* SORDIDO, *hesitates, goes.*) Mrs, you are well-loved, I can see it . . .

LIVIA: Yes, but for most of mankind it renders me comprehensible as a dumb Arab . . .

SORDIDO: A stranger even, catches it, some signal like the sailors' flags which reads 'I come well satisfied . . . !'

LIVIA: It's true, and who are you, unnecessarily ragged, feigning the artisan? What are you, a graduate in some obscure science? It won't do in this state to parade your education. Learning, like love, is for the sewers.

SORDIDO: It's the sewers that I live in.

LIVIA: When all above is poison, the sweetest things must flourish in old cracks . . .

SORDIDO (*looking around*):   Please, this is the gutter we are standing in and cops all around us dressed as men — (*He performs spontaneously.*) **Long live the Duke! The Duke a wondrous man, adore the duke there! Adore him you bastard! Roll on his nuptials, etcetera!** He has a big cock, did you know it? Shh! I also pretend to be mad.

LIVIA: I like you. You are not innocent.

SORDIDO: I am made for the age. I carry my brains in my fingers and write nothing. All knowledge lies in instinct, the fugitive carries the truth behind his teeth, don't lend me a book I will be spotted, **man with a book there!** (*He smiles.*) Now sleep with me, if I have entertained you. This offer comes exclusive, since I was a man I've done no more than kiss, and that but faintly . . .

LIVIA: Entertained me, yes you have, but the other, thanks I will not.

SORDIDO: Oh, mingey loyalty to some idle cove, I hate that.

LIVIA: Not loyalty, but hunger for one only, that's proper chastity. I swear nothing to priests or civil servants.

SORDIDO: He has worked wonders on you . . .

LIVIA: And me on him. I'm not his instrument. And yet I am.

SORDIDO: Unfair world, he muttered ritually . . .

LIVIA: No democracy in love.

SORDIDO: None, and I'm no democrat. The word stinks like fish forgotten on the slab. This wedding will drive me to a murder — (*He performs again.*) **Long live the duke! His charm, his love of fun! Adore him you mean-minded bastard!** The more democracy is clapping the more I feel some growl start here — (*he indicates his stomach*) and all my cheeks aswamp with bilious acid, swallow, swallow, choke!

LIVIA: It was not arbitrary, your coming across.

SORDIDO: How could it be? In this state we are all linked who hate, by little quirks and signs, and eyes to eyes direct when looking down would be collusion with the great unanimous approval. The word which characterizes everything is **yes** and no is only fit for whispering — (*He grabs a passer-by by his lapels.*) Say yes!

MAN: Yes . . .

SORDIDO: He says it! See! (*He turns back to* LIVIA.) You are a no, or you could not fuck like that . . . good day . . . (*He bows.* LIVIA *goes off.* BIANCA *and the* WIDOW *appear, indulging a crowd.* LEANTIO *also, suddenly from a new direction*).

LEANTIO: Hide me, sir!

SORDIDO: Turn edgeways then, I'm not broad.

LEANTIO: Hide me and later I'll explain it.

SORDIDO: No, use me do and fuck explanation.

LEANTIO: Is that the duchess of the state?

SORDIDO: In everything but title . . .

LEANTIO: Hide me!

SORDIDO: I do, I do, but I must breathe out and naturally I shrink a little . . . there, I puff up . . . (*They stare at* BIANCA.)

LEANTIO: She goes — what does she do — tell me —

SORDIDO: Shopping.

LEANTIO: Shopping, why? She needs nothing.

SORDIDO: What's need to do with shopping?

LEANTIO: She forever decks herself out . . .

SORDIDO: I hear beneath it all she has a body but none's seen it . . .

LEANTIO: Who says?

SORDIDO: She is a virgin, sir. The paper says so.

LEANTIO: Look! The poor go ahh, go ahh, go ahh . . . she is pretty, they are poor, she grins and they go ahh . . .

SORDIDO: The acme of artificiality.

LEANTIO: No, she means it, which is worse . . . Turn! She comes by here!

SORDIDO: I charge for this, most mobile tree trunk. Forgive me, I must clap, I have my act to think of . . . (*He applauds* BIANCA, *who smiles, passes.*)

LEANTIO: They simper at her beauty, but what do they think?

SORDIDO (*darkly*):   They see her naked in their mind's eye . . .

LEANTIO: No, they think her pure, they cannot envisage such whiteness on its back and yelping.

SORDIDO (*staring after* BIANCA):   You imagine with authority.

LEANTIO: Her love is crude. Is crude, I tell you. (*They watch her depart.*) There, she clears off leaving the rabble disputing in their rags which bonnet suits her best, like fifty popes had sprayed their misery with water . . . (*He turns to* SORDIDO.) I thank you. I was seeking my mistress who went out only for some oranges . . .

SORDIDO: I understand your impatience. Was she smooth and clear-eyed, full of pride in body? It stands out miles, this quality . . .

LEANTIO: Yes. Are you much experienced with women?

SORDIDO: I've slept with none, but I imagine. (*He goes to leave.*)

LEANTIO: Wait, you prince of scrim and flannel . . . (SORDIDO *turns.*) The hag was my mother, and the duchess was my wife . . .

SORDIDO: It's an offence to say so. None have had relations with her but the Duke.

LEANTIO: Well, I tease . . . (*Pause. Their eyes are locked.*)

SORDIDO (*smiling*):   I know it. So much loathing could only come from ripped-up love. They say a fool brought her from Venice and lost her in a week. You are the fool.

LEANTIO: I struggled miserably with the misapprehension she desired me. Desire she did not.

SORDIDO: Desire? Now that I cannot understand. You mean she — no what is it, this desire? Old men will dribble at her wedding, is that it? And bollocky youths make crude eyes, ramming out their arses, is that it? **And dukes go thump, thump, thump into her belly, is that it!** (LEANTIO *clasps him round the shoulders, laughing.*)

LEANTIO: I think I love you! You hate all, and who else can be trusted but him who hates with such discrimination?

SORDIDO: I am Sordido, and you may find me in odd attics scratching with the dead men, or swallowing fine wines in the horticultural extravaganza known as Isabella's house . . . (LEANTIO *starts to go.*) Plot with me. (*He stops.*) I shall burst into the wedding and take the impeccable by force. My first and only entrance to the gateway of all life and death. In her washed matrimonial skin, all scented for the state and bishops' twittering, I'll force her. Down on some polished marbles in foams of lace and splitting fabrics I'll fuck her place! (*Pause.*) There, forget I spoke. Only a vision. I am liable to visions. Comes of poverty and weird alcohols . . . (LEANTIO *is deeply stirred. He looks long into* SORDIDO, *and* SORDIDO *into him.*) Sometimes your life comes to you in the street, drops at your feet like birds dead in the frozen winter. Plop! The crux of your life. And you were only out for oranges . . . (*He lingers, leaves.* LIVIA *hurries in, eating an orange and carrying a bagful.*)

LIVIA: This crowd of gaping gobs has separated us! (*She kisses* LEANTIO.) The genuflecting poor! And filthy hands applauding riches! Was there ever a spectacle more like to make lovers ashamed of love? I felt like smacking them out of their servility. (*She holds out the bag.*) Oranges. (*He does not take one.*)

LEANTIO: I met a man . . .

LIVIA: I also! Do take one, they are so sweet!

LEANTIO: And the man chilled me with a dream.

LIVIA: Look, how huge they are!

LEANTIO (*sending the bag flying*). Piss your oranges! (*They roll across the street. Pause.*)

LIVIA: What dream, Leantio? (*He stares.*)

LEANTIO: A dream not fit for telling. (*He takes her arm.*) Let's get to bed and drown evil in perspiration —

LIVIA: Wait.

LEANTIO: Smother me in your hollows —

LIVIA: Wait, I said —

LEANTIO (*turning angrily on her*). Wait, what for! Wait, you who never waits? What is this hanging back, you with your barmy appetite for love, legs ever open for my fist and now won't shift, why! (*Pause.*)

LIVIA: My flesh is not a pond to drown your fears in. (*Pause.*) Desire's truth, Leantio, and compels it speak. All the rest is fucking. Our union is not a place for hiding in, or a sink to vomit temper. (*Pause.*) What dream, and who was he?

LEANTIO: A dream of Bianca raped. On her wedding morning. (*She goes to him, takes his arm.*) I dare not see more of him! He visits Isabella's house, or you discover him in cellars, so he says, which cellars do you think? A man in black and alive with hate. **He made me long for vegeance on the doll who was my wife.** The dying embers of that instinct he fanned with his imagination, let's go . . . !

LIVIA: Find him.

LEANTIO: Find him?

LIVIA: The man who shakes you so. And drag his dream into the daylight . . .

LEANTIO (*staring at her*). What are you? Livia? (*She extends a hand to him. He does not take it.*) Can't . . . walk beside you but . . . can't touch . . . (*She leads off. He follows. As they leave, the* CARDINAL *appears, watching.*)

CARDINAL: They walk with space between them. The flesh cool and the veins not hammering . . . what's done that? (*He picks up an orange, contemplatively.*) An idea . . . ! Oh, God, an idea has come between them! Oh, easy lust or nagging marriage, this we know and manage, but imagination . . . ! **Birth of an idea there!**

Scene Six

The fort at Rouens. A party enters.

LIVIA (*mocking*):   Here's a fort to terrify an enemy! The walls
are thick with ivy and the cannon in the ditch. As for the
garrison, it's nettles!

SORDIDO: Attention, nettles!

LIVIA (*to* LEANTIO):   I did not know the reach of the
Duke's contempt for you until this minute . . . he might have
smacked you for a cuckold, public in the gob, as give you
this derogatory honour. Loose stair there!

WARD (*gazing around*):   Leantio, exquisite appointment!
Where will you pitch your pennant? A peasant has the
flagpole for fencing cattle in! (*Laughter*)

LIVIA: My skirt's his flag, flapping in the foul wind which
blows off Florence. Smell, smell that! (*She breathes in,
leaning over the parapet.*) Stink of nightclub and brassy
odour of the stock exchange!

WARD (*breathing deeply*):   Duke's crevices.

SORDIDO: Officers' fart and dying breath of doormen.

LIVIA: Vomit of the debutante.

SORDIDO: Great stench of black-gummed deference.

LEANTIO: Why gather here? Where is the virtue in it? (*He
turns away.*)

LIVIA (*staring at the distant city*):   Look, the city glows in
dusk . . . throbs with the pulse of money . . . we stand outside
it and with one finger eliminate corruption . . . (*She holds up
a finger before her eyes.*)

LEANTIO: This is a futile picnic, dancing defiance from a
distance . . .

LIVIA (*turning away*):   But laugh we must! Must laugh at wit
of dukes, who give decrepit forts to men with decent grudges!

SORDIDO: Laugh, yes, because our joke is better.

LEANTIO: What joke? The ruination of Bianca?

LIVIA: Ruination, why? We save her.

LEANTIO: Save her! By rape! Since when was rape salvation?

LIVIA: Leantio, whole cliffs of lies fall down in storms. By
this catastrophe she'll grope for knowledge her ambition
hides from her. And simultaneously, Sordido's crime will
rock the state off its foundations, which is erected on such
lies as ducal marriages.

LEANTIO: I've hated her, God knows the length of my
loathing, yet I would not have my basest urgings played
to —

LIVIA: Oh, he is so decent, forcing down his feelings!

LEANTIO: What did you love me for?

LIVIA: **Your hunger. Not your decency**. (*She holds* LEANTIO
passionately.) What we have found in love doesn't come
to clerks with consciences, all 'does this please you' and
'forgive me, does that hurt?' No, but taking, from the
depths of unkind longing! We liberate her from herself, and
at the same stroke, unleash contempt on all we've come to
hate.

LEANTIO: Where is the realism in all this?

LIVIA: **Realism I hate the word**. (*She contains her fury*.) Shall
we, who have come to knowledge and own truth, not act on
it? Shall we shrivel up in sarcasms, giggling at the satires of
the radicals and make content with sympathizing, doling
cash to rebels we're too posh to meet? I have thrown my
money to the poor while hating charity, and laughed at
criminals while hating crime, and now I act! It kills the soul
not to exploit an inspiration! (*Pause*.) Oh, I irritate him with
my earnestness! Forgive me, I see enthusiasm is only welcome in the bed . . .

LEANTIO: Enthusiasm? Enthusiasm's madness, or its sister,
what's enthusiasm doing here?

LIVIA (*contemptuously*): Leantio, the clerk . . . ! The clerk is
showing through the skin . . .

LEANTIO (*stung*): You hate Bianca and dress up revenge as
politics!

LIVIA: Hate her? No, I pity her. It's you who hates.

LEANTIO: Pity? You? Pity's not a quality I'd pin to you.

LIVIA: Pity, yes. Pity her who uses cunt as property, to buy
her way up floors of privilege. When Sordido's forced his
pain on her she'll learn the thing she sells can just as well be
stolen . . . (*Pause*. LEANTIO *paces*.)

LEANTIO: We rob her of her rights . . .

SORDIDO: Her right to nay. Her right to yea, she can keep
that.

LEANTIO (*paces, turns*): This rape — this rape you call
deliverance —

SORDIDO: Rape, indeed, and not the first time . . .

LEANTIO (*turning on* SORDIDO): Who raped her pre-
viously, me?

LIVIA: You? Never you. The Duke. With my connivance. I wrapped her for his lust and tied the ribbon, while you sweated in a foreign port.

LEANTIO: It was seduction, though I shudder to imagine, seduction it was, surely —

SORDIDO: **Violation**. (*Pause*) Violation, yes, which came by wealth and power. And her protesting mouth was stopped, not by a fist, but greed and glamour suffocated it. By her squalid ambition was repulsion choked. And now, against the Duke's degraded appetite, my purity claims access to her ravaged territory. (*Pause. LEANTIO stares at him.*)

LEANTIO: It's death.

SORDIDO: I risk death for her privacy. And stealing her toy virginity, all the poor of Florence grab their rights, who had been meant only to swoon with insatiable envy ...

WARD: While he, immaculate rebel, among her moist wound intrudes, I'll shout out **oh, exquisite robbery!**

LIVIA (*laughing, embracing the* WARD). Here comes your wife, delighted with this mossy tower and thinking it a perfect place to picnic!

WARD (*going to intercept her at the top of the steps*): Beloved! The steps are shattered, mind your ankle!

LIVIA: Through her I will arrange Sordido's entry to the palace. Hurry, leave us ... ! (SORDIDO *and the* WARD *hasten down.* LIVIA *turns to* LEANTIO.) Who would have thought I might descend to trickery again? Old skills don't die. Sad truth. (*She caresses him.*) And yet, a thing is vile, not in itself, but only in relation to its usage —

LEANTIO: Not so, that's cruel misuse of reason —

LIVIA: **Of course it's so**. (*He turns from her. Pause.*)

LEANTIO: So, this is the infant of our exceptional love ... You labour for a child as hideous as this ...

LIVIA: You are so precious, who half-killed me with his passion once ... (*Pause. She takes his head in her hands.*) Oh, listen, our love plunged through all layers of affection, burst longing, split open desire, struck seams not of comfort but of truth! We humiliate our long adventure if we draw back from its message!

ISABELLA (*entering*): Oh, pretty place!

LIVIA (*disengaging from* LEANTIO): I knew you'd love it! (*She goes to* ISABELLA's *side.*) Niece, all's well with you if you adore your husband — (*She turns back to* LEANTIO.) Do leave us to speak a little, private thing ... ! (LEANTIO *goes out.*) He wants to love you, chaste and passionate, it's true! Is he not kind to you, in preparation? Confirm it, he has not for whole weeks teased you.

ISABELLA: No, he has been weird and considerate . . .

LIVIA: Exactly! His scheme — of such excessive romance I could blush for him — is to marry you at Bianca's wedding!

ISABELLA: Marry me? We are already married!

LIVIA: Oh, that, no, this one he calls proper. It's the way with these leathery cynics to want white weddings and lace underthings who bawl the dirtiest. (*Pause.*)

ISABELLA: Two weddings? One for the mass . . . one secret . . .

LIVIA: Yes! And this with consummation! But one thing. He will have Sordido there as witness, then to depart, no more the irritation to your happiness.

ISABELLA: Sordido . . .

LIVIA: Smuggle him in, as Gentlemen to you. He'll kiss hands and vanish. You'll hear no more from him.

ISABELLA: Dear Aunt — (*She goes to embrace her.* LIVIA *recoils.*)

LIVIA: No, you only wound me with your gratitude, I merely repeat your loved one's own suggestions. Now, downstairs and join them at the barbecue . . . (ISABELLA *skips away.*) Nothing's lost . . . for all my travelling in love, through hurricanes of difference . . . I believe I'm even better at it . . .

Scene Seven

The Palace. BIANCA *is bridal.*

BIANCA (*posturing at a mirror*): What do you think?

CARDINAL: Think . . .

BIANCA: To see me thus. Do you think — she is pretty as a doll — she is so pretty she is — scarcely human — or rather, at some point she is naked under that? (*She walks, turns.*) Do you think, she is a confection of femininity, or rather — I would give my life to kiss her arse? I only ask. I have never been a duchess before.

CARDINAL: I think — you are not a woman at all — but a symbol of the state.

BIANCA: You have a wonderful intellect.

CARDINAL: I have lived my life with symbols. I am wearing symbols. I worship them. I finger them before I sleep.

BIANCA: It is a strange way to spend a life, always the thing that isn't, and never the think that is. I think your head must ache. And not just your head. Ache . . . ache . . . (*She hurries to him, anxious, proud.*) Look what I've done! Look at me! Am I not perfect? Say I'm perfect, you who has been since his cradle, celibate, tell me I am perfect!

CARDINAL: In all ways.

BIANCA: I think this is the absolute of joy! And everything hereafter, downhill. After you have anointed us, and all trumpets and all beggars and all cavalry have pranced and wept and bellowed and spat spit and coughed phlegm and shat their dung and splintered glasses and all old women cried for what they never knew and all the ugly railed at what they never were, I shall on the eiderdown, among cracking of braid and tearing taffeta, go down for his lips, and all the power of the state will huddle at my little, florid entrance . . .

CARDINAL: The state made flesh . . .

BIANCA: There you go — symbols again! Still, if it keeps you sane . . . (*He turns to go, bowing.*) You know, I think there must be poverty, if not of life, then mind. Or we could not love ourselves so much . . . (*He goes out. The* WIDOW *enters, adoring.*)

WIDOW: You dazzle, darling. Brilliance splashing through my cataracts. If I were a man, I'd say fuck God, why kneel to him, this is perfection. And it is . . . (*She weeps.*)

BIANCA (*holding her*): I am everything, aren't I? I am everything. There must be me, mustn't there? There must be me, or they would all —

SORDIDO: Despair? (*She turns.*)

BIANCA: You mistook your entrance. Chamberlains and ushers in the hall.

ISABELLA (*entering, crossly*): You should not be here!

SORDIDO: No, this is my entrance —

ISABELLA: No, you go — (*She goes to lead him.*)

SORDIDO: **This is my entrance**. (*He advances on* BIANCA.) I am so immaculate for this. I am not some fetid courtier or mortgagee who labels himself Duke by virtue of some thousand hired guards, no, were he even half-legitimate he could not quarrel with my right **I am thirty and pure**. No dirty walls resounded with my roar as I thumped the belly of the prostitute, am I not good for this, and fit to be your mate? You are no virgin, after all, I flatter you with my infatuation . . .

BIANCA (*sensing his intention, to* ISABELLA): Fetch my officer, who stands outside.

SORDIDO: Drag him in by all means, he has no throat to cry alarm.

ISABELLA (*horrified*): **What is this?**

LIVIA (*entering*): I must, who makes dreams come to life, witness the occurrence. Don't call me hypocrite, what I have dealt in I attend right to the finish.

WIDOW (*recognizing her*): Oh, lady, I know you! We played chess when I was your neighbour!

LIVIA (*her eyes fixed on* BIANCA): Is that so? The moves I don't recall . . .

BIANCA: Why are you here?

LIVIA: Did I not work your seduction by the governor of this place, and now unwork it . . .

BIANCA: You tremble . . . more than me . . .

LIVIA: Yes . . .

BIANCA: Is this my murder, then?

SORDIDO: Shout help and see. As for gasps, I make allowances . . . (*He goes towards her.*)

WIDOW: Oh, fucking Jesus, they are going to throw her in a heap!

BIANCA: Run, then, and save me! (*The* WIDOW *staggers towards the door, meeting* LEANTIO.)

WIDOW: Oh, son, I thought you had a fort . . . (*She turns back.*) I won't go, dear. I think they'll throttle me. And I've never seen this done . . .

BIANCA (*to* LIVIA): You are a woman. Intervene!

LIVIA: No, sweet and perfumed thing, we have the same sex, but are not equally women. It's a false sisterhood you seek in me.

BIANCA: Oh, utter vileness to wreck this wedding . . .

SORDIDO: No, this is the proper matrimony! The people marry you! (*He seizes her.*)

LEANTIO: Oh, dear girl wife, who clung to me in perfect innocence, in shadows of her father's wall —

LIVIA: **It is not her.**

LEANTIO: I hate this life which wrings such changes! (*He weeps on* LIVIA.) Give me the lie of innocence, always the lie —

LIVIA: No, life is alteration, the shedding of all things until at death there's no regret, but all's been spent, discard, discard or petrify! (ISABELLA *runs off.*) Stop her!

SORDIDO (*emerging*): Is that love? Is that?

WIDOW: Search me what love is, son . . .

SORDIDO: **I say it is**.

WIDOW: It is, then . . .

SORDIDO (*to* LIVIA): She loves me . . .

LIVIA (*seeing his madness*): Yes . . .

SORDIDO: **Does I say**. (*He looks around.*) She is a miracle, beneath. It was as if I knew her, and always had. I could die now, and not protest . . . (*The* DUKE, HIPPOLITO, *the* CARDINAL *burst in armed.*)

DUKE: Oh, my property! They stamp about my loveliness! Look, her clothes cling round his boots! Die, you thing of shit and sewerage! (*He kills* SORDIDO.) I am defiled! (HIPPOLITO *goes to attack* LIVIA.) Not her! Keep her for torture! Dogs to lick her womb!

ISABELLA: Bianca! Where is Bianca!

DUKE: See to her, I cannot . . . cannot come near such a pitch of muddy squalor as my bride is now . . .

CARDINAL: Can she stand? Or is she injured?

DUKE: **I don't know I haven't looked**. (*He sees* LEANTIO.) You, I understand. So when you die I'll think, through all his twitching, as the skin peels off his flesh, he gloats to know he wounded me, his enemy . . . (*To* LIVIA.) But you, envious and unwomanly, such a refinement of horror as you deserve will tax the most senior torturer's imagination. I'll send to Turkey, or to China, for the pain that suits you best . . .

LEANTIO: Mother, even you will suffer . . .

WIDOW: Me? I've got no politics.

CARDINAL: The blind man also feels the storm.

WIDOW: **I only came 'ere for a decent dinner**.

DUKE (*to* ISABELLA, *who is attending* BIANCA): How is she? She must go through with it, or government is mocked. Sentries are fainting in the heat and mobs of dirty unemployed press on one another's backs. She must go through with it!

HIPPOLITO: All who've witnessed this, kill off. And what's not known will start no rumour.

DUKE (*seeing* BIANCA, *staggering*): Oh, my shame and my —

BIANCA (*seeing* SORDIDO's *body*). You stabbed him . . .

DUKE: **I slew the thief.** (*He extends a hand to her.*) You are not damaged?

BIANCA: Damaged . . .

DUKE: You seem — ruffled but — not imperfect . . .

BIANCA: Imperfect — I — (*She shudders, falls into the* DUKE's *arms.*)

HIPPOLITO: Press her . . . ! Tell her, on her own two feet. Her coach is squealing on its springs and you should be at the cathedral.

BIANCA: **No** —

DUKE: Be sweet now, you are not so very —

BIANCA: Not so very, no —

DUKE: Some spirit for her, to bring back colour in her cheeks — look, the bastard scratched her — **powder it!** (*He turns away, in disgust.*)

BIANCA (*as* HIPPOLITO *comes to examine her*): **Don't touch.** (*She fingers the place.*) Why did he? Was I too beautiful for him? I think he would have snapped my spine, my loveliness enraged him so. Did he hate beauty?

LIVIA: Yes, to see it sell itself —

DUKE: **Powder her cheek.** We are too late already —

BIANCA: No. (*Pause. He stares at her.*) No.

DUKE: I would remind you, lovely as you are —

BIANCA: Are? Liar. You mean were.

DUKE: I would remind you, lovely as you —

BIANCA: **Were** —

DUKE: You are not flesh alone but also state, as I am, also **State**.

BIANCA: You did not mention that behind the statues, I thought you then pure male but now I find —

DUKE: **Mention it? You knew it, hypocrite!** The rod that thrust between your skirts was double thick with wealth and treble thick with power, you flowed for it! (*Pause*)

BIANCA: Yes . . . and that's not love, is it? Is it? (*She looks at the* CARDINAL.) Oh, what am I, then? When I go — when I tremble for a man, for this man and not for that one, what is it made of, love?

CARDINAL: A discourse on the origins of passion I more than most, would dearly love to hear deliberated, but in the street all Florence wonders what —

BIANCA: Oh, fuck Florence . . . (*She smiles.*) Well, of course, I have . . . (*She goes to* LIVIA.) Dear woman, your eyes are gates damming back the torrents in your soul . . . (LIVIA *holds her.*) I forgive you . . . the selling of me to this merchant of men . . . and I forgive you twice . . . the undoing of my knotted womb which swelled and gushed to base desire . . . (*To* DUKE *etc.*) I'll not act the coronation. (*She holds* LIVIA.)

HIPPOLITO: This is real shit we're plunged in.

DUKE: Shut up.

HIPPOLITO: I tell you, we —

DUKE: Do up your gob, you quivering bastard!

HIPPOLITO: Ridicule can topple empires . . .

DUKE: I do so hate — at moments of the deepest crisis — clever dicks delivering homilies! (*He walks a little, stops.*) I ask her once again, and if she won't must stab her and say the violator did it. So I'll convert this farce into a tragedy, and win more pity than contempt. I'll be the black-clad mourner of all Europe, and all future cruelty will be explained away by pain.

HIPPOLITO (*in awe*):   Oh, God, the brilliance of him . . . !

CARDINAL (*aghast*):   But she — her beauty — she is so —

DUKE: Oh, he trembles at the well of love! On your knees to her spoiled fundament! (*He thrusts the* CARDINAL *aside.*) Bianca, adored woman and picture of purity, come now and kneel in sight of all and seal our love. (*He extends a hand. Aside to the* WIDOW.) Get pins, do up her garments. (*Pause.* BIANCA *does not respond.*) Never mind the love, then. Kneel anyway. (*His hand remains.*) Come on, we had incredible nights and will again. (*Pause. She still refuses.*) **No act that two could do was not attempted by us, what is this!** (*Weeping, he turns to the* CARDINAL.) Oh, on her funeral my weeping will be real, I shall go naked through the streets behind her coffin . . .

BIANCA: I must be truthful. In cunt. If nowhere else, then there. For all the lies we carry, and must carry, lies of politics and kindess, the small lie and the big, I don't protest. All the things we handle leave us stained, but there I do want — **futile, pursuit, who knows — I** do want truth. Not hungering for what my father tutored me was male, or nurses giggling at the soldiers' strut, but what my stripped emotion commands me. And him, utterly anonymous on the floor, did break some bond, for if I loved power, and power was my

dream of male, he had it, too. **Help me understand my needs**.
(*Pause. They stare at her.*)

DUKE: Yes, will do, and work it out at leisure in our villa,
dwarfs and maniacs if that's your craving . . .

BIANCA: Oh, God, I never felt so cold, such a deep cold and
so alone . . . (*She goes to disrobe.*) Get these clinging weapons off me and I'll wander.

DUKE: **Wander? Wander!** Never wander! You have fucked
your entrance into politics, never wander more, you are
collared for your lust!

CARDINAL: They are frothing in the streets, and turning
over toffee apple stalls . . .

DUKE: Wander, no . . . (*He puts his hand to his dagger.*)
Forgive me, Lord of Governments, who lends His mercy to
him stretched between love and responsibility . . . (*He goes
towards* BIANCA.)

LIVIA: Don't kill her for confusing your costume with your
sex . . .

DUKE (*striking her*): **Hate! Hate the knowing woman!** (*He
stares at her.*)

HIPPOLITO: Act then . . . (*The* DUKE *turns to* BIANCA.)
Act . . . (*Pause.* LEANTIO *goes to move, but* LIVIA *restrains
him.*)

LEANTIO: Oh, my life's love . . .

HIPPOLITO: Act, or the market will be trampled and money
bleed to death . . .

CARDINAL: I think, if Christ stood here, his wounds would
open to hear money made your god . . . !

HIPPOLITO: **Act!**

DUKE (*touching* BIANCA's *exposed neck*): Oh, this perfect
neck all white with cruelty, it rots — all — calculation —
Bianca . . . ! (*He slides down her, to his knees, sobbing.*)

HIPPOLITO: Oh, somebody govern! (*He goes to take the
dagger from the* DUKE, *but the* WARD *enters.*)

WARD: No rush . . . (*He goes to the body of* SORDIDO.)
Beloved, uncharitable thing. If every stab was gob what a
roar of derision would thunder out your corpse! **Do you think
it hurt him to be killed?** He hated life, it was absurd to him.
His sneering lip! He flung words like shards of glass against
the flashy whore and schoolgirls blushing with false innocence, monarchs, tramps, all their posturing he slashed. I
shall be so alone . .

HIPPOLITO (*inspired*): Govern the state.

WARD: Why? You take me for a cynic, and therefore fit to rule? I'd no more force decisions on the rest than throttle babies in their prams, which I considered once, for humour . . . (*He looks at* LIVIA.) Let her.

HIPPOLITO: Her? She's been seen skirts-up in the alley.

WARD: Good. Let her govern. She knows, and she hates money. Let that be your manifesto! **I love and I hate money**. Quote it, publish now!

HIPPOLITO (*pursuing his intuition*):   You, for all your mockery, you have the wisdom, think!

WARD: I am too good an actor. I would tell the truth in such a way to make it unbelievable, and then they'd all rejoice to swallow simple lies! No, she is the fittest for a dynasty.

HIPPOLITO (*hurrying away*):   Oh, catastrophe!

BIANCA: Is also birth . . .

CARDINAL: What?

BIANCA: Catastrophe is also birth. Out the ruins crawls the bloody thing, unrecognizable in the ripped rags of former life. Ghastly breaths of unfamiliar air! Like the infant, expelled from the silent womb, screams red its horror, then tastes oxygen. I have to find my life! (LIVIA *goes to embrace her.*) **Don't touch**. (*She freezes.*) Too new to be suffocated by your impulsive sisterhood. I'll bruise. I'll crush in your embrace . . .

WIDOW (*staggering*):   Take me, someone!

LEANTIO: Oh, you waddling bag of rheumatism and sinking flesh, can't you get enough of life? (*The* WARD *tugs her away, then stops, seeing* ISABELLA.)

WARD: Isabella? What of you, then? (ISABELLA, *does not reply, but goes to* BIANCA, *stands by her.*) Isabella? (*She does not reply. He goes out. There is a cacophony of running feet, yells off. The* CARDINAL *goes to make his escape.*)

LIVIA (*seeing him*):   Get Christ out of your pocket! He knew money strangled love, and love's corpse stifled imagination, and dead imagination was the ground from which more money grew. Money, death, and money! (*The* CARDINAL *starts to go.*) **Don't go**.

CARDINAL (*turning violently on her*):   Love! To hear you speak of love who engineered this agony! **Murder of words**. (*He goes out.* LIVIA *reaches a hand to* LEANTIO.)

LIVIA: Leantio, down to the street now. And tell the people we have broken lies and tread the pieces. (*He stares at her.*) Leantio . . . down to the street now and —

LEANTIO: **Stay by her**. (*He looks at* BIANCA.) Must . . .

BIANCA: I do not want it, Leantio. Little spasm of male pity. Male violence, male pity. The blow. The charity. Get off . . . !

ISABELLA: Escape, or we shall never!

LIVIA: Rags, tattered trousseau in the alleys, run! (*Suddenly* BIANCA *strikes* LIVIA *in the face.* LIVIA *reels, as does* BIANCA *from the force of it. Pause.*)

BIANCA: Thank you . . . (*They stare at one another, then* ISABELLA *hurries* BIANCA *away. Pause,* LIVIA, LEAN-TIO *apart and still.*)

DUKE: New duke! (*He points to* LEANTIO.) New duchess! (*He points to* LIVIA. LIVIA *and* LEANTIO *go to hurry out.*) Don't love . . . ! Don't love . . . !

MINNA

'Oh, stifle this laughter, Tellheim! I implore you!
It is a terrifying laughter which betrays a hatred of
humanity . . .'

G.E. LESSING, *Minna von Barnhelm*, 1767

CHARACTERS

MINNA VON BARNHELM	A Woman of Twenty-five
FRANCISCA	Her Three Maids
JUST	A Discharged Soldier
TELLHEIM	A Discharged Officer
THE HANGED	Two Unlucky Civilians
LANDLORD	Of the Inn at Grosshayen
WERNER	A Discharged Officer
COUNT VON BRUCHSALL	Minna's Guardian
VOYAGERS	To the Isle of Cythera
CUPID	An Infant God

ACT ONE

Scene One

An encampment in Saxony. Tents, ropes. A hanged man, a hanged woman, revolve in the breeze. A sprawling soldier tightens a drumskin. He idly hits it with a stick. Four women enter, dressed as bundles. MINNA walks up and down, anxiously. The others watch, holding hatboxes, valises, etc.

MINNA: This was a mistake. (*Pause*)
A mistake obviously and yet (*Pause*)
A mistake that had to be made (*Pause*)
Error. Error. My forte. And magnificence.
All fingers point in one direction and still she (*Pause*)
Yes
Smother me
Plaster me
Immerse me in good counsel still I
Swimming ponds of kindness still I
Minna
The little figure in the snowstorm of sound advice
Shake
Shake
Down float the words of warning
The greater the unanimity the more inclined she is to
Yes
Demurr
Minna
Self-destructive
Minna
Idiot
Von Barnhelm

I agree
Perhaps she aches to die
Minna
Perhaps she does . . . (*She stops pacing, she addresses the soldier.*)
Where are the officers? (*He ignores her.*)
The officers, where are they? (*He is as if deaf. She turns to her maids.*)

Leave me if you wish! Abandon me! I am so grateful to you, you have excelled the highest standards of devotion, merci, merci, merci, always I will think of you, go quickly or I'll cry . . . ! (*She turns away. They do not move. She peeps.*)

You have not gone?
You persevere with such a mistress as I am?
Oh, do you love me so implacably?
Am I irresistible to you?
I am!
Obviously I am! (*They run to her. They embrace as nearly as possible in their bundles. They turn as if in a dance.*)

JUST: **Take your clothes off shoes there wigs there keep it neat now naked yes naked I said that's an order and in silence who said you could speak hands by your sides so what it's cold it's winter who said you could.** (*The women stare at him. He taps the drum with a finger, testing its tension.* MINNA *walks curiously to him, looks.*) **I do the talking round here stand up lie down stand up again don't look at me look at the ground the mud the puddle is what you should look at not me and when I.** (*Pause. The women look at one another.* JUST *climbs to his feet.*) My master is expecting you.

MINNA: Impossible, I am a surprise.

JUST: He expects surprises. (*He starts to go out.*)

MINNA: Wait! (*He stops.*) What do you mean, he is expecting me, it is seven years since I —

JUST: Von Barnhelm? Minna? (*She stares.*) My name is Just. I am his servant. And I knew you would appear . . . (*He bows.* MINNA *looks to the maids.*)

MINNA: Advice!
Advice! (*The* FRANCISCAS *immediately erupt into a cacophony of advice.*)

FRANCISCAS: Turn round at once / Write a letter / Wait at the inn and / The situation is so very / And then let him in but / Wear a flimsy garment in bright red / Refuse / Refuse to entertain him until he / Flinging yourself at his feet say / Back to Grosshayen quick / Be ever so severe / And that big hat with flowers on / Just cry / Be absolutely rigid with contempt / And cry until / (*Pause.* MINNA *walks up and down, reassured by this routine. She stops.*)

MINNA: And more!

FRANCISCAS: Black is your colour / Say I was merely passing and / White hat and gloves / No make up / None / Command him with that severity you have / Back to Wiesbaden quick as your legs can carry you / He'll fall at your feet and / Run / (*They stop. A wind blows.* MINNA *looks at them.*)

MINNA: Sometimes you hear a door close in your life, as if some draught of history had caught it... (*Pause*) How lovely our life was...! And we did not appreciate it, obviously! Sometimes we thought it boring and routine but now...! It will shimmer on the margins of our dreams, a Heaven wilfully abandoned...! (*Pause*)

FRANCISCA: Minna... go home... (*Pause.* MINNA *glares at her.*)

Go home...

MINNA: And yet, we part even with perfection...

FRANCISCA: Please...

MINNA: Why, when I know full well this man is not happiness... (*An officer appears, stops. Her back is towards him and she does not turn.*) You are not happiness, are you? (*She turns to face him. He bows.*)

JUST: **Kneel down I said you heard me kneel and face the ditch where she was kneeling you kneel there eyes straight ahead and silent silent yes goodbye** (TELLHEIM *emerges from his bow. His eyes meet* MINNA's. *A rush of memory and confusion.*)

FRANCISCAS: Seven years / She was a girl and now / Seven / I could draw him with my eyes shut / Seven of impatience and / Could press his lips from clay / Despair / His lips particularly she / (*Pause*)

MINNA: Happiness... what's that...? (*She laughs, she turns swiftly to* FRANCISCA.) He had blue eyes!

FRANCISCAS: We're tired / This pilgrimage has stained our lives / Fields burned and cities / Who could have witnessed this and still survived unscathed / It isn't him, Minna / But us / Who've changed (*Pause.* MINNA *looks back to* TELLHEIM.)

TELLHEIM: Minna . . . I will speak little . . . as I did before
. . . few words in case I lie . . . you know my horror of exaggeration . . . and my belief what cannot be said simply cannot
be properly said at all . . . Minna . . . I think the word
love stands alone and requires no props of metaphor . . . is
purest unaccompanied . . . therefore I'll say this once and not
much more . . . I love you . . . (MINNA *gazes on him, ponde-*
ring.)

FRANCISCAS: Something has happened . . .

TELLHEIM: Yes . . . A war . . . (*Pause. MINNA turns swiftly*
to FRANCISCA.)

MINNA: Advice!

FRANCISCAS: Beautiful / Oh, Miss / Was ever a thing better
expressed / No grossness / Coarseness poetry or slang / But /
Truth / And his eyes, simple and direct / His eyes / Truth
surely comes / Like this

MINNA: But they were blue . . . ! (*She searches FRANCI-*
SCA with her own eyes.) His eyes . . .

FRANCISCAS: **So what . . . !** (*The FRANCISCAS giggle*
with excitement, embarassment and pleasure. MINNA turns
resolutely to TELLHEIM.)

MINNA: Your brevity is much appreciated. Not necessarily
by me, I have a weakness for hyperbole. And your sincerity
is obvious, though so is my confusion, **Tellheim are you**
altered (*Pause*) Darling, I kept you like an altar in my heart
and laid my youth there, day after day laid down and
smoothed like banknotes, no balls, no parties, and men who
looked at me might just as well have flung their glances at
stone walls, **Are you altered or is it me**? (*She looks. She wills*
herself. TELLHEIM laughs.) My brown-eyed love . . . ! (*She*
goes to embrace him, but her bundles keep him at a distance.
Her arms fall. Pause.)

TELLHEIM: Madam, you are intangible . . .
Which is correct, for I'm not a fit subject for your adoration
any more . . .

MINNA: No? Why not? (*Pause*)
            Why not, Tellheim? (JUST *beats out a fast tap on*
            his drum.)

THE HANGED: Minna . . . !
                        Minna . . . !
                        Is it true you never take advice?

MINNA: As true as God and all that happens I say yes to.

THE HANGED: Tellheim will be the death of you.

MINNA: Indeed! I expected nothing less of such a man!
THE HANGED: Minna . . . !
                       Minna . . . !
MINNA: What I have chosen, I adhere to.
THE HANGED: Minna . . . !
MINNA: Yes, and cleave! **Cleave!**
THE HANGED: Death's not half of it.
MINNA: So be it, **I have marched five hundred miles of murder
    to be here, this also was campaign** (*She turns abruptly.*)
THE HANGED: Minna . . . !
                       Minna . . . !
MINNA (*turning irritably*):   What!
THE HANGED: He *is* Tellheim . . . (*The drum stops.* FRAN-
    CISCA *goes to* TELLHEIM.)
FRANCISCA: My mistress, where shall she sleep? Since you
    were expecting her, provision has been made, I dare assume?
    (*Pause*)
                       Comforts. (*Pause*)
                       Privacy. (*Pause*)
                       Etcetera. (TELLHEIM *looks at her, then
    indicates with a hand.* JUST *picks up some of the bags. He and
    the servants depart. A faint wind.*)
MINNA: I read so much it is quite possible you'll find me
    difficult to love. You have lived, but I have studied, and I
    won't concede you anything in experience. My little bedroom
    was the site of slaughter also. Do not laugh at me. I mean,
    blood flows in libraries . . . (TELLHEIM *looks at her. Sud-
    denly.*) Have I aged? For months I plucked grey hairs as if
    — why does one do such things — as if your love might
    suddenly recoil to know I am a girl no longer. Tell me you
    like grey hairs. Tell me all you see is what you wanted.
    (*Pause*) Philosophy I particularly liked, but algebra oh,
    algebra is my best friend, wherever we have been the walls
    are chalked with — and the roads — smothered in equations!
    I love you and these bundles kept us chaste! That was my
    idea also. (*She laughs.*) No man could come near us, as you
    have seen! In these we passed whole regiments of deserters
    unviolated, true! (*Pause*) Am I talking too much? But some-
    one must, for you are silent.
TELLEHIM: As ever, Minna.
MINNA: As ever, yes! An example of my algebra, and do say
    this appeals to you, the elevation of a howitzer! The elev-
    ation of *a* howitzer is *c* squared over *a* squared over *b*, *b*

being the weight of the projectile, but taking the trajectory as *y*, the rate of fall might be expressed as *x* over *b* — and these bundles depressed the spirits of the most determined ravisher believe me, Francisca for some reason they — not me — were forever lending their attentions to — I stared them out, I defied them — I'm talking too much it is fear, Tellheim . . . (*She hangs her head. Pause.*)

TELLHEIM: I did not hate the war, Minna . . .

MINNA: No . . . ?

TELLHEIM: How easy it is to say you hate a war . . .

MINNA: Yes . . . I suppose it is . . .

TELLHEIM: We long to wear the badges of civility even if our hands are red.

MINNA: Yes.

TELLHEIM: I did not hate the war. Nor do I hate the consequences of it. (*His gaze takes in* THE HANGED. MINNA *registers this.*) You see, I do so want to be truthful, Minna.

MINNA: Yes! Do be truthful if you can!

TELLHEIM: And this truthfulness may horrify you.

MINNA: Well, yes, perhaps, but — (*She smiles.*) How odd! We are both warning one another, we are both issuing these threats, as if appalling danger lay in this. It is anxiety, surely. It is a form of love? (TELLHEIM *goes out.* THE FRANCIS-CAS *enter.* MINNA *turns to them.*) Undress me, now. Unwrap me from my innocence I must discard all things that kept me from my love . . . (*Music.* THE FRANCISCAS *unwind* MINNA *from her bundle, spinning her round. The dance ceases. A crow caws. The* FRANSICAS *depart.* MINNA *is not naked but stands in a dark, formal, modern suit and blouse. She looks into the audience. She laughs.*)

Scene Two

The inn at Grosshayen. The LANDLORD *enters with a single glass on a tray. Some time in the 1950s.*

LANDLORD: You're not the first.

MINNA: No.

LANDLORD: Nor the last, I daresay.

MINNA: No.

LANDLORD: And may I say at once you are not welcome.

MINNA: Say it by all means.

LANDLORD: Not at all welcome. I put the tonic in. We don't like strangers. We do not even like each other. And ice, but I'm out of lemons.

MINNA: Thank you. (*The* LANDLORD *turns as if to go, stops.*)

LANDLORD: Your underwear is white. (*Pause. His back is turned to her.*)

Miss Barnhelm.

MINNA: I heard you.

LANDLORD: Is it? The white ones you've got on today? (*She is still.*)

You could be my worst enemy. And killed my child. You could be everything I loathe and still I'd crave to know. (*Pause*)

LANDLORD: Absurd the thing called love.

MINNA: It is love, is it? My underwear is love?

LANDLORD: **Love yes why not love idiot**. (*Pause*)

What time do you like breakfast? (*Pause. She swallows her drink.*) I cleaned your room myself this morning I'll do Miss Barnhelm's I said to the maid she knows me she pities me and I'm religious in my own way handling your garments in the wardrobe is not unlike old women stooping to the relics of the saints dinner is at seven no need to book though we have parties here sometimes I hate myself of course the parties come like you to plough the past but then I think at least I am redeemed by honesty I am not toxic with some secret urge some are you know by speaking it you find relief do you require a newspaper at breakfast I don't read papers myself but you are a woman of the world what world however Grosshayen's good enough for me Grosshayen is a world also not a nice one possibly. (*He hesitates, turns to go, stops.*) So is it —

MINNA: Yes.

White today.

The LANDLORD *goes out. There is a sudden eurption of shattering glass, breaking windows, a cry, then a cacophony of yells. The* FRANCISCAS *rush in from all directions. They are also dressed clerically.*

FRANCISCAS: Oh, Miss / Enough of this / Someone will be / We say no to all intimidation / Back to the city quick / All the more reason to defy / It's not undignified to quit / Exactly the tactics I predicted / Pack the bags now / Oh, Miss / Resist / Another day / Lives at risk / (*They await her opinion. Pause.*)

MINNA: I'm brave. (*Pause*) This bravery is pure prejudice, I admit. (TELLHEIM, *in modern dress, enters. He stands silently.*) An absence of philosophy perhaps, for whilst I read philosophy I merely use it to shelter in, I wrap myself in concepts, I am a bundle of suffocating propositions which serve to immunize me against doubt. A self-righteous prig, Minna von Barnhelm, and humourless, no doubt. Do sit down and stop smiling, Major Tellheim, every day you wear that smile which is designed to make me feel naive, presumably? (*He sits at a bare table.*) But the naive are necessary, don't you think sophistication might only blur the stark colours of justice, a word I do not fear at all, do you, justice? It's algebraic, crime, punishment, and justice, I think. (*Pause*) I've come to prosecute you . . . (*Pause*) Murderer . . . (*Pause. She closes her eyes.*)
       Shh . . . (*A cruel wind blows through a landscape.* JUST *enters with a pile of books.*)

JUST: Grosshayen is an island. Listen! Always the sound of the sea! (*He poses, head on one side. Then he dumps the books on the table. The sound of traffic on roads.*) Metal! Metal sea! And when you breathe, the spray! (*He breathes.*) Carbons, oxides, blowing off the coast! (*He dusts the books with his cuffs.*) As for the sunsets! Madam, did you see the sun more veiled in mystery than he is here? He glows through fogs and soots more lovely than some blazing thing in the South Seas. For the subtle, obviously, Grosshayen. For the artists. The explorers of the soul and eye . . . (*He looks at* TELLHEIM.) Miss Barnhelm asked for the regimental diary. What have we to hide?

FRANCISCA (*casting a glance along the spines of the books*):   It's not all here . . .

JUST: No, three are missing, but don't conclude anything from that.

MINNA: Why not?

JUST: In five years the regiment was annihilated several times. You can't recall the men, why imagine you can recall the diaries?

MINNA: That sounds clever, Mr Just —

JUST: Clever? Is it clever to die? I never saw much that was clever in it —

MINNA: You are trying to belittle me —

JUST: But then, I never died myself, perhaps when your body is chewed in seven pieces there is a certain cleverness in that —

TELLHEIM: Just —

JUST: Head this way, legs that, intestines hanging off the treetops, that's cleverness, perhaps —

MINNA: **You are using your pain to mock me, Mr Just**. (*Pause.* JUST *smiles.*)

JUST: No, it's an island, this, between three major routes. All night the traffic flows . . . oranges from Jaffa . . .

Dutch boots . . . (*Pause*)

Do you require anything else, Miss Barnhelm? (MINNA *shakes her head. He goes out.*)

FRANCISCAS: A liar / A liar, obviously / This place swims in deceit / His eyes / His eyes / That sunken look / And now a missing book /

MINNA: But Tellheim had blue eyes . . .

THE HANGED: Minna . . . !

Minna . . . !

MINNA (*irritably*):   Yes . . . !

THE HANGED: The Monster of Grosshayen watched us die

MINNA: I know

THE HANGED: And laughed . . . ! (*Pause*)

Why did he laugh?

MINNA: I don't kow . . .

THE HANGED: Why? (*Pause.* TELLHEIM *stands up.*)

TELLHEIM: May I make a suggestion? I think Tellheim does exist. I think this blue-eyed Major survived the war, and having survived the war, survived the peace. Among so many Tellheims, none of whom can strictly be described as innocent, this blue-eyed Tellheim is distinguished by imperishable guilt. Whether he suffers from this guilt or merely experiences it as an affliction stemming from the attitude of others, we cannot tell . . . (*Pause*) Yet . . . (*Pause*) Let us ignore the colour of my eyes. Let us proceed on the basis that Tellheim's eyes were of an indeterminate colour. The case against Tellheim will thus be constructed on a false premise but how much might be learned even so, of wickedness, its peculiar satisfactions and so on. Much useful experience

might be gained from prosecuting one who is, essentially,
incapable of the offence for which he stands indicted. But
perhaps other offences might be laid at his door, given he is,
if not Tellheim, still . . . (*Pause*) Tellheim . . . (*Pause*)

THE HANGED: Minna . . . !

                Minna . . . !

MINNA: Shut up! You are so impatient! How I detest your
impatience!

THE HANGED: He is so clever the Butcher of Grosshayen!

MINNA: **And me**

        Am I not clever also (*Pause. She leans on the desk.
She looks at* TELLHEIM.)

        How philosophical you are . . .

        And algebraic, Major . . . (TELLHEIM *bows
slightly, goes out.*)

FRANCISCA: Minna . . .

MINNA: I have found him, haven't I? I know I have.

FRANCISCA: Minna . . .

MINNA: **It's him**

FRANCISCA: Yes

MINNA: And everything he utters is a trap, even the language, a bottomless hole down which the innocent fall
spreadeagled in the draught **Not me however I am unintimid-
ated on the contrary he fears me**. (*Pause*) Don't you think?
Francisca? (*Pause. She looks at her assistant.*) Why do you
look at me like that? Do I exaggerate? **I do I do exaggerate**.

FRANCISCA: Yes, you do . . .

MINNA: Then leave me if you want to. Resign. You
wouldn't be the first. And as you say, it's dangerous here,
someone will be hurt, rest assured of that. In any case, who
needs you, I have always been alone —

FRANCISCA: Minna —

MINNA: Oh, yes I have, solitary, solitary, solitary, and out
of loneliness I've hewn the shelter of my sensibilities — (*A
fractional pause.*) No, that's rubbish, I've never been alone,
never in my life! (*They all laugh.*) I haven't, have I? I was
loved by everyone! To tell the truth, I have been smothered!
(*She laughs. They watch her, smiling. The smile fades.*) Are
you devoted? Francisca? Are you devoted to me?

By way of reply, The FRANCISCAS *hurry to her, enclose her
in an embrace, a knot of affection. The sound of shattering glass,
and jeering. The distant tunes of a waltz. The* FRANCISCAS

run off. MINNA *is left standing in her underclothes, hands by her sides.*

Scene Three

The LANDLORD *enters with a tray. He stops, stares.*

MINNA: Wrong room again.
LANDLORD: These doors are all the same
MINNA: Yes, but
LANDLORD: Why don't you lock the door if you
MINNA: I don't like Grosshayen
LANDLORD: Or tell me to go you don't tell me to go I notice
MINNA: I need to say that do I
LANDLORD: Grosshayen isn't nice but perhaps you aren't either

If you don't lock the door it's obviously an invitation (*Pause*)
I'm enslaved by beauty. What I call beauty.
Pity me. (*Pause*)

MINNA: All right, I will
LANDLORD: **There's someone in here with you**
Oh, Miss Barnhelm . . . !
Oh, Miss, Miss . . . ! (*He shakes his head in despair.*)
Someone touches you
Someone
Where I cannot
Where I may not
Goes at will (*He sobs.*)
And this is the best room far and away the best
I cleaned the windows
Not the best there is one other but
Oh, you are not nice
Would you like the other I can get the other probably
Not nice, are you?

MINNA: I don't know . . .

LANDLORD: No, you aren't at all by the way you can depend on me

MINNA: To do what?

LANDLORD: Oh, listen, Miss von Barnhelm, sarcasm is so poor, I mean I will die for you . . . are you smiling, don't smile I will die for you and whoever is here with you smiling will not that is the difference between us a significant difference possibly (*He turns to go.*)

MINNA: I am nice, Oskar. Now take whatever you fancy from the top drawer and good night. (*The* LANDLORD *shakes his head, and goes out. A long pause. A hand is seen reaching for* MINNA *in the dim light. It remains extended.* TELLHEIM *enters, in an overcoat . . .*)

Scene Four

TELLHEIM *stands in the landscape of Grosshayen. A wind. Traffic.*

TELLHEIM: She loves me . . .

JUST (*entering*): That is my impression, Major.

TELLHEIM: This love does not however, appear to affect her concentration in the least.

JUST: No.

TELLHEIM: She is convinced I am guilty.

JUST: Her convictions have no legal status, Major.

TELLHEIM: None at all, but conviction, like any abraisive substance, wears down resistance. I am beginning to believe in my own guilt. Or rather, in the guilt it is assumed Tellheim must suffer.

JUST: We are all susceptible to the vehemence of others. Truth hardly enters into it. But you love her also, which may or may not be to our advantage.

TELLHEIM: I do, I think . . .

JUST: You think . . . ! Major, the signs hang off you like a madman with a sandwich board.

TELLHEIM: Oh . . . ?

JUST: Oh, he says . . .

TELLHEIM (*reproachfully*):   Just . . .

JUST: You are transformed.

TELLHEIM: Just . . .

JUST: Well, I say transformed. Most people would find you marble, ashlar-faced as ever, but to one who knows your every nuance as I do, you are aflame. A schoolboy kissed by a priest. A child too intimately fondled by its aunt. No, you are in a riot, Major. A silent riot, naturally. A riot strictly contained within the eyelids . . . (*Pause*) I don't know which of us is the more inhuman. You, who thrived on danger, who, the more exposed you were to death, the more incandescent you became, or me . . . who trembled, shuddered, whose dissolution was inhibited only by faith — faith in you — I whimpered, I was I think, nine parts a dog, hair on end, white-eyed, but like a dog also, fixed to the spot by fidelity . . . (*Pause*) A saint and a dog, but never quite human, either of us. (*He affects a laugh.*)

    But you're the intellectual, and I . . . !

    I —

TELLHEIM: You need not stay with me, Just (*Pause*)

    Perhaps I offend you by the very invitation to desert me, but —

JUST: Yes. (*Pause*)

TELLHEIM: Yes, then I must offend you, or repress the thought which gave rise to the offence, and that I refuse to do —

JUST: Of course —

TELLHEIM: To repress an idea once conceived, no matter how horrific, is not I think a sign of friendship or integrity —

JUST: Of course not, tell it all, sir, injure . . . !

    Wound away in the name of honesty!

TELLHEIM: Just, there is a danger now in Grosshayen which you need not expose yourself to —

JUST: **I define my obligations**. (*Pause*)

   There was danger always. Danger of one kind or another. And every danger I have shared with you —

    And now I sound sentimental which I know you hate — (*He erupts.*)

    You are trying to rid yourself of me because my loyalty offends you —

TELLHEIM: Offends me?

JUST: **You resent me, you resent the embodiment of unselfish love which I am, you want to think the world is cold as wells, it is your philosophy and I am the living impediment**

Admit it

Admit it

My   devotion   is   incomprehensible   to   you ... !
(*Pause*)

Please don't discharge me I will become a criminal mad and criminal and finish in some institution with a single light bulb in a room please please (*He stops.*)

And anyway, you need me. (*He recovers.*)

Who cleans your shoes? You don't know one end of a shoebrush from another **and ironing shirts** . . . ! (*He scoffs.*)

Miss Barnhelm will not lift a finger for you, Major, I know her type, it is you who will stand at the ironing board, fathoming the proper temperature for petticoats . . . (*He laughs.*) I know . . . ! (*He laughs. Laughter off, as from a party at a fête. A* CUPID *enters.* JUST *and* TELLHEIM, MINNA, *are still. The* CUPID *parades, slowly to the sound of the fête. It goes off as the* FRANCISCAS *enter, circa 1767.* JUST *goes out.* MINNA *stretching her arms to receive the gown they are carrying.*)

FRANCISCAS: Miss / The Major is out walking on the heath / So silent, isn't he / He smiles but / Smiles and yet / Politeness but we wonder if / The war perhaps was worse than people said / Miss Oh Miss / Thank Heaven you are clever / Such melancholy would drive some girls out their heads / (*They fling the gown over* MINNA *and dress her.*) And as for Just / Some servant him / A funny name to start with / We go ugh / Ugh we go when we see him / Why should the major want that for his valet / Just what's so special about Just / He has an artificial limb! (MINNA *is dressed. The* CUPID *wheels in a large mirror in which she examines herself.*)

MINNA: Do you like him? (*The* FRANCISCAS *are silent.*)

The Major, does he appeal to you? (*Pause*)

I ask you quite sincerely and you must give me your sincere opinion in return, that's friendship, isn't it, and we are friends, notwithstanding you are my servants, notwithstanding anything. (*Pause*) Francisca.

FRANCISCA: No. (*Pause. for the first time* MINNA *turns from the mirror to examine* FRANCISCA.)

MINNA: You do not like the man I love.

FRANCISCA: I —

MINNA: The man for seven years I have sustained a terrible devotion for you say you —

FRANCISCA: I —

MINNA: For whom we have crossed broken landscapes and slept in burned out barns you dare to say you —

FRANCISCA: Yes! I dare! (*Pause*)

MINNA: Good. (*She smiles.*) Good, because you are such a common and mundane creature that for such a man to win approval from you could only mean. Would mark him down as utter — (*Pause*) Excellent! (*Pause*)

FRANCISCA: Perhaps it is your will you follow, Minna, rather than your heart and —

MINNA (*ignoring her*): No! One must acknowledge that exceptional men rarely win the approval of common humanity, and how should they? It would demean the very quality of distinction would it not, if it came stamped with approbation like some —

FRANCISCA: Shh —

MINNA: Some common product of —

FRANCISCA: Shh —

MINNA: Emblazoned with the imprimatur of the servant class, no, you are ideal for me, Francisca, ideal because whatever you approve I know I have to shun, you are the very barometer of banality . . . ! (*Pause.* FRANCISCA *takes* MINNA's *hand.* MINNA *emits a sob and a smile.*) Am I unkind? (*Pause*) Oh, leave me if you wish! Find a better mistress, there are many, many, I feel sure, I am depraved and —

FRANCISCA: You are not depraved —

MINNA: **I am depraved and** —

FRANCISCA: I do not wish to leave you —

MINNA: Depraved and suicidal —

FRANCISCA: But you will drive me away —

MINNA: **A monster of selfishness and low-living**. (*Pause*)

FRANCISCA: You are nothing of the sort.

MINNA: Sinful . . . Sensual . . .

FRANCISCA: Rubbish.

MINNA: Francisca I am! (*She glares.*)

FRANCISCA: Yes. Of course you are. Your body is a — (*Pause*)

> Plank
> Of
> Trodden

>   Crime
>   Sordid
>   Stained
>   And

MINNA (*brightly*): I am invited to dinner! Dinner, he says!
(*She tosses a card in the air. FRANCISCA retrieves it and
reads it.*) His handwriting suggests a madness, don't you
think? An uneven character warped by the writhing of a
shattered soul. It is obviously dangerous to come near such
a man and yet. (*Pause*) You must come, too. (*Suddenly*) **I do
resent you sometimes you know no more of life than me I at
least have had experience of books** (*Pause*)

>   Don't laugh.
>   Never laugh or I shall dismiss you on the spot.

FRANCISCA: Yes.

MINNA: I can laugh. I can find myself ridiculous but I'm the
mistress, so . . . (*Pause. The* CUPID *passes by idly. The
wind.*)

>   I feel in Grosshayen — (*Pause*)
>   One is — (*Pause*)
>   Nowhere . . . (*Pause*)
>   I feel Grosshayen is — (*She looks at* FRANCISCA.)
>   The end of things . . . (*The distant sound of
>   couplings, trucks.* MINNA *jumps up*.)
>   And sexuality, what is it but a metaphor?
>   What is it?
>   What?

But a metaphor and stay until I signal you and if I do not
signal you don't interpret that to mean I have forgotten you,
it merely means I have decided to be seduced another night
instead withstand all hints and urges on his part sit there no
matter how absurd you feel, Francisca, thank you. (*She
kisses her and goes out.* FRANCISCA *looks at herself in the
mirror. The other* FRANCISCAS *shake out* MINNA's *garments
and fold, then go out,* TELLHEIM *is discovered, watching*
FRANCISCA.)

TELLHEIM: Some men would be your mirror . . .

FRANCISCA (*unmoved*): Would they . . .

TELLHEIM: Uncritical. Unethical. Unpartisan.

FRANCISCA: Yes . . . (*She plucks an eyebrow.*)

TELLHEIM: Some men . . . (FRANCISCA *makes up*.)

FRANCISCA: My mistress fears you, Major Tellheim. Correctly, in my estimation.

TELLHEIM: Yes, Miss Barnhelm does. Do you? (FRANCIS-
CA *stops. She faces him.*)

FRANCISCA: There are fears which need to be obeyed,
Major, but others... (*Pause*) Others are merely the sugges-
tive currents of new life... the trembling of the rock pool at
the incoming tide... (*She gets up, she tosses down a lipstick,
and goes out, sweeping up another of* MINNA's *discarded
dresses as she goes.* TELLHEIM *is still, fixed in thought. The
sounds of boats rowed on water, and fêtes. A party appears,
silently, clad in black as if in mourning. They hold an assort-
ment of cases and bags.* TELLHEIM *looks at them. They are
still. They return his searching look.*)

TELLHEIM: The hotel's there... (*He lifts a hand to point.
They do not move, but stare like cattle. As if by an atavistic
instinct,* TELLHEIM *goes among them. He taps them on the
shoulder. As he taps each one, he or she departs, leaving the
bags. It is a neat, practised administration. A band is heard,
playing a march badly...* TELLHEIM *is still...*)

Scene Five

MINNA *enters, following* JUST, *who transports a campaign
table and a cloth over his shoulder.*

JUST: The camp! The camp! What is the camp but a picnic?

MINNA: It's a place without privacy, certainly...

JUST: And if the camp is a picnic, what is the battle but a
dance?

MINNA: I don't know, Mr Just...

JUST: I say to the Major, as the cannonade begins,
　　　 Sir, shall we dance? (*He bursts out laughing.*)
　　　 He laughs, no matter how often I repeat it!

MINNA: The Major is a kind man, possibly...

JUST: Kind? No, it's funny. (*He lays out cutlery.*)
　　 The manoeuvring of troops is no more nor less than the
rehearsal of a minuet. Do you watch battles? Women do.

MINNA: I haven't had that privilege.

JUST: Time enough! The peace is only a suspension of the
war. The wars have different names, The Seven Years' War,

The Thirty Years War, The War of Someone's Eye or Ear, but it's the same war, believe me, Miss. The war needs. The war calls. Irrelevant, the pretext . . . (*He turns to go, stops.*)
    I have this tongue. (*Pause*)
    What a tongue it is.
    Look.
    Tongue. (*He projects it. He retracts it.*)
    Miss Barnhelm. (*He looks at her fixedly, then assumes his old disposition.*)
My mother said she wished it had been taken out at birth! How cruel I was to her! I was her equal in quarrelling at four and by six I could reduce her to a puddle of humiliation. What a thing it is! What versatility! (*He projects it again.*) In fact, given my body is something less than perfect in its proportions, it's obvious some God of Compensation pitied me — excessively, the Major says! I am superabundantly fluent, and sometimes conduct four dialogues at once. This makes me a servant of dubious value but the Major is a charitable man and in return I exempt him from my cruelty. Him alone, I promise you . . . (*He turns to go. He catches sight of* TELLHEIM *who is perfectly still. He proceeds.* MINNA *is addressed by* THE HANGED.)

THE HANGED: Minna!
                       Minna!
MINNA: Oh, listen, you claim too much attention!
THE HANGED: We suffered, so we know —
MINNA: All right, you know, but what you know I might perhaps be forgiven for not knowing!
THE HANGED: Minna!
                       Minna!
                       We'll educate you!
MINNA (*placing her fingers in her ears*):   Perhaps I do not wish to know. Has that occurred to you? Perhaps the things you know will spoil my evening . . . (*She removes her fingers.*)
THE HANGED: Don't hate yourself. That is his weapon. That is how he breaks your soul . . . (*Pause. The wind. They turn on the ropes.*)
MINNA: Hate myself? **Hate myself** . . . ! (*Pause.*)
                 No, one must give serious consideration even to the most outlandish
                 Hate myself
                 Not
                 One

        Bit
        No
Of course this vehemence might be construed as certain
evidence I'm only smothering what pains my mind to recog-
nize but
        Silly
        Silly
        Francisca! (*She waits.* TELLHEIM *reveals himself.*)
TELLHEIM: Forgive me, I sent her away. (*He takes*
MINNA's *hand and kisses it.*)
MINNA: Sent her away . . .
TELLHEIM: Servants, by and large, whilst not inhibiting our
conversation, might — (JUST *enters with a napkin and tureen.*)
MINNA: But he's here . . .
TELLHEIM: Just? (*He seems to ponder.*)
        Yes . . . he is . . .
        Which surely shows how little I regard him as a
        servant!
MINNA: It was quite wrong of you to —
TELLHEIM: In his case, service is of such a special order —
MINNA: **Quite wrong of you and an infringement of my**
(*Pause*) Now I sound querulous and —
TELLHEIM: Please, Minna, take a seat —
MINNA: I am not fragile or anxious, merely —
TELLHEIM (*drawing out a chair*): Here, I think —
MINNA: Tellheim. (TELLHEIM *stops.*)
        Listen when I speak. (*He looks at her. Suddenly they*
        both laugh.)
What a marriage! What a marriage we shall be! Rarely
placid! Often stormy! (*She sits.*)
I speak of marriage since marriage precisely is the purpose
of my voyage! (*Pause*)
        Voyage . . .
Why did I say voyage? Tellheim? Perhaps it felt like a
voyage to love. Perhaps Grosshayen is an island . . . Tell-
heim? The Island of Love? (*He looks at her over the table.*
JUST *remains holding the tureen.*) I wanted you. And I shall
have you. It's my will . . .
TELLHEIM: Yes, Minna . . .
MINNA (*inspired*): One of my equations concerns the reci-
procity of love, shall I say?
TELLHEIM: Yes, say . . .
MINNA: I take *a* to represent myself —

TELLHEIM: *a* . . . ?

MINNA: *a*, yes, I am *a* — (*She stops, laughs.*) Naturally *I* am
a! I suppose I could be *x* but I am *a* — (*She laughs again.*)
Obviously, one perceives the world from one's own perspective —

JUST (*impatiently*):   Soup?

TELLHEIM: Please, be *a* . . .

MINNA: And you are *b*, thus —

JUST: Soup?

TELLHEIM (*not removing his eyes from* MINNA):   Fetch a
blackboard!

MINNA: I am not sure it is so complex as to require —

TELLHEIM: Blackboard and the easel! (JUST *puts down the
tureen and goes out.* TELLHEIM *remains looking at*
MINNA.) I think you like your voice.

MINNA: I like it, yes. But do you?

TELLHEIM: It has not changed. You use it more, however —

MINNA: Yes, I do! And you say less! It's obvious we are
made to compensate each other! (JUST *enters with board and
easel.*) **Do you think I will be distracted from you, Tellheim?
Idiot!** (JUST *puts down the easel rudely and goes out.*
MINNA *swiftly goes to the chalk.*)

Let *a* be Minna von Barnhelm, a woman of wit and no
significance, and *b*, Major Tellheim, war hero and economist
of language who would rather remain silent than waste
his breath on metaphysics — (*she scrawls*) *a* plus *b* in this
equation equals *c*, *c* being — (*she scrawls*) harmony. (*There
is a pistol shot. She stops.* TELLHEIM *gets up, and walks out
in the direction of the shot.* MINNA *is quite still, expectant.
A pause.* TELLHEIM *returns and resumes his seat.*)

TELLHEIM: Harmony, what is that? (*Pause*)

MINNA: The state of satisfaction resulting from the dissolution of two competing egos, Major.

TELLHEIM: Dissolution? Is that not a change, Miss Barnhelm, resulting in the destruction of the original substan-
ces?

MINNA: Obviously, Major.

TELLHEIM: And the agent of this destruction, what is that?

MINNA: Love, obviously. (*Pause*)

TELLHEIM: So love destroys us?

MINNA: Obviously, yes . . . (*There is a second shot.*) TELL-
HEIM *reluctantly gets up, goes out.* MINNA *is still. A pause.*
TELLHEIM *returns.*)

TELLHEIM: Everything is obvious to you, whereas nothing is obvious to me. One of us is gifted with insight, clarity, translucency, while the other struggles in obscurity. One of us is certain, the other full of doubt. One goes forward. One hangs back.

MINNA: I feel sure great love is made from such unlikely combinations.

TELLHEIM: Certainty again! Miss Barnhelm, I — (*There is a third shot.* TELLHEIM *leaps to his feet, holds the edges of the table in white-knuckled hands.*)

> **Stop that** (*He is seized by a tremor.*)
> **Stop**
> **Stop**
> **Stop that**
> **Stop**
> **Stop** . . . (*He recovers. A wind ripples the tents.*)

MINNA: My darling . . . (*She extends a hand, which* TELL-HEIM *does not take.*)

> I made my heart a place for you . . . (*She leaves her open hand outstretched.*)
> Do enter in . . . ! Or you will wander, wander, all that remains of your life . . . !

A massive cloth, fine, silent, descends in front of them, falling like a curtain. On this descending shape can be discerned the plan of a camp, fences, huts etc. As it crumples on the floor it sends up a cloud of dust which settles over them in their stillness. The CUPID, *also dusty, perambulates, departs. Two of the* FRANCISCAS *are discovered in the clearing air.*

FRANCISCA: Gross — hayen / Minna / Your home and grave / Between the trees / Minna / We love you but / In / Differing degrees / (*Silence.* MINNA's *peeling laugh is heard. Not from her mouth. A man enters.*)

WERNER: Hello? (*All is silent. He advances, stops.*)
> Hello? (*The sound of footsteps on stairs, hurried.*)
> I have a room . . . !

LANDLORD (*appearing at the foot*): If I like you.

WERNER: If you like me?

LANDLORD: If you satisfy me. I'm not obliged to take all comers, am I? There are occasions one prefers one's rooms empty. One is particular. One hesitates. One waits for the guest to prove his suitability.

WERNER: Funny hotel . . .

LANDLORD: And you? You might be a funny guest for all I know.

WERNER: In some respects we are all probably a little —

LANDLORD: Oh, please, no philosophy. (*He looks at* WERNER.)

           I'm not sure.

WERNER: You're not sure.

LANDLORD (*miserably*):   Oh, I don't know, this is a difficult profession —

WERNER: I'm clean, I'm orderly, I'm —

LANDLORD: But not a woman, are you? (*Pause*)

WERNER: Not a woman, no . . .

LANDLORD: I could give you the room, I could get you to sign the register, give you a key, and then along comes a woman who wants the room. Too late. You're already in there. (*Pause*)

WERNER: Is there no other room that —

LANDLORD: I've got any number of rooms, thank you. But there are coach parties, women travelling in cars —

WERNER: Yes —

LANDLORD: Walkers, anything — I have to think about it it is a most — I hate the job in many ways and these are critical decisions!

WERNER: Perhaps you are too chivalrous, Mr — (*He hesitates.*) Keeping so many rooms for women —

LANDLORD: It is not chivalry, Mr —

WERNER: Werner —

LANDLORD: Not chivalry at all . . . (*Pause.* WERNER *looks around.*)

WERNER: Grosshayen . . . (*He shakes his head.*) It always was a funny place . . . (JUST *enters, with a dish on a tray for* MINNA *and* TELLHEIM. *He stands.*)

LANDLORD: Funny? Everything is funny to you. What are you, well-balanced, Mr Werner?

WERNER (*shrugs*):   I try to keep a —

LANDLORD (*walking away smartly*):   **All right, it's on the third floor, Mr Werner!** (WERNER *looks about him.*)

MINNA: Obviously, Tellheim, I'm here to be seduced. (*She gets up.*)

           And all this —
           algebra —
           is obfuscating things!

This discussion belongs, surely, not to the preface, but to
the epilogue ... of love ... ? (*Pause.* TELLHEIM *is
unmoved.*) The doing precedes the speaking ... ? (*He merely
looks. The church clock on Grosshayen tower chimes.*)

WERNER: I'll carry my own bag ... ! (*He hurries up the
stairs after the* LANDLORD.)

THE HANGED: Minna ... !
            Minna ... !

MINNA: Shh! No more words. Today. (JUST *takes*
MINNA's *face in his hand. She shudders.*)
            Francisca! (*He draws it back.*)
            Fran — cisca ... ! (*He puts his lips to hers, drawing
            her backwards. Two* FRANCISCAS *appear.*)

FRANCISCAS: Oh, Miss / A man's appeared / Out of the
blue / The perfect witness / Turning up on cue / Or possibly
a trick / They are so / And without a conscience / Will only
speak with you / He says / (*The* CUPID *enters, pushing the
mirror, as* JUST *lays* MINNA *firmly over the table, so that
she watches herself, yielding, and objectified.*)

MINNA: Oh, Mr Just, your tongue ... was not appreciated
by your mother ...

Scene Six

*From the darkness of the stage, a figure approaches, dressed in
the clothes of 1767. He is unhurried, the proprietor of the
landscape. He stops, seeing* MINNA.

COUNT: Oh, Minna ... Minna always was too clever for men
... (*He looks around him, at the trees.*)
            Nothing's the same!
            Grosshayen!
            Grosshayen still!
            But nothing's the same! (*He takes a pinch of snuff,
            and goes out,* JUST *and* TELLHEIM *also.* MINNA
            gazes at herself, disarrayed.)

MINNA: Francisca! (*One of the remaining* FRANCISCAS
         hurries in, stops, stares.)
         I am depraved . . . (*The maid goes to cover her.*)
         Don't touch! (*Pause. She still examines herself.*)
         Obviously, depraved . . . (*She sits up.*)
         Or is it not obvious? Perhaps it's only obvious to
         me . . . (*She pulls her hair, idly.*)
         I should know, shouldn't I? If I'm depraved or not?
         Francisca? (*She looks at her.*)
         Oh, you are not Francisca . . . ! Where is she?

SECOND FRANCISCA (*shrugs*):   Gone . . .

MINNA: Gone?

SECOND FRANCISCA: Miss. (*Pause*)

MINNA: But that's disloyalty . . . ! To me . . . !

SECOND FRANCISCA: Miss. (MINNA *stares.*)

MINNA: She has been kidnapped, obviously! Or fallen into a
ravine, are there ravines here?

SECOND FRANCISCA: I haven't seen a ravine, Miss —

MINNA: Swamp, then! She heard a bird, and lured by its
song, was drawn into the forest where everybody knows bogs
and marshes, hardly discernible to the eye, have sucked so
many to their deaths, Grosshayen's swamps, they're legendary, are they not, Francisca?

SECOND FRANCISCA: Miss.

MINNA: **The swamps of Grosshayen**. (*She glares.*)

SECOND FRANCISCA: Miss. (*Pause*)

MINNA: I think to fall into a swamp whilst following a bird
is — foolish in the extreme and not untypical of that young
woman whose frivolity was — (*Pause*) More than I could
stomach and yet one must pity, mustn't one, a servant who
adored with such fidelity, do up my dress now, what happened here was — oh, I cannot tell you!

SECOND FRANCISCA (*attending to her*):   I'm too foolish, I
suppose —

MINNA: His tongue . . . ! And I — (*Pause*) What is the
point of telling you? (*The servant shrugs.*) I'll tell you anyway! (*She hugs her suddenly.*) Oh, I am so dependent on your
love! Tragically dependent, Francisca! **He put his face down
there** . . . ! (*They gawp at each other.*)
         Depravity, surely . . .
   Oh, Francisca, if *c* is Heaven, and *b* is love, might *a* be —
wickedness, perhaps?
         I am a ruined woman!

Aren't I?

Say! (SECOND FRANCISCA *looks at her.*)

SECOND FRANCISCA: You are nothing of the sort. Now,
lift up your arms and —

MINNA: **You are all as bad as each other!** (*The* SECOND
FRANCISCA *removes the dress from her.* MINNA *sits
crossly in her underwear. She is aware of the* LANDLORD,
who has insinuated himself into the scene.)

You keep bringing me drinks which I have not ordered.
Why? Do you think I can be made into an alcoholic?

LANDLORD: I am your friend, Miss Barnhelm.

MINNA: Really? I think you want to wreck my liver. You
have something to hide and think I can be distracted by a
constant stream of liquor.

LANDLORD: Everyone has something to hide, Miss Barnhelm, that is the human condition, surely? (*Pause*)

MINNA: Not my condition, Oskar . . .

LANDLORD: No? (*He stares.* MINNA *is suddenly insecure.*)

MINNA: **What is Tellheim?**
   What?
      You know. (*The* LANDLORD *goes out. The* SEC-
OND FRANCISCA *holds out* MINNA's *modern, legal dress.*
WERNER *stands at the edge of the light.*)

WERNER: Miss Barnhelm!

MINNA: Wait! (*She looks at herself in the mirror. The* SEC-
OND FRANCISCA *clothes her, zips her.* MINNA *holds her
hand unexpectedly, tightly.*)

You are my friend . . . (*Pause. She reflects.*) Is that a
question, or an order . . . ? (*She laughs.*) What does it matter?
Say yes in any case.

SECOND FRANCISCA: Yes . . . ! (MINNA *looks at her.*)

MINNA: I am so easily satisfied! (*She turns. The* SECOND
FRANCISCA *goes out.*) Come in, Mr Werner . . . (*He enters.
She pulls her dress, looking at herself. He waits, watching.*)

WERNER: I have to speak.

MINNA: Good.

WERNER: Miss Barnhelm, Grosshayen is a graveyard . . .

MINNA: That is something everybody knows.

WERNER: Garden
         And
         Graveyard
         House
         And

MINNA: Why, Mr Werner? The urge to speak. The imperative that cannot be denied?

WERNER: Because I know.

MINNA: And knowing . . . compels telling . . . ?

WERNER: Miss Barnhelm, I was Tellheim's adjutant.

MINNA: Perhaps you have reasons for telling, reasons which
are obscure or dishonourable, and these you are more than
satisfied to leave unexamined, or to obliterate under this
unconvincing objectivity, Mr Werner? Knowing compels telling, but precisely why?

WERNER: **Miss Barnhelm this is not relevant to testimony, is
it?**

MINNA: Allow me to be the judge of that, Mr Werner.

WERNER: **Many would escape justice if the motives of their
accusers were put under the microscope Miss Barnhelm!** (*He
shudders, pause.*)

MINNA: No one is immune from justice, Mr Werner.
   We will prise them from the very cracks and crevices of
silence, from mountain tops among the Andes where they
count the hours with their native concubines, or concrete
rooms in Arctic complexes where they sit unshaven over
stoves, we will strip them off their bedsteads, Mr Werner,
and drag them bumping by their heels down flights of stairs,
nailing them in crates where they will crouch like bears, sad
bears bewildered in the freight compartments of great aero-
planes, pitiful, pitiful the torturer, what was your relationship to Tellheim, then?

WERNER: I was his friend.

MINNA: His friend? He had friends, then?

WERNER: Many friends, yes.

MINNA: Many friends! The Tellheim we are seeking spoke to
no one, other than professionally or —

WERNER: Oh, many, many friends and —

MINNA: **Don't interrupt me.** (*Pause*)

WERNER: Interrupt you? Did I?

MINNA: I like to finish my sentences. (*Pause*)

WERNER: Yes.

MINNA: If I am allowed to complete my sentences it will
enable you to think of better answers.

WERNER: Better answers . . . . ?

MINNA: Yes. More truthful ones.

WERNER: I want to tell the truth, Miss Barnhelm.

MINNA: You want to, yes. But Tellheim had no friends.

Everybody testifies to it. (*Pause*) Perhaps you did not know
Tellheim.

WERNER: I knew Tellheim —

MINNA: *A* Tellheim, yes —

WERNER: No, *the* Tellheim —

MINNA: One Tellheim among many —

WERNER: I knew him, I said —

MINNA: The Tellheim who runs the newsagents in Fursten-
burg? I've met him —

WERNER: **The torturer Tellheim. Tellheim of Grosshayen. I
knew him**. (*Pause*) I was his biographer.

MINNA: Biographer?

WERNER: Yes. I was writing his biography . . . (*Pause. The
wind. The sound of shattering glass and jeering youth. The*
LANDLORD *enters.*)

LANDLORD: I keep losing my windows . . . because of you
. . . but I don't mind . . . (*Pause. He waits.*)

MINNA: I'm not in my room . . .

LANDLORD: No . . .

                Thank you . . . (*He starts to go, turns.*)

   When Louis XVI died, they drank his blood . . . (*He
shrugs.*) Understandably . . . they jostled one another round
the guillotine. Scrapped for bits of hair . . . and licked his
blood . . .

MINNA (*laughs, shrilly*): I'm certain I should have done the
same! Lips to the cobbles . . . tongue to the block . . . lap . . .
lap . . . (*The* LANDLORD *goes out.* MINNA *laughs, turns
suddenly to Werner.*) I can be kissed, Mr Werner! I can be
kissed!

Snow falls. TELLHEIM *and* JUST *are seen in long coats,
bearing shovels. They go to a spot and dig.* JUST's *rapid drum
tap. The* CUPID, *on a wire, flies over the stage. The* THIRD
FRANCISCA, *in costume of 1769, enters laughing with a picnic
hamper and a rug. She spreads it on the snow.*

Scene Seven

THE INTERLUDE

MINNA *puts a coat loosely over her shoulders. She goes near to where* TELLHEIM *and* JUST *are digging. Suddenly, they stand back as a gust of light and wind roars from their excavation, throwing litter and detritus high into the air.* MINNA *goes warily to the rim and looks in. In a silence, modified only by a slight wind, she descends. A voice is heard calling her name.*

COUNT (*as an aristocrat of 1769*):   My daughter!

My daughter! Where is she? (*He is seen approaching from the depths of the stage.*) I call her my daughter, of course she's my niece, but what are relations but fences to be ridden, hedges to be leapt, walls to be scaled etcetera.

> **Uncle**
> **Uncle**
> **There's a word**

Oh, problematic this avuncularity!

And a kiss is a kiss, let the world examine it, speculate, you mundane trespassers for whom the lawn is sacrosanct, speculate . . . ! (*He is followed by the picnic party, all of 1769.*)

> Oh
> Here
> She
> Is
> Before the mirror
> Perched and perfect
> Minna
> Minna

Dear! (*The* CUPID *turns the mirror to show* MINNA *seated, 1769. The* COUNT *leans over her shoulder.*)

> Permit me place my rutted mask beside your
> Oh my spoiled and ragged!
> Is it not a vile offence to make them even proximate but

I am an uncle after all (*The party laughs.*)

> And oh, I have decayed since my last look
> Minna

Minna (MINNA *takes his hand.*)
There is a boy lives there of clear-eyed soul (*He peers at himself.*)
Can you detect him, Minna?
Scandalous decrepitude . . . (*Pause*)

MINNA: It's nice, your mug. (*She kisses the* COUNT *swiftly on the cheek.*) And anyway, you have less of a quarrel with your face than I with mine. Francisca! This hideous foundation cream has brought me out in spots! (*The* SECOND FRANCISCA *hurries in. The party play, picnic.*)

FRANCISCA: Spots, where?

MINNA: A rash of them.

FRANCISCA: Rash, where . . . ?

MINNA (*pointing to her cheek*): **Just here the rash miss look**.

COUNT: Oh, for such a rash . . . ! (*He turns to go.* MINNA *grasps him by the arm.*)

MINNA: Don't go, father . . . (*The* COUNT *stops.*) Run your fingers over me . . . (*He touches her, sensitively, her hair, her neck.*) You have the worst face in the world. It is, is it not, **diabolical**? (*The party laughs.*)
    It is, it is! (*She jumps up.*)
        I am ready now, to die . . . ! (*She stops.*)
    Did I say die? Dance, I meant. Dance, obviously, no one dies on the Isle of Venus, do they? Does anybody die on Cythera? (*She hurries off, followed by some guests. The* SECOND FRANCISCA *is about to follow. The* COUNT *takes her hand.*)

SECOND FRANCISCA: No, I am your daughter's maid . . . (*She also goes out. The* COUNT *stares at himself in the mirror. He is aware of a man behind him, young, in Prussian uniform of 1769.*)

COUNT: Men envy me . . .

TELLHEIM: Yes . . .

COUNT: Knowing my relations with my niece . . .

TELLHEIM: Yes . . .

COUNT: **Rich and carnal Count von Bruchsall fucks his niece** they say that, don't they?

TELLHEIM: Yes, they do . . .

COUNT (*turning to* JUST, *who, liveried, is passing with a tray*): **Don't they**?

JUST (*stopping*): Whatever you say, sir.

COUNT: No, you say it.

JUST: If you insist, **Count von** —

COUNT: Shh. (*He waves a hand.*)
How little they know of our pains . . . (*He goes to* JUST.)
Obviously, I wanted to corrupt her, but how impossible that
is . . .

JUST: Is it?

COUNT: Oh, yes, you know how impervious she is . . . You
have ears, and you have eyes, and this little body which
insinuates itself through doors . . .

JUST: Yes . . .

COUNT: You know it all . . . off you go now Mr Just . . .
(JUST *goes out.*)
Tellheim, there is nothing quite so painful to a man like me
as the knowledge nothing you might do to a woman alters
her, that she is, for all your pandering, unspoiled, that she
returns from each erotic expedition, anodyne, immune . . .
(*He looks at* TELLHEIM.) We carve ourselves on one
another as boys dig their miserable initials in the bark of
trees . . . some permanence . . . some epitaph!

TELLHEIM: Perhaps the flesh always returns to its shape
whereas the mind . . .

COUNT: I like the flesh, Tellheim . . .

TELLHEIM: Yes . . . it is finite, however . . . flesh . . . (*The*
COUNT *looks at* TELLHEIM, *quizzically.*)

COUNT (*changing mood*): Do you not adore Grosshayen,
Captain? I have expended several fortunes on this estate. The
little temples, for example, cost more to age than to create.
There are specialists who apply history to them with a brush!
Decay is costly!

TELLHEIM: Yes, and yet we cannot wait.

COUNT: We can't! We can't wait! (MINNA *hurries in,
distraut.*)
Minna!
Minna!

MINNA: No, go away, don't touch! (*The* COUNT *bows,
withdraws.*)

SECOND FRANCISCA (*entering*): Dearest, dearest . . . !

MINNA: Go away!

SECOND FRANCISCA: If you insist.

MINNA: No, don't go away . . . (*She hesitates, then flings
herself into* SECOND FRANCISCA's *arms.*) I don't like
dancing, I only think I do!

SECOND FRANCISCA: Very well, don't dance —

MINNA: **But that is true of everything!** (*She stares into* FRANCISCA's *eyes.*)

Everything, on close inspection, is so — unutterably poor . . . (*Pause*)

And everybody . . . (*Pause*)

SECOND FRANCISCA: Yes . . . ! (*She shrugs.*) It's true! We are poor! Why pretend otherwise? Perhaps, therefore, close inspection is not wise. And the mirror, possibly, is not your best friend . . .

MINNA: No, Francisca, you are . . . ! (*She laughs.*) You alone tell me, you alone demonstrate, the world is not a pit . . . (*She holds* FRANCISCA's *hand.*)

SECOND FRANCISCA: Yes . . . that is an onerous responsibility, Minna . . . if I must be . . . everything that's *not* the pit.

MINNA: Yes. It's hard on you. I ask too much. Please, don't feel an obligation to me. I'd hate that. Abandon me, if that's your wish, I am a burden on everybody's patience, obviously, abandon me, by all means.

SECOND FRANCISCA: I will. One day, I will . . . (*She kisses* MINNA, *and goes out.* MINNA *stares after her. Distant laughter. She sees* TELLHEIM, *examining her from a distance.*)

MINNA: The Isle of Love! (*Pause*)

Cythera. (*Pause*)

The Isle of Love and Venus was born here! (TELLHEIM *looks at her.*)

Not really but (*Pause*)

Not really silly but it sounds much nicer than Grosshayen doesn't it I think so but it's possible I'm (*Pause*)

You say Cythera (*Pause*)

Captain

Please . . .

TELLHEIM: Cythera. (MINNA *laughs.*)

MINNA: Now, you said that in such a way, such a deliberately unerotic way, as if you wished to make it absolutely clear I have no power over you, your speech was ugly with resistance! I know the type! I know the motive! Say it again but this time do allow the sibilants to breathe, the word is like a wind in trees, do surrender to me, Captain, you know you want to so why resist, it is your *better* self that longs to be subordinate, not the contrary, I promise you! (*Pause*)

TELLHEIM: Cythera . . . (*Pause*)

MINNA: Yes. (*Pause*) Your voice is beautiful . . . I could listen to you — (*She smiles.*) Not all day long, no, but . . . (*She laughs, teasingly, stops abruptly.*) I don't like people and the reason is quite simply — (*Pause*)

TELLHEIM: They do not take instruction properly? (*Pause*)

MINNA: Yes.

        Exactly that.

        That.

        Precisely.

TELLHEIM: It seems they prefer making their own mistakes to being correctly led by others.

MINNA: Yes.

TELLHEIM: Cy — th — era . . .

MINNA: Idiots.

TELLHEIM: Cy — th — era . . .

MINNA: Fatuous and contemptible . . .

        Idiots . . .

TELLHEIM: I hope the war will not spread so far that it touches Grosshayen, Miss Barnhelm, for whilst your uncle's garden depends for its effect on being suspended on the very rim of chaos whilst still obedient to order, war is —

MINNA: What do you know about war? (TELLHEIM *smiles.*)

TELLHEIM: War tends in its effects to —

MINNA: Have you been to war, I thought you had only recently received your officer's commission?

TELLHEIM: Favour the annihilation of such subtle distinctions . . .(*He bows his head.*)

MINNA: So what? Like me, you probably have an imagination, and this imagination is the perfect substitute for experience, in fact **exceeds it in horror** I have had so much sex from him you would not believe it . . . (*She smiles. The bursting of a window*, MINNA *screams.*)

Scene Eight

MINNA: **Franc — cisca** . . .

A wind scatters the snow off the stage. The sudden ringing of a choir. WERNER runs down the iron staircase but cannot advance. His shoes clatter. The LANDLORD enters, stop, drops his tray, is still. A silence. JUST enters from the depths of the stage, holding open an old army greatcoat. MINNA goes to him, puts her arms into it. She walks through a moaning wind to the excavation. She does not look down. The CUPID papsses once on a wire. The sound of traffic on the motorways. MINNA smothers pity, and self-pity . . .

MINNA: Now, that was deliberate . . . (*Pause*)
          One plunges in a swamp and now one's murdered. (*Pause*)
    Deliberate yes because to be murdered takes a little just a little imperceptible perhaps but still a little — (*Pause. She looks at JUST.*)
          Wouldn't you say — complicity? (*She looks forward again.*)
          Acquiescence
          And
          Collusion? (*Pause*)
    I think you could say without extreme exaggeration this — being murdered — was an attempt on her part to spite me, yes, blame attaches to the murderer obviously but less obviously it attaches also to the victim **say if you agree** and as for servants servants as a class the species known as servant if I might be permitted to so generalize **who can trust them certainly I never did** to turn your back on anyone round here is suicide one must conclude therefore she willed her death. (*Pause*)
    Francisca was a traitor to me. Yes. To me. A traitor **and yet possibly — I do not hesitate to indict myself** — that surely is a sign of my better nature — **were I a nicer person she would not have felt this need**. (*Pause. She looks at JUST again.*) This appalling need to punish me . . . were I nicer . . . were I at all nice . . . Mr Just . . . (*Pause*)
JUST: Not the faintest chance of finding out who did it . . .
MINNA: No. . . .
JUST: To involve the police even —

MINNA: Oh, fatuous, Mr Just . . . (JUST *bows.* TELLHEIM *comes forward.* JUST *kisses his cheek as he passes.* MINNA *turns to* TELLHEIM *with a smile.*) Oh, now I need you more than ever . . . ! All my spiritual and emotional energy must now be concentrated purely on you! Can you stand it! Or will you wither, like a green leaf on which a child directs the sun's rays through a magnifying glass? Will you wilt, and smoulder, Major Tellheim? (*He takes a step towards her.*) **I am a child! I am a child!** (WERNER *completes his descent of the stairs, calling to her.*)

WERNER: Miss Barnhelm! Run! Save your life! (*He stops, seeing them kiss. He retreats silently up the stairs. A pipe plays. Water drips, as in a thaw.* THE HANGED *turn on their ropes. The kiss endures . . .*)

ACT TWO

Scene One

A brilliant day. MINNA, *in a froth of finery, of 1769, is pushed on a swing by the* THIRD FRANCISCA. *The* LANDLORD *passes through in female underwear, exciting no notice.* JUST *watches, with a tray.*

THIRD FRANCISCA: Listen / The past goes by / And must be ignored / The cries of suffocated life / Need not be heard / Minna /

MINNA: Just . . . !

THIRD FRANCISCA: By you /

MINNA: Just . . . !

THIRD FRANCISCA: Listen / That protest from the leaves / Is only audible because you stirred / The sleep of centuries /

MINNA: Do you like me?

THIRD FRANCISCA: And the swags on ornamental urns are pad-locked . . .

MINNA: Francisca, he doesn't say!

THIRD FRANCISCA: To the absurd / Only / To them /

MINNA: Tellheim, he does not say! (JUST *arrests the swing as* TELLHEIM *enters.*) Which is cruel, so cruel, isn't it, because he knows I need to be admired, he knows my appetite for uncritical affection! Tell him, instruct him, to adore me! (*She jumps down.*) Now.

TELLHEIM: Obviously, I can instruct him, but —

MINNA: That's adequate. I am prepared to go through life without convincing proofs of anything. The words alone. Delivered with conviction. Approximate. And satisfy me. (*She looks at* TELLHEIM, *then turns to* JUST.) Just?

JUST: I cannot seriously believe you've failed to register, Miss Barnhelm, my adoration of you which is expressed in such a variety of ways —

MINNA: Yes —

JUST: Such a range of manifestations —

MINNA: Yes, but say it —

JUST: And nuances, it hardly calls for —

MINNA: It does call for —

JUST: Articulation —

MINNA (*petulantly*): It does! It does! (*A leaden pause. The* THIRD FRANCISCA *goes.*)

JUST: I have a deep affection for you . . . (MINNA *looks at him.*) This affection, in its sediments and stratifications, Miss Barnhelm, frustrates the power even I possess to speak and drives my tongue like some humiliated hound to cower in its kennel . . . (*Pause. She tosses her hair.*)

MINNA: Good. (*She looks to* TELLHEIM.)

        Good. (*She smiles.*)

   So you killed my maid from pure envy, Mr Just? If so, I can't protest. (JUST *looks into the distance*)

   If so, I must swallow my wrath, for love kills love. (*He puts his hands in his pockets.*)

   Posession swamps possession . . . (*She teases him.*)

   So greatly did you long to serve me you could not tolerate a rival **that's all right by me and anyway she stopped me all the time** (*Pause*)

   By mild mockery and so on by gentle admonition little tugs on reins and so on **I saw through it all I said to myself Just will trample that regime miss it's only a matter of time**. (*She laughs, shaking her head.*)

   The truly insane are those who most assiduously seek advice, do you not think so, Tellheim? Who listen with a glutton's gaze to sympathetic warnings? No, I cannot thank you enough for ridding me of someone who was under the absurd illusion she had my best interests at heart. The times I tried to separate myself from her, the stratagems I invented to prod her into quitting, but would she? (*She shakes her head.*)

   Thank you. Now I can be myself. Already I am different. Something — (*Pause*)

        Someone — (*Pause*)

        Grows inside me (*Pause*)

        To whom I never gave a name . . . (*Pause*)

Till I met you . . . (*Suddenly*)
You are the same Tellheim your eyes are blue (*She shudders, she runs off.* TELLHEIM *looks after her.*)

TELLHEIM: Poor child I (*Pause*)
Dear Heart I (*Pause*)

Yes Just even I require illusions even I cannot divest myself of all some rooms remain unentered some doors still holding on obscure landings but the storm will thrash them obviously and howling winds scour the floors out the windows whirl the treasured items of a sentimental life yes Just thank you thank you

JUST: **You are failing to resist her** (*Pause*)
TELLHEIM: Yes (*Pause*)
It's true she does corrupt me (*Pause*)
Not by kindness for she has none something else (*Pause*)
I think she has the authentic spirit of a murderer . . . (*Pause*)
An enthusiasm, which I never had . . . (*A severe and urgent knocking on* MINNA's *door.*)

Scene Two

The THIRD FRANCISCA *is discovered hoeing the ground with care. A fog of early morning. The knocking repeated.* MINNA, *invisible behind the mirror brushes her hair . . .*

MINNA: She is not here!
LANDLORD (*off*):   Not there . . . ?
MINNA: Minna von Barnhelm. Only her clothes. (*Pause. The* LANDLORD *enters.*)
LANDLORD: I'll speak with the clothes, then. (*He enters. He looks for* MINNA.)
MINNA (*still concealed*):   I was a girl. And the girl did not know Tellheim. (*The* LANDLORD *finds her garments on the bed. He crawls to them.*) Could not know him, and remain a girl . . . (*He smothers himself in her clothes.*) This girl expired, therefore. This girl died or love would die instead . . .

LANDLORD: Miss Barnhelm —
MINNA: Dead!
LANDLORD: Miss Barnhelm —
MINNA: **Dead I said**
           The
           Algebraic
           Infant . . .
THIRD   FRANCISCA (*meeting   resistance   with   her   hoe*):
     Hey . . . !
LANDLORD (*going out*):   **Cythera**
                          The
                          Isle
                          Of Venus!
THIRD FRANCISCA (*throwing down her hoe and pulling at
     the earth*): Hey . . . ! (JUST's *drum, frantically tapped.
     Music. The* THIRD FRANCISCA *begins to drag from the
     ground metre after metre of frothing finery. The* CUPID *flies
     by on its wire. As the stage fills,* WERNER *is seen walking
     calmly with two ledgers under his arm. The music and percus-
     sion stops. A silence. A wind.*)
WERNER: We killed without anger. Anger, when it did
     appear, was itself not real. This inauthentic anger was em-
     ployed merely as a means of facilitating things, and as a
     consequence I think did not always convince those
     against whom this anger was directed. A peculiar condition
     therefore manifested itself, in which those about to die sensed
     a certain absence of conviction in their killers, an absence
     which nevertheless could not and would not obstruct the
     essentially mechanistic nature of their fate. It was as if
     emotion here could only be imitated. Its abolition was the
     precondition of activity and yet it lingered, in the form of
     stagecraft, dissimulation, and the like. Some days I was
     convincing. Some days not. This could have been the effect
     of the weather, or if I had been with a woman on the
     previous night . . . (*Pause. THIRD FRANCISCA enters.
     joins* MINNA.)
MINNA (*behind the mirror*):   Francisca . . . ? Is that you?
     (THIRD FRANCISCA *does not reply.* MINNA *emerges
     from behind the mirror, severely coiffured and in her black,
     legal dress. She looks at her.*)
           I dressed myself. (THIRD FRANCISCA *ignores
her.*)
           So what?

I dressed myself . . . (THIRD FRANCISCA *is utterly still.* MINNA *looks at her, long, dispassionately.*)

WERNER: And we were never bored. In retrospect this absence of boredom is hard to understand given the monotony of the routine. (MINNA *turns away from* THIRD FRANCISCA.) I was in fact, elated, as I never was in peacetime doing work with similar routines. I hurried there. I felt compelled. And if the task became more difficult — from the point of view of its demands on our resources — the urgency to fill the quotas, for example, I experienced a corresponding satisfaction, a pride in defiance rather as a child who runs against an escalator and I think this must explain the laugh . . . (*Pause*)

MINNA: The laugh?
What laugh? (*The sound of a peculiar laugh from behind the hedge of netting. A bright summer light floods the stage.*)

Scene Three

TELLHEIM, JUST, *the* COUNT, *are discovered in the garden of Grosshayen. They wear costume of the 1950s.*

COUNT: Minna!
My thin my pale one your body is a bag of weapons he who kisses you might tear his lips or lose a finger in the crevice of your arse . . .

MINNA: I'm not well . . .

COUNT: And your breasts are little purses clinking from your ribs, no man loves such aridity I warn you . . .

MINNA: No man, uncle . . .

COUNT: But then the war has stripped the fat from everything. The war and the peace together. The breakers and the makers. The undertakers and the midwives. Poor Grosshayen, recognizable but only just. I copulated on that mound. First I made it, then I copulated on it! (*He laughs.*) Seven hundred cubic metres. Still there the mound! But not the temple.

JUST: The temple was surplus to requirements, obviously . . .

COUNT: A sort of tower was erected there instead.

JUST: A timber tower, yes.

COUNT: Gone now! Timber tower! Temples of Archadia! Gone! Gone . . . !

JUST: Not entirely gone, Count . . .

COUNT: Fragments of. A little archaeology. And there I copulated also! (*He points.*) Yes . . . I find my bearings rather as a dog recalls a landscape, by recollecting where it raised a leg! (*They laugh.*) Minna, you were party to it, I believe.

MINNA: To what was I a party?

COUNT: The copulation.

MINNA (*looking*): Yes. I was.

COUNT: Smile then, my dear.

MINNA: I am already smiling, Uncle.

COUNT: One would never know it! Smile however, in your own fashion, I never criticize. Have you observed that, Major Tellheim? That I never criticize?

TELLHEIM: I am not Major Tellheim, Count.

COUNT: What? Not Major? Not Tellheim? Which? (TELLHEIM *smiles.*)

TELLHEIM: Count, I am uncertain both of my rank and of my identity . . .

COUNT: You may be, sir, but she's not! Minna! Is this the man you love?

MINNA: Yes.

COUNT: There you are, then! Take her word for it. A bitch will know her mate in a park of aniseed, I daresay . . . ! (*He laughs again.*)

MINNA: A bitch will, yes . . . (*She looks at* TELLHEIM.) Major . . .

WERNER: The ashes were spread on the cabbages. And this produced a crop which even the most seasoned horticulturalists declared extraordinary. From the point of view of size they were grotesque, but perhaps grotesque only from this point of view, that anything experienced beyond its normal dimensions at first appears grotesque, it seemingly offends against an innate sense of scale, but what is this scale? It is only that the tolerances have remained unstretched which creates in us the idea of the normal. The normal also moves. Thus the cabbages were metaphorical, and their amazing size shocked only if one failed to acknowledge that they too were aspects of a world which had become accelerated . . . (*Pause.*

become accelerated . . . (*Pause. He stares ahead. The* COUNT *casually begins to undress.* TELLHEIM *and* JUST *sit, eyes closed, faces tilted to the sun, in dark glasses, idle as hotel guests. The* COUNT, *immaculately, hangs up his shirt, his jacket.* MINNA *sits, chin on hand, staring into the distance, resigned as a bored mistress. The* CUPID *passes silently. Birds sing . . .*)

MINNA: The worst thing about the world, I think . . . (*Pause*) How hard it is to say the worst thing . . . I must cease making these preposterous claims . . . (*Pause*) Is that it does not stop . . . (*Pause*) Isn't that a slap in the face of sensibility? (*The* COUNT *is folding his tie.*)

COUNT: Odd, isn't it, that even with a woman, I fold my tie. And always did! No haste or hunger ever made me neglect this simple discipline, for silk does crease . . .

MINNA: I understand that. That is a characteristic of me also.

COUNT: Yes, I remember it! How well she folds her clothes! Even as a child!

MINNA: Yes.

COUNT: Undress, then. Or lift your hem. I'm not fussy about nakedness, which is rarely beautiful, I have observed . . .

MINNA: You have observed, have you . . . ! (*She laughs.*) Oh, I am your niece! Your very phrasing is my own . . . dear man . . . (*She shakes her head.*)

COUNT: Minna, was I a proper parent to you? (*Pause*)

MINNA: A proper parent? (*Pause. She appears to reflect.*) Well, not proper . . . merely . . . excellent. (*The* COUNT *grins.*) Proper's a lot to ask, and having observed the properly brought up I must say it is not something I aspire to. (*Pause*) Nothing you did was proper, but also, nothing you did was I not a willing collaborator in, so the proper can be set aside and —

> **Oh, don't apologize**
> **Don't** (*A shot rings out.*)
> **Please**

TELLHEIM (*jumping up*): **Stop that!** (*another shot*)
> **Stop that**
> **Stop**
> **Stop** (*and another*)
> **Stop that**
> **Stop**
> **Stop**

JUST *holds* TELLHEIM *tightly in an embrace to comfort him. The* COUNT *is peculiarly still. The wind. The oars.* MINNA *goes to the* COUNT *and places her hands on his face, looking into his dying eyes.*

MINNA: Oh, Tellheim, he is under the impression that I hated him . . . ! He sees in his last, shrinking look the triumph of an injured woman . . . not true . . . not true . . . (*The* COUNT's *eyes close. His body is rigid.* MINNA *looks to the* LANDLORD, *who is discovered waiting attentively.*) He did not wrong me . . . never . . . (*She drapes the* COUNT's *jacket over his head. The sudden eruption of drum taps.* JUST *is galvanized by horror.*)

JUST: Master / The woman's mad / Master / To kill for nothing whatsoever / And a father / What / What / Have we here? (*He masters himself, he smiles.*)
      Miss Barnhelm . . . (*He shakes his head.*)
      Hilarious . . .
      By such actions to assume . . . (*He pretends to pity.*)
      You might achieve equality with me . . . (*Pause.* MINNA *stares at him.*)

MINNA: I'm bad. (JUST *smiles with bemused contempt.*)
      After all, it isn't numbers, is it? It's not algebra. (*He looks at the floor.*)
      Not the act. Nor the quantity. Is it? I ask you. (*She turns her head to* TELLHEIM.)
      Not the volume or the quality, is it Tellheim? (TELLHEIM *ignores her.*)
      But the deadness in the heart . . . surely? (*Pause*)
      Badness Major . . . (*She laughs.*)

MINNA: Francisca . . . ! (*Pause. No one appears.*)
      Oh, I so love to be alone . . . ! I so love the silence that runs back from the cliffs like waves . . . self returned to self . . . ! Minna and more Minna yet . . . ! Self to the power of n . . . Mirror . . . ! (*She turns, sees herself, laughs, sobs.*) Mirror . . . ! (*She goes to her image and presses her body against it, hanging her hands over the frame.* JUST *turns to* TELLHEIM.)

JUST: Do you want your life wrecked? Say so if you do. Wreck by all means, only let me know because I have a small investment in this servitude, insignificant to you perhaps but oddly a preoccupation of my miserable existence —

TELLHEIM: Just —

JUST: **Shut up I'm talking** come apart by all means, spars, rudders, rusty engines on the rocks, plates protruding from the water, yes, brains in the seaweed who's stopping you not me I only gave a life to it and life we know is nothing but a —

TELLHEIM: Just —

JUST: **Do I bully you all right I bully what are servants for to keep mad masters from the room of manacles I have guarded your mind for fifteen years** all right betray me all right betray and dream the consequences you won't dream hard enough I promise you **life without me** — (*He emits a howl.*)

I'm threatening you

I'm threatening you

I do when I become enraged and rage is fear you said so take me in your arms will you take me in your arms or something . . . (TELLHEIM *does not. A cruel silence.* JUST *shrugs.*)

She . . .

She . . . (*He breathes.*)

Take me in your arms your servant . . . (TELLHEIM *does not.* JUST *recreates himself. Pause.*)

No.

No.

Because a falseness hurts you like a burn. A charity scalds you. An emotion manufactured, even to alleviate another's pain, racks your soul. (*Pause*)

Great man.

Great man I always thought it pure privilege to serve **Why don't you put a hand to a dying dog** . . . ? (*Pause*) Whose loyal eyes seek yours . . . ? (*Pause*)

Dinner is baked hake you savage bastard . . . (*He goes out*, TELLHEIM *walks a little.*)

TELLHEIM: Cy — th — era . . . (*He shouts.*) Landlord!

LANDLORD (*entering*): Major, you summon me at all times of day and night I must remind you it is not my practice to obey these peremptory (*Pause*)

Yes? (*Pause*)

I personally attend only the ladies' rooms so if you require (*Pause*)

What can I get you? (*Pause*)

I don't like you under my roof, there was a time I felt it as an honour not now however the world has altered and Miss Barnhelm is obviously unwell (*Pause*)

The bar is closed or possibly not open yet (*Pause*)

She is under my protection as indeed all guests have the right to be thank you for your cheque but as usual it isn't dated (*Pause*)

For what my protection's worth . . .

TELLHEIM: Put the Count in his grave.

LANDLORD (*shocked*): Put the —

TELLHEIM: Fetch a trolley or a —

LANDLORD: **Put the Count in** —

TELLHEIM: Yes, that's what I said —

LANDLORD: **You have to date the cheques or they** (*Pause*)
I don't know where to dig. Your spade hits bits of others.

TELLHEIM: Yes. Grosshayen's like that —

LANDLORD: **Only because you**
Only because of your (*Pause*)

We always have this and at one time I didn't mind it quite amused me if it wasn't the date then the signature was missing (*Pause*)

Doesn't he have a vault? A mausoleum with those shelves of marble and things that look like hatboxes with entrails in? (*He sniggers. He looks up.*)

Coats of arms? Hearts in jars and . . . ?

TELLHEIM: Rotted.

LANDLORD: Yes . . . (*Brightly*) The pants and things . . . it's just the same . . . they fade . . . so you bleach them and the bleach rots the fibres . . . (*He shrugs. He smiles. He curses.*) All right, so time goes by, but — (*Pause*)

TELLHEIM: Yes, I understand the deterioration of all things. Love. Garments. Obligations.

LANDLORD: It's hard to make a living what with —

TELLHEIM: I'll move into the smaller room —

LANDLORD: Currency's all over the place and —

TELLHEIM: The view over the water I was fond of but —

LANDLORD: What with shortages — (*Pause*)
Thank you. (*Pause*)
Thank you, Major. (*He goes out.* MINNA *turns abruptly from the mirror.*)

Scene Four

MINNA: She's gone . . .
Francisca . . .
Into a corner . . . and stood on a chair . . . (*She looks up* to THE HANGED.)
You know!
You know how it's done
And fell the two feet necessary to obliterate the world
I don't hold it against her
The spectacle of love in others can be oddly nauseating and I did not like the way she brushed my hair
As if
The hair was laughing at her
Passion in the absolute does that
It does
Make others wince at their own solitude . . . (*Pause. She turns* to TELLHEIM.)
I have a witness, Major Tellheim. (WERNER *walks slowly from the back of the stage. As he does so, the* LANDLORD *enters pushing a porter's handcart. He drops the handles by the* COUNT's *body and proceeds to load him.* TELLHEIM *sees* WERNER *and he spontaneously opens his arms.*)

TELLHEIM: Paul . . . ! (*His arms fall.*) With trousers wet from stepping in the water! Paul! The ferryman has no respect for dignity! It is pure ill-will on his part that he will not use the landing stage! With so many servants the pleasure of a task loyally performed is spoiled by petty malice. Perhaps these servants are descendants of men once masters in a different time in whom some damaged pride still manifests itself in little spites . . . (*Pause. They look at one another.*) Paul, you have not aged.

WERNER: You neither.

TELLHEIM: No! Me neither! (*He looks to* MINNA.) This is Paul Werner. The war brought us together but peace exposed the contrasts in our character. I was intimate with Paul, but intimacy owes more to circumstance than predilection. Have you not found that, Minna I am often horrified to think of intimacy, which we crave but which is only an illusion. One

more trick of the world. One more laugh of the world. Every
time we lay aside an intimacy we weep for ourselves, we weep
angrily, as if one had been cheated in a shop, as if one had
permitted oneself to be ridiculed . . . (*The* LANDLORD *has
loaded the* COUNT *and is moving off.*)

MINNA (*to* TELLHEIM):   You do know Sergeant Werner,
then?

TELLHEIM: No. I merely recognize him.

LANDLORD (*calling to* TELLHEIM):   I'll shift your trunks
while I've got the cart, Major? Save you?

TELLHEIM: Save me, by all means, yes . . .

LANDLORD: I'll have no trouble letting that room. People
who come here always say, that one with the balcony, that
one with the French windows that's occupied, is it? Unfortunately yes, I say, a most distinguished person in that room.
The ones who come to mourn, they want a nice room,
naturally. Them and the lawyers! (*He goes out.*)

MINNA: Mr Werner, I must ask you formally to identify this
man.

WERNER: Yes.

MINNA: Is he the Major von Tellheim about whom you have
made extensive statements now forming part of an indictment for crimes against humanity?

WERNER: Yes. (MINNA *sits at the table. She covers her face
with her hands. The empty swing crosses the stage, to and fro
in a wind. A voice is heard.*)

JUST (*off*):   Can I sit on the swing?
           Can I sit on the swing? (TELLHEIM *turns to see*
JUST *entering, dressed as an eighteenth century female ado-
lescent.* JUST *waits, with increasing impatience.*)
           Please!
           Swing me, please!

TELLHEIM *catches the swing, stills it. With a cry of triumph,*
JUST *scrambles onto the seat. He is a parody of Fragonard as*
TELLHEIM *propels him into space. A clatter of percussion.*

JUST (*with infantile ecstasy*):   Dig that hole you bastard dig I
said no not with that that is a spade who said you could the
spade is not for digging with your hands dig with your hands
and you polish the spade the spade has marks on it oh horrid
dirty spade I do hate that a spade should shine a spade
should gleam and you transport the earth he digs not in your

hands your mouth yes mouth I said on all fours like an animal oh have you seen an animal digging its grave I never have until today stop stop you stop and you take over yes I saw you smile not smile I say it was it's your grave now yes you and you make him go faster yes it's hardly moving that grave is it your grave hardly moving ride him yes ride him as he digs and (*He stops. A shot.*)

> **Stop that**
> **Stop**
> **Stop** (*Another*)
> **Stop that**
> **Stop**
> **Stop**

JUST *dies, but the swing continues its motion. The sound of oars and lutes. A crowd dressed for a fête champêtre appears from the depths of the stage.*

TELLHEIM: Poor Just, how he loved to persecute . . . a common persecutor who thrived on the pain of others. How he lacked the subtlety to actually argue with God . . . (*The dim sounds of picnic.*)

> Minna . . .
> I love you . . .
> But I shall make you silent . . . the words will die in your mouth . . . (*He suddenly covers his face.*)
> **Run, Minna, or you will never leave this place . . . !**

(MINNA *stares at him. The noise grows. The party approaches chattering inanely. Suddenly turns to them with a surge of gaiety; and bows.*)

> Tellheim! (*They laugh, ecstatically.*)

THE CROWD: Cyth — era!

TELLHEIM: Tellheim of Grosshayen! (*The* CUPID *flies, the crowd applauds.*)

> He
> Who
> Thrashed
> God!

THE CROWD: Cyth — era!

TELLHEIM: Who turned off love as if it were a light, observe my servant's innocence . . . (*The crowd laughs unaware* JUST *is dead.*) His innocence hangs like a little sun . . .

he cared for me but am I not the sworn enemy of existence?
Am I not the final rebuke of God? This woman knows! Oh,
still here, Minna? Still hoping against hope? I bound God
here in wire and burned Him, I was more pitiless than pebble
more blind than sand to mouths which hung like torn sheets
of incredulity

> **They could not believe their eyes**
> Minna, still here?
> Tellheim
> Caned
> God
> On
> These
> Little
> Acres
> I supervised
> I supervised
> The hell that none deserved for hell is unde-
> served to be hell, surely . . . ?
> Incomprehensible the punishment for being . . .
> Minna
> You've not gone

I cannot make love, Minna, to play God's game in copulation He would be smiling with contempt Behold Tellheim has
danced my minuet whose last step is demeaning death

> **Run Minna run**
> There are children and the condolences of mar-
> riage over there

And when your heart aches he will stroke it this kind
husband and when the world sits on your pride he'll lick
your tears and when the clouds appear to mock you with
their numbers he will explain the origins of the universe by
reference to picture books

> Relief
> By
> Mutual
> Consent
> **I've seen it**
> **Minna . . . .**
> I've seen it done
> Even
> At
> The

Oven
Door . . .
God's mockery of
God's
Oh, everywhere His laughter
Can't get it out my ears . . . ! (MINNA *stares at him, pitifully.*)

MINNA: How could you . . . How could you make yourself impossible to love . . . Oh, the man I've sought so long is the enemy of life . . . (*A wind stirs the branches.*) **I shall be also, Oskar . . . !** (*The* LANDLORD *comes.* MINNA *extends her arms to him. She shudders. He hesitates. He looks for assistance.*)

LANDLORD: Mr Werner, I — (MINNA *falls in his arms.*) I — I — (*He places his hands reluctantly on her head.*) Don't . . . touch . . . flesh . . . (*He touches her. He goes out. She addresses the crowd, brightly.*)

MINNA: I know why you are here! You come in search of Venus, and it's certain that she does live here, yes, it is her birthplace and being sentimental never stays away for long, a night out here or there but — sensible woman — keeps one foot in reality — (*The crowd laughs with delight.*)

    I am the same — yes — a realist to the core — (*and again*)

    Not easily misled, or if misled, not misled for long — (*They laugh.*)

    I know! I am identical! Now you will recognize her by three things — (*They clap.*)

    She does not smile — (*They moan sadly.*)

    What's amusing about love! (*They are shocked.*)

    No, don't look for a smiling goddess, that will be someone else, Second — (*She is intimate, secretive.*)

    She — (*Pause*)

    Has bad breath — (*They gasp.*)

    It's true it's true

    The reason being — (*They are complaining.*)

    Do you want to know the reason — (*They are quiet.*) It's — anxiety . . . because . . . great love . . . she knows . . . is . . . pain . . . she is not shallow, Venus . . . she suffers . . . all the time . . . oh, all the time . . . and this . . . is . . . not good for the health . . . you understand . . . thirdly — (*Pause*) Almost certainly . . . she'll be found before a mirror . . .

gazing at herself . . . because Venus is actually ashamed . . . (*They sigh with disappointment.*) No, no, it's true . . . don't laugh . . . she is so beautiful and yet . . . her beauty does not command . . . its powers are not infinite . . . poor woman . . . she looks at herself with disbelief. She hates herself . . . ! (*They look bewildered, hostile.*) Off you go, now! Remember Grosshayen is an island and Venus cannot swim — oh, that's a fourth thing, I am profligate with clues! (*The crowd hurries away, laughing.* MINNA *is still, deep in thought, her eyes rise at last, to* TELLHEIM.) Tellheim, what am I? (*Pause*)

TELLHEIM: One thing I've yet to destroy . . . (*Pause*)

MINNA: Yes . . . Oh, yes . . . ! I've found you, and I must die. The very fact you love me assures you I must die . . . (*She shakes her head.*) Your war with God is never ended . . . and I thought — (*She laughs.*) I could — what — mediate? (*Pause*) I'm not afraid of death, I must say this, vulgar posturing apart, fatuous rhetoric notwithstanding, I've no more left to do, my twenty-five years **were ample**. (*She goes idly to* JUST, *takes his head in her hands, letting it fall again.*) Fear, in the end, is something one grows tired of. Tired of fear, yes. Bored with fear. Quite enough fear, thank you, I've seen old women twitching with impatience for their final hour **you kill me and I'll kill you**. (*She looks at* TELLHEIM. *He wavers, visibly.*) Oh . . . ! (*Pause*) He does not . . . he cannot . . . contemplate . . . his own extinction . . . **The devil does not want to die** . . . ! (*She laughs. She calls for the* LANDLORD.) **Oskar!** (*She frowns angrily at* TELLHEIM.) Don't spoil a pitiless life by showing pity for yourself, don't wreck my faith — (*Turning, whimsically.*)

>These fir trees really are not Cythera, are they?
>Fir trees are a canopy of death — **Os — kar!**
>Fir trees you wouldn't want to look for Venus in,
>or run naked through unless — (*She lets out a cry of despair and comedy.*)
>Unless —
>I was fucked there at thirteen — (*She points.*)
>And there at eight — (*Again*)
>**No fir trees then** . . . ! (*She laughs.*)
>Crimes and crimes, sir! (*The* LANDLORD *appears silently with a tray of drinks, she studies him a long time.*)
>Drinks . . . (*She shakes her head . . .*)

He's brought us . . . drinks . . . ! (*Laughter comes from the woods. The* LANDLORD *nods in the direction.*)

LANDLORD: Be riotous tonight . . .

MINNA: Yes . . .

But the bar receipts . . . ! (*Cries from the woods. She listens a while.*)

Go and bring us the guns, Oskar . . .

LANDLORD: Guns, Miss Barnhelm?

MINNA: Yes. You know. (TELLHEIM *walks up and down, his hands in his hair, taut with tension.*)

LANDLORD: Guns . . . ?

MINNA: Guns, yes, guns . . . ! (*The* LANDLORD *turns to go.*)

And leave the drinks . . . (*He hesitates.*)

LANDLORD: The reason I prefer —

MINNA: Yes —

LANDLORD: Underwear is — (*Pause*)

MINNA: I know, Oskar. It never disappoints. And you shall have it. All of it, I promise you. (*He turns to go.* THE HANGED *erupt into an exclamation, like birds shrieking.*)

THE HANGED: Minna / Minna / They have found Venus in the woods / And she /

MINNA: Venus . . . ?

THE HANGED: In the woods / Miss Barnhelm / And /

MINNA: Venus . . . !

THE HANGED: Beat her with sticks . . . ! (*The roar of euphoric party-goers. They enter in black, as if mourning, dragging with them a naked woman. It is the* FIRST FRANCISCA.)

MINNA: But I'm Venus . . . Me . . . (*She turns in bewilderment. The* LANDLORD *greets the party.*)

LANDLORD: Grosshayen welcomes the bereaved, and its solitary hotel provides the high standards of comfort and that solemn atmosphere so necessary to a proper contemplation —

MINNA: **Me I said** —

LANDLORD: Guided tours of the camp area begin each day after breakfast in the car park and coffee can —

MINNA: **Venus is me**. (*The mourners examine* MINNA, *bewildered. She stares at the kneeling figure of the* FIRST FRANCISCA *as if grappling with an impossible truth.*)

TELLHEIM: Miss Barnhelm is collecting evidence for the Commission on Atrocity, and I am fully cooperating. Already five hundred thousand words of testimony have been accumulated and these will form the basis of a prosecution which —

MINNA: **I must be . . . to love him** . . . (*She turns to* TELLHEIM.)

> I defy you . . . I defy you to break me with any sin . . . (*She looks to the* LANDLORD.)
>
> The guns, I said . . . (*The* LANDLORD *is stiff, as if petrified, as is the party.* MINNA *takes a drink from the tray and swallowing it, flings the glass, which tinkles in the darkness . . .*)

To die will not be easy. Tellheim knows. However compelling the arguments in favour of. The logic, or the algebra. And this partly reflects the structure of the body, Tellheim knows . . . (*She takes a second glass, swallows the contents, flings it away again.*)

> God designing us to withstand accidents, and technology is fallible, Tellheim knows — (*She turns abruptly to the kneeling woman.*)
>
> **Why did you hide from me I thought you dead.** (*She turns away again.*)

And we cling to things, we cannot lever off our fingers from the world we love it so no matter what its ugliness, we battle one another for the last gasp of air, Tellheim knows — (*She turns to the* FIRST FRANCISCA *again.*)

> **You deserve to be beaten I should have beaten you myself** . . .

FIRST FRANCISCA: I am Tellheim's love . . . (*A profound pause.*)

MINNA: He does not make love, silly. Only his servant does . . . (*Pause*)

FIRST FRANCISCA: Minna —

MINNA: **Don't be silly don't be a silly child falling in swamps and now this preposterous why do you want to irritate me**. (*Pause*)

> I am his lover. I am evil, Francisca, and therefore close to him. (*Pause*)
>
> You on the other hand, are good . . . (FRANCISCA *looks pitifully at* MINNA. *Pause.*)

Deny her statement, Tellheim. Her silly statement, deny it, please . . . (TELLHEIM *does not. Suddenly the mourners erupt into life, chattering and laughing inanely. They proceed*

*to climb up the staircase to their rooms. In the following
silence, the* CUPID *enters with a gun, and stands patiently.
Seeing this,* MINNA's *hand goes involuntarily to her mouth
as she emits a strange, disembodied laugh.* WERNER, *emerging from the shadow, identifies it.*)

WERNER: That's the laugh . . . (MINNA *looks at him.*)

MINNA: Is it . . . ? Is that the laugh . . . ? (*She seems to
ponder, then suddenly turns to the* CUPID *with an out-
stretched arm, demanding the gun. The* CUPID *does not
accede.*) Come on . . . it's love . . . you know it is . . . (*She
goes to him, and relieves him of the gun.* WERNER *swiftly
picks up the* CUPID *in his arms and goes off with him.*) Oh,
Mr Werner . . . ! How sensitive . . . ! (*A popular march is
heard.* TELLHEIM, *with a fatal determination, takes the*
FIRST FRANCISCA *in his arms, kneeling by her, and kisses
her profoundly.* MINNA *watches this in the mirror, coolly, as
if she contemplated a picture in the tranquillity of a gallery . . .*)
Minna . . . your little heart has died and become — a whelk
. . . ! Calcinated, brittle as a whelk . . . pity the whelkheart of
dear Minna . . . pity her . . .

FIRST FRANCISCA: I do . . .

MINNA: For what, Francisca . . . do you pity your poor
mistress . . . ?

FIRST FRANCISCA: Her cleverness . . .

MINNA: Yes . . . Oh, yes . . . weep, then . . . (*She watches
them in the mirror.*) That isn't weeping . . . (*She swings abruptly and lets off a round, wildly, unaimed.*)
　　　　　Missed!
　　　　　Typical Minna! What a state she's in . . . ! (*She fires
　　　　　another.*)
　　　　　And that was accidental . . . ! (*A cry comes from the
　　　　　top of the stairs.*)

LANDLORD: Hey . . . !

MINNA: It's all right . . . !

LANDLORD: Stop that, I've people here who've come to
mourn —

MINNA: Everything's under control! (*He withdraws.*
MINNA *takes the gun more determinedly.*)

TELLHEIM: Minna . . . she's done no harm . . . (*For a
moment,* MINNA *holds the gun poised, then her arms
falter. Despair suffuses her.* THE HANGED *laugh in a terrible staccato rhythm which stops abruptly. They turn in the
breeze . . .*)

MINNA: And those who do no harm . . . are they immune,
Tellheim . . . ? (*She looks pitifully at* TELLHEIM.)
>The ground is made of them . . . (*Her look is one of
>lost love. She discovers a will, forced over despair.*)
>**This isn't Tellheim . . . !** (*She shouts off.*)
>**Pack the bags!** (*The second and third* FRANCIS-
>CAS *appear in modern dress.*)
>His eyes were brown . . . ! (*A burst of satisfied
>laughter comes from the mourners, dining above . . .
>She looks at her hands, raised, gazing from one palm
>to the other.*)
>And I'm. . . .
>Oh. . . .
>Solitary . . . (*She looks to her assistants.*)
Consign all Mr Werner's testimony to the bog, where it will
sink . . . into the sediment of Europe's griefs . . . (*They go to
move.*)
>**Evil requires goodness**
>Oh, isn't that its poverty . . . ?

MINNA *goes to where* JUST *hangs on the swing, and puts her
face close to his. She kisses his dead face. A march builds to
a crescendo, along with the clatter of knives and forks.
Echoing above it, the incredulous laugh of* MINNA VON
BARNHELM . . .

JUDITH

A Parting from the Body

CHARACTERS

JUDITH   A Widow of Israel
HOLOFERNES   A General of Assyria
THE SERVANT   An Ideologist

The tent of a general. HOLOFERNES *alone.*

HOLOFERNES: Tonight I must talk about death. For example, its arbitrary selections. This I find impossible to assimilate. This I find agony to contemplate. Its fingering of one. Its indifference to another. Its beckoning to one. Its blindness to another. This haunts me, this casualness. This gnaws my curiosity. I might say this quality in death has governed my emotions and made battle precious. Come in. For while victory is the object of the battle, death is its subject, and the melancholy of the soldiers is the peculiar silence of a profound love. Do come in, I detest the way some hover round the door, do you think I am deaf? This certainly lends me a quality which some describe as tenderness. Because I walk among the dead they will ascribe to me feelings of shame or of compassion. This is not the case. Rather, I am overcome with wonder. I am trembling with a terrible infatuation. Come in, I said. (JUDITH *enters, kneels, is still.*) This sensitivity they find hard to reconcile with cruelty, for which I also have a reputation. But cruelty is collaboration in chaos, of which the soldiers are merely the agents. It is not without philosophy. And some generals talk of necessity. They talk of limited objectives. There are no limitations, nor is there necessity. There is only infatuation. I hate to be bothered when I am thinking about death. Come in! (*A* SERVANT WOMAN *enters, kneels.*) What a racket even bare feet make for the contemplative mind. Tomorrow the dead will clog the ditches, so I must think. It is perfectly natural to think, however little thought affects the outcome. (*Pause.* JUDITH *produces a bottle. She uncorks it, with a characteristic sound. Pause.*) I do not drink, which if you were not a stranger, you would know. Obviously you believe in rumours, for example, the rumour that cruel men are degenerate. The opposite is the case, I promise you. (*A long pause.*)
THE SERVANT: I heard — futile now, I see — I heard — you liked women. (*She looks at* JUDITH.) Don't you like women either?

HOLOFERNES: Tonight I must talk about death.

THE SERVANT: She talks about death! (*She looks* at JUDITH.) Don't you? All the time she does. Death this, death that. I say to her, you melancholy thing, I don't know what made you like it. No, she is utterly morbid. Aren't you? (*Pause. JUDITH stares at the ground.*)

HOLOFERNES: I think you are a poor liar, and she is shallow. I think you have brought me a bitch as a present, a thing that giggles. On some nights I should certainly not cavil, but tonight is different. Tonight —

THE SERVANT: You want to talk about death! Of course you do, and she can, can't you, she's shy, that's all, I promise you on this particular subject she can spout for hours, can't you, go on, show the gentleman how much you. Go on. How well you. Judith. Show him. (*Pause. Suddenly HOLOFERNES seizes the SERVANT, fixing her tightly in an upright posture, between life and death. Pause.*)

HOLOFERNES: Those who die tomorrow, let us think of them.

THE SERVANT: Yes —

HOLOFERNES: The speed of their final thoughts, the torrent of their last reflections —

THE SERVANT: Yes —

HOLOFERNES: We fight on false presumptions, the first of these being that death will pass us by, I mean the wilful suspension of all logic is what permits the battle, though the battle is itself quite logical —

THE SERVANT: Yes —

HOLOFERNES: We ache for the pain of our companions, I am certain of it, soldiers nourish the secret hope their friends will die, does that horrify you, I only — (*the SERVANT chokes*) — seek the truth of battle, does that horrify you, I only probe the ecstasies of pain —

JUDITH: You are killing my property. (HOLOFERNES *is still, rigid.*) My property can't breathe. (*Pause*)

HOLOFERNES: I do not wish to fuck tonight.

JUDITH: No. You wish to talk.

HOLOFERNES: And anyway, this area is out of bounds, didn't you know, it is forbidden to civilians.

JUDITH: Yes.

HOLOFERNES: There are notices everywhere, or can't you read? What possible use are you to me if you can't read, tonight of all nights, when I must argue death, what use is the company of the illiterate?

JUDITH: I could be illiterate and still —

HOLOFERNES: Converse?

JUDITH: I might —

HOLOFERNES: There is no wisdom in the illiterate, I assure you, none —

JUDITH: Oh, I don't know —

HOLOFERNES: No, listen, don't repeat untruths which are merely sentimental —

JUDITH: I wasn't being sentimental, only —

HOLOFERNES: It is a fallacy that ignorance can harbour truth, and you are **so unwelcome**, take this away! (*He releases the* SERVANT, *who slides onto her knees.* JUDITH *does not move. The* SERVANT *breathes deeply in the silence.*) I do like women, but for all the wrong reasons. And as for them, they rapidly see through me. They see I only hide in them, which is not love. They see I shelter in their flesh. Which is not love. Now, go away. (*Pause*)

JUDITH: Let me speak. I cannot promise anything I say will be original. But I'm not unread. And if I say things which don't accord with your experience, it may serve to sharpen your own perceptions. No one can always engage with his equals, sometimes it's beneficial to hear an unsophisticated point of view. And anyway, how do you know you have an equal?

HOLOFERNES: I have no equal in the field I've made my speciality.

JUDITH: Which field is that? Murder or philosophy? (*She is suddenly pained at her cleverness.*)
            No, that was —
            Give me another chance to —
            That was —

HOLOFERNES, *as if oblivious to her, sits in a canvas chair, looking away, as if in thought. In the silence, the cry of a sentry in the night.*

HOLOFERNES: It is of great importance that the enemy is defeated.

JUDITH: Oh, yes!

HOLOFERNES: Or is it? Perhaps it only seems so.

JUDITH: Seems so?

HOLOFERNES: Always the night before the soldiers die I think — perhaps this is not important, after all. Perhaps it would be better if the enemy defeated us. I mean, from a universal point of view. Perhaps my own view is too narrow.

JUDITH (*thoughtfully*): Yes . . .

HOLOFERNES: Fortunately this consideration only occurs to me after I have made the plan of battle, never before. It is as if the thought were released by the certain knowledge I shall win.

JUDITH: Yes, but is it certain?

HOLOFERNES: Yes. No matter what the preparations of the enemy we shall win. For one thing, they believe we shall win, which alone ensures that they will lose. Take your clothes off now. As for this gnawing sense I have described that victory lacks authenticity, this disappears with the sunrise.

JUDITH: Take my clothes off . . . ?

HOLOFERNES: I think it is the persistence and proximity of Death, who lurks in all the interstices of life and cannot be abolished, which justifies the military profession. I think it is abhorrent only to those who lack the intellectual courage to recognise it for what it is — the organization of a metaphor. Did you not want to take your clothes off? What else did you come for? Hang them on a chair. I long to be married, but to a cruel woman. And as I lay dying of sickness in a room, I would want her to ignore me. I would want her to laugh in the kitchen with a lover as my mouth grew dry. I would want her to count my money as I choked.

JUDITH (*in confusion*): I cannot. (*She shakes her head.*) I cannot — simply —

HOLOFERNES: No.

JUDITH: As if —

HOLOFERNES: No.

JUDITH: If you would —

HOLOFERNES: Yes?

JUDITH: Just — touch — or —

HOLOFERNES: Touch?

JUDITH: Or —

HOLOFERNES: Murmur?

JUDITH: Something — just —

HOLOFERNES: I can see how difficult it is for you. Unfortunately I only wish to talk about death. It is you who came to be naked.

JUDITH: Yes, but — naked lovingly.

HOLOFERNES: Lovingly naked?

JUDITH: Yes.

HOLOFERNES: Tomorrow many will be naked. And so humiliated in their nakedness. So cruelly naked and smeared with excrement.

JUDITH: **I can't undress with you** —

HOLOFERNES: Their arses, their silly arses show —

JUDITH: **This is so much harder than I thought.**

HOLOFERNES: Yes, and you have hardly begun. (*Pause. She glares at him. She controls her panic. She turns to the* SERVANT.)

JUDITH: Take my clothing.

THE SERVANT (*smiling*): I've done this before. For Judith. And not only Judith!

JUDITH: He wants me naked. So.

THE SERVANT: All sorts of girls.

JUDITH (*undressing*): Naked I must be.

THE SERVANT (*taking a garment and laying it over her arm*): Some could and some couldn't.

JUDITH: Naked and unashamed.

THE SERVANT: Because undressing is an art.

JUDITH: As if I were not the object of his gaze, but simply the object of my own . . .

THE SERVANT: Properly done, it's most effective —

JUDITH: As if I were before the mirror and not before — (*She freezes.*) **I can't.** (*Pause*)

THE SERVANT: You've done it before.

JUDITH: Still, I can't.

THE SERVANT: Why ever not? Silly! (*Pause. The* SERVANT *looks to* HOLOFERNES.) She can't . . . I'm sorry . . . she is very sensitive . . . Idiot! No, she is though. She is magnificent but. (*She shakes her head.*) There you are, people are like that, one day flinging it all off and another — it must be you. It must be your. Whatever you have got. That's doing it. I mean. You are a most peculiar man, and I say that with all respect, with every admiration, you throw a girl off her — you would make a prostitute uneasy — and that's not as difficult as you would think, it really isn't, I've known exasperated prostitutes. (*She turns to* JUDITH.) Put this on again, you'll —

JUDITH: No. (*Pause*) I'll stay like this. Half-naked. (*Pause*) I am a widow, I don't know why I mention that. To earn your sympathy, perhaps.

HOLOFERNES: I have no sympathy.

JUDITH: No, I didn't think —

THE SERVANT: Why should he?

JUDITH: I suppose I —

THE SERVANT: He never knew your husband, why should
he —

JUDITH (*to the* SERVANT): **Just get out**. (*Pause. The* SER-
VANT *prepares to go.*)

HOLOFERNES: No. Stay. (*The* SERVANT *looks to*
JUDITH.) Wouldn't you prefer to stay? Admit you would
prefer that.

JUDITH: Perhaps she would, but I —

HOLOFERNES: No, no, it's me that has to choose, surely?
It is my night, not yours. Tomorrow I. Tomorrow they.
Flesh on all the hedges. No, it's me, surely? (*Pause. The cry
of a sentry in the night.*) I am a man who never could be
loved. I am a man no woman could find pitiful. Pity is love.
Pity is passion. The rest is clamour. The rest is just imperative. (*The* SERVANT *looks at* JUDITH. *A silence.*) When I
see my soldiers drag a woman in the thorns, her white legs
thrashing the air and her squeals oddly harmonious with the
squeals of passing transport, I ask myself who is the most
pitiful, knowing as I do how sorry for themselves all soldiers
are, and how they smother misery among the clods and
nettles and disordered clothing of their victims. I find it hard
to reprimand them. After all, what is an army? It is the mad
life licensed. It is not harmony, is it? It is not harmony on
the march. (*Pause*) When a woman loves a man, it is not his
manliness she loves, however much she craves it. It is the pity
he enables her to feel, by showing, through the slightest
aperture, his loneliness. No matter what his brass, no matter
what his savage, it creeps, like blood under a door . . .
(*Pause*)

THE SERVANT: It's going to be difficult tonight. I felt as we
came in here, it's going to be difficult tonight.

JUDITH: I must admit, Holofernes is not what I expected. I
am neither awed nor intimidated, and I can say in perfect
honesty, he is not what I expected. It makes things different.
It doesn't make them worse. I should dress, in order that —
(*She goes to reach for her clothes.*)

HOLOFERNES: No.

JUDITH (*stopping*): I think if we are to engage with one
another in —

HOLOFERNES: No.

JUDITH: It is very hard to be — to collect one's thoughts and —
HOLOFERNES: I also will be naked. (*Pause*)
JUDITH: Yes. Well, that would — that might —
THE SERVANT: This isn't what we expected. Is it? This is far from what —
JUDITH: Be quiet. (*Pause*)
It doesn't help. (*Pause*)
Be quiet. (HOLOFERNES *gets up. The* SER-VANT *goes to receive his clothes. He removes them item by item.*)
THE SERVANT (*laying them over her arm*): What lovely stuffs . . .
HOLOFERNES: Dead men's stuffs.
THE SERVANT: Oh, really?
HOLOFERNES: An army is not honourable, is it?
THE SERVANT: I wouldn't like to say if it is honourable or —
HOLOFERNES: No, it is not honourable, so I make no pretence at honour.
THE SERVANT: I respect that, I really do, and that's a nice piece, too, dead men's, is it? Lovely weave. (*She looks at him.*) You're not that strong, are you? You're not what I'd call powerful. But wiry, are you? Probably you're very fit?
JUDITH: You talk too much.
THE SERVANT: Do I? It's nerves. (*To* HOLOFERNES.) You're stopping there, are you? That's it? (HOLOFERNES *is lightly clad. He does not reply.*) That's it. (*She goes to lay out the clothes.*)
JUDITH: Tomorrow, when you have defeated Israel, as you say you cannot fail to do, how much will you destroy?
HOLOFERNES: All of it.
JUDITH: And the children?
HOLOFERNES: Them I'll enslave.
JUDITH: And the men, you'll —
HOLOFERNES: Cut their throats.
JUDITH: The old men, and the —
HOLOFERNES: If they have throats —
JUDITH: You'll cut them.
HOLOFERNES: Some of this cutting I will do myself.
JUDITH: That's no less than I expected.
HOLOFERNES: I do not distinguish myself from the army. I am cleverer than the army, but not better than the army. I

do things they could never do, such as to plot the disposi-
tions. But this does not relieve me of my compact with their
vileness. If vileness it is.

JUDITH (*shrugging complacently*): Some would say so.

HOLOFERNES: Some would. I never pay regard to some's
opinion. Neither do I laugh at myself. Sometimes, like
tonight, I think I want to see a woman naked, but usually,
seeing her, I realise it is not what I wanted at all. Generally
speaking, I am unhappy until I see the happy, and then I
understand the reason for my condition. If I had allowed you
to be naked, or you had allowed yourself, I should have
dismissed you long before now.

THE SERVANT: Lucky, then! Lucky you —

JUDITH (*hissing*):   **You — make — this — so —**

THE SERVANT: Sorry —

JUDITH: **Pitifully — mundane — and —**

THE SERVANT: Sorry —

JUDITH: **Sit — and — watch.** (*The* SERVANT *obeys. A
pause.*) I also am unhappy. I believed I was unhappy because
I was widowed. But my widowing merely licensed me to
show myself for what I am. Everyone else must laugh and
smile and greet each other, hoisting their children in the air
and acting the perfect neighbour, whereas I am privileged to
wear a melancholy face. Many envy me for this, and men are
drawn to unhappy women, as perhaps you know, being
subtle. I'm subtle, too. None subtler. She's right, however,
you are not well-built. Your power comes from elsewhere,
obviously. Am I talking too much? You have revealed so
much I feel I should also, but perhaps that's wrong. You
might wish me to be silent. You might wish to imagine me
rather than to know me. That is the source of desire, in my
view. Not what we are, but the possibilities we allow to
others to create us. Silence, for example. Might be judged as
mystery. (*Long pause. They look at one another.*)

HOLOFERNES: I can't be loved.

JUDITH: So you said.

HOLOFERNES: So if you were thinking of loving me, you
would do well to reconsider. (*Pause*)

JUDITH: Yes . . . (*Pause*) Yes . . . I came here thinking . . .
what did I think . . . I —

THE SERVANT: You thought —

JUDITH: **I said to be quiet, didn't I**? (*Pause*) I came here
thinking — obviously — thinking — I love — I — (*Pause*)

Never mind, love will do — (*Pause*) Love the — object — may I call you an object — the object Holofernes — the strategist, the general, the theorist, the murderer, the monster, the hero Holofernes. All those things, which are easy to love. Which are almost a substitute for love. But love is more difficult, it's — **please don't make me go yet.** (*Pause. The* SERVANT *looks anxiously from* JUDITH *to* HOLOFERNES. *The cry of the sentry. Pause.*)

HOLOFERNES: Let us talk about death.

JUDITH: Yes.

HOLOFERNES: Its ridiculing of life.

JUDITH: Yes.

HOLOFERNES: Its mockery of purpose, its humiliation of —

JUDITH: Yes, yes. (*Pause.* HOLOFERNES *looks at her, while she stares at the ground.*)

HOLOFERNES: We exist for one reason.

JUDITH: One reason? I thought we existed for no reason at all.

HOLOFERNES: To reproduce ourselves. (*Pause.* JUDITH *affects a gasp.*)

JUDITH: That's odd! That — coming from you — is particularly odd because — the pain you've given — and the things you've — to people who have never — and now you say — it is odd. Really, it is odd. I think you have such a beautiful manner. Quite unpredictible.

HOLOFERNES: Given we have no purpose but this eminently absurd purpose it would seem to me it is neither more creditable, nor more dishonourable, to slaughter than to kneel on the cold floor of a monastery. Naturally, I speak from Death's perspective. What other perspective is there?

JUDITH: Yes, but if life is so very — is so utterly — fatuous, should we not comfort one another? Or is that silly? (*Pause*) You think I'm silly. You're right, I'm only saying this to — I'm spewing the conventional opinion because — when this is such a special night, I really should forbid myself the conventional opinion, even if it is correct, which it may be, even so, however conventional it might be — **and all I wanted was to lie with you.** (*Pause*)

HOLOFERNES: And would that be easier?

JUDITH: Not easier, but. (*Pause*) Not easier at all. (*She draws her garments round her.*)

THE SERVANT: I always said, with love don't ask too many questions. Love's silent, I said. Or it speaks in rather ordinary words. (*She turns to* HOLOFERNES.) Tomorrow you'll be different! You'll have done the killing of a lifetime! Tomorrow you won't know yourself! 'Did I go on about death?' 'Was I miserable?' **Off with yer skirt, darling!** (*She chuckles.*) No, I've seen it. We picked the wrong night. (JUDITH, *with a surge of bravado, gets up.*)

JUDITH: All right, let's fuck.

THE SERVANT: Oh, dear . . .

JUDITH: I mean, all this — what is all this? You're a general, I'm a widow, so what? You kill thousands, I stay at home, so what? Don't think I haven't met your type before. I have. You want me to plead and pander. I will do. I can do that. You want me to say how much I, how magnificently you, all right, I will do, I'm far from educated, so I'll stop pretending, and anyway, nothing you say is original, either. Do I insult you? Do I abolish your performance? It needs abolishing. (*Pause. The* SERVANT *turns away in despair.* HOLOFERNES *stares at her, without emotion. The pressure in* JUDITH *dissipates. She shrugs.*) I am reckoned to be the most beautiful woman in the district. So I thought I had a chance. (*She goes to pick her clothing off the floor. She stops, and lets out a scream. The scream ceases. She remains still.*)

THE SERVANT: I said to Judith, are you really up to this? Yes, she said. It'll hurt you, I said, one way or another. I know, she said. You'll never be the same, I said. I know that, too, she said. But you can know a thing and still not know it. Now look at us. (*Pause*)

HOLOFERNES: And yet I want to be. (*Pause*) I, the impossible to love, require love. Often, I am made aware of this. (*Pause*)

THE SERVANT: You are? (*Pause*)

HOLOFERNES: This lack.

THE SERVANT: You are, are you?

HOLOFERNES: This lack asserts itself in a distinctive way.

THE SERVANT: Yes?

HOLOFERNES: **Do you think I can't see you**? (*The* SERVANT *is transfixed.*) **Your mask. Your fog. Do you think I can't see you**? (*Pause*) The way in which it asserts itself is as follows. Frequently I expose myself to the greatest danger. I court my own extinction. Whilst I am exhilarated by the conflict I am also possessed of the most perfect lucidity. So absolute am I in consciousness, yet also so removed from fear of death, I am at these moments probably a god.

Certainly that is how the enemy perceives me. It is only when the action is over, and I am restored to the weary and sometimes damaged thing that is my body, that I sense a terrible need; not for praise, which I receive in abundance, but of that horror in another that I might have ceased, and had I ceased, she also could not have but ceased. I am not the definition of another's life. That is my absent trophy. I think we live only in the howl of others. The howl is love. (*Pause*)

THE SERVANT: I think, with you, the problem is your strength. Do you mind this? Do you mind if I lecture? I think you probably are perfect. You know too much, which is like armour. Shall I go on? I've seen the hardest whore panic when she could not detect a weakness in the customer. You must give people rights. You must give them their powers over you. Like I step off the pavement for a beggar if he curses me. What has he got? Nothing. Nothing but his curse. So I yield him that. I give him his paltry power. So with you, you must give the woman something to hold over you. You are too perfect. There! End of lecture! (*She turns to* JUDITH.) Are you feeling better, darling? She is not a whore. She is a widow and not a whore. Only with you around, she felt like whoring! (*She laughs. A silence. The cry of the sentry. Suddenly* HOLOFERNES *clasps the* SERVANT *in his arms, desperately, sobbing quietly. The* SERVANT *looks to* JUDITH. *As suddenly,* HOLOFERNES *releases her.*)

HOLOFERNES: You say I am not weak. I was weak once. None weaker. I crept through life. I staggered from sickness to sickness.

THE SERVANT: I didn't mean that kind of —

HOLOFERNES: I ran from other boys and hid in corners. I sought no company, or the company of girls whose games appeared less brutal, falsely, but. I stammered with shame when asked to speak, even though my mouth was full of language. I lived always in the shadows, hating the sun's glare because it exposed me to the scrutiny of others. **There was none weaker than me**. (*Pause*) But being weak, I discovered cunning. I learned to say one thing, knowing it would satisfy the expectation, whilst carrying on a second and more secret conversation with myself. I led people away from my true intention, my speech became a maze, I used speech to trap my enemies, my speech was a pit, I lived in speech, making it a weapon. And also I learned to run. I practised running, so when speech failed, I could out-distance them. That is how I, the runt, became a general. The mind of the weak-bodied is so terrible, is so out-landish and so subtle. He has made a spiked thing of it, to impale your innocence. (*Pause*)

JUDITH: You mean, nothing you say is true? (HOLOFERNES *looks at her*.) I don't mind that. I am perfectly able to lie myself. **I am almost certainly lying now in fact**. (*Pause*)

No, that's —

I'm glad because —

That puts my mind at rest — (*She laughs*.)

Excellent! Because so much is false when men and women are together, so much! I have always thought, when men and women are together, all this is false! And you say — you confess — all is trickery, all is deception, façade and affectation! Excellent! Forgive my hysteria, it was the pressure, the sheer suffocating pressure of sincerity. And now I am light! I am ventilated! A clean, dry wind whirls through my brain! I intend to kill you, how is that for a lie? And that must mean I love you! Or doesn't it? Anything is possible! I think, now we have abandoned the search for truth, really, we can love each other! (*She looks to the* SERVANT.) The relief! (*She laughs again*.) The relief of knowing you are simply an element in a fiction! I think before this moment I never was equipped to love. (*She extends her hand to* HOLOFERNES.) Take my hand! Take my widow's hand in your murderer's hand, my mothering hand in your massacring hand! (*He extends it. She holds it, looks at it*.) It's so white! It's so well cared for. Poets are much grubbier, but they also murder. (*Pause. She kneels beside him*.) Do you like me at all? Of course your reply will be a pack of lies, but. Say anyway. (*Pause*) I spent hours on this get-up. Like a bride. Which is another lie. My lips are not in the least bit red, I am rather pale-mouthed actually. Lies everywhere! Do you like me, though? When you told me you could not help yourself lying I fell in love with you. That was the moment. My husband betrayed me all the time, with girls, but this will be different, won't it? Why girls? Was he ashamed of something? Lie, do lie! (*Pause*)

HOLOFERNES: I know why you're here. (*Pause. The* SERVANT *stares*.)

JUDITH: I know why I came.

HOLOFERNES: I know what you intend.

JUDITH: I know what I intended.

HOLOFERNES: I know it all.

JUDITH: I knew it all. (*Pause*) I knew it all. And now I know nothing. (*He looks into her.*)

HOLOFERNES: We love, then.

JUDITH: Yes.

HOLOFERNES: And I, who is unlovable, I am loved.

JUDITH: My dear, yes . . . (*Pause*)

THE SERVANT: One of them is lying. Or both of them. This baffles me, because whilst Judith is clever, so is he. Whilst Judith was renowned for being subtle, what else is he? And only six hours to the battle! (*She comes forward.*) The battle begins at dawn. It begins with shouting. They shout for twenty minutes. Yes, a twenty-minute shout! Then they let fly the javelins. Then they shout again. I've seen it. Four times I've seen it. Four times I've run for my life. Our General says we will learn from our mistakes. He says this with a monotonous regularity. We have learned, say the soldiers. We've learned to run the moment we see Holofernes. They look for him. His little form. They see him move his staff — like this — and this — and every movement of his staff brings down an unexpected blow. I run. I jump on the nearest wagon. I whip the horses. Off I go. Fuck the war and fuck the wounded. The whores are miles ahead. The sign of a lost battle is the fleeing whore-carts. Sometimes they pass through towns hours before the army. That's the signal to pack up and go. The whores outrun the cavalry! What strategists they are! What sensibilities! (*To* JUDITH *and* HOLOFERNES.) Shall I leave you, or — (*She sees they are embracing.*) Oh, one of them is lying, but which! (*Pause. She looks from a safe distance, sitting on a pile of clothes.*)

JUDITH: You kiss strangely. I don't criticize, but how strangely you kiss!

HOLOFERNES: And you.

JUDITH: Me?

HOLOFERNES: Your mouth smothers mine, as if it were a hunger. But it might also be — a violence.

JUDITH: And yours is hard. You keep your lips tight-sealed, which might be wonder, or perhaps, are you ashamed? Don't be ashamed. I like your lips.

HOLOFERNES: I can't be loved . . . !

JUDITH: You are! You are loved!

THE SERVANT: How brilliant she is! How ecstatic she is! She convinces me! But she must be careful, for with lying, sometimes, the idea, though faked, can discover an appeal, and then we're fucked! It's true! I've seen it! I've seen everything!

JUDITH: Shh! (*The* SERVANT *sits again.*) He wants to sleep. (*The* SERVANT *looks puzzled.*) Don't you? You want to sleep . . .

HOLOFERNES: Yes.

JUDITH: And I know why . . . (*To the* SERVANT.) **I do know why**! Dear one, you want to sleep because this also has been a battle. Tomorrow we will make love. (*She turns angrily on the* SERVANT.) **It has been a battle for him!**

THE SERVANT: Yes . . .

JUDITH: A terrible battle for him. To love. To give. (*To the* SERVANT.) And you stare, because he won't make love. You stare, because he does not pull me to the floor. I hate the way you stare! You do hate men! How you hate them!

THE SERVANT: Me?

JUDITH: Yes. For you they have no modesty, their modesty is a sign of impotence. I do hate the way your lip is half-bent in laughter, in contempt, whore!

THE SERVANT (*puzzled*): Who's stopping him sleeping? I'm not!

JUDITH: Whore!

THE SERVANT: Abuse away, dear —

JUDITH: That is real whoring, it is real whoring when a woman mocks the modesty in a man! (*Pause. In the silence, the sentry cries, and* HOLOFERNES, *wrapped in* JUDITH's *arms, sleeps. A long pause, without movement.*)

THE SERVANT (*abandoning her persona*): Judith . . .

JUDITH: Shh . . . (*Pause*) Listen, his breathing, like returning tides . . .

THE SERVANT: Judith . . .

JUDITH: Shh . . . (*Pause*) His moving, like slow cattle on the road . . .

THE SERVANT: Judith . . . his sleep is restoring him for slaughter . . . his strength is the extinction of our race . . . Judith . . . his breath is our oblivion . . . his dreams are our pain . . . get the sword down, Judith . . . his luxury is our murder . . . Judith . . . his tranquillity is our scream . . . the sword's up there . . .

JUDITH: I've seen the sword.

THE SERVANT: Good. Unsheath it.

JUDITH: I hear you. I hear you very clearly.

THE SERVANT: You have a child.

JUDITH: I have a child, yes.

THE SERVANT: Take down the weapon, then.

JUDITH: Yes.

THE SERVANT: Your child sleeps also. Her last sleep if you —

JUDITH: I am not hesitating.

THE SERVANT: You aren't hesitating? What are you doing, then?

JUDITH: I don't know, but you need not urge so. I am not hesitating.

THE SERVANT: You say you are not hesitating, but it looks like hesitation. Take the sword down or I will.

JUDITH: I am absolutely not hesitating.

THE SERVANT: No, but — (*She goes to reach for the sword.*)

JUDITH: **Do not take the sword down**.

THE SERVANT: Israel commands you. Israel which birthed you. Which nourished you. Israel insists. And your child sleeps. Her last sleep if —

JUDITH: **I am well drilled**. (*She glares at the* SERVANT. *The sentry cries. Pause.* JUDITH *goes to the sword.*)

THE SERVANT: Excellent. (JUDITH *unsheaths it.*)
Excellent.
My masterful.
My supreme in.
My most terrible.
My half-divine. (JUDITH *raises the weapon* over HOLOFERNES.)

HOLOFERNES (*without moving*): I'm not asleep. I'm only pretending. (*Pause. The sword stays.*)
My dear.
My loved one.
I'm not asleep. I'm only pretending. (*Pause.* JUDITH *closes her eyes.*)

JUDITH: Why?

THE SERVANT: Don't discuss!

HOLOFERNES: Because I must win everything.

THE SERVANT: Oh, don't discuss! Israel dies if you discuss!

HOLOFERNES: I can win battles. The winning of battles is, if anything, facile to me, but.

JUDITH: My arm aches!

HOLOFERNES: But you.

JUDITH: Aches!

HOLOFERNES: Love.

JUDITH: My arm aches and I lied!

HOLOFERNES: Of course you lied, and I lied also.

JUDITH: We both lied, so —

HOLOFERNES: But in the lies we. Through the lies we. Underneath the lies we.

THE SERVANT: **Oh, the barbaric and inferior vile inhuman bestial and bloodsoaked monster of depravity!**

HOLOFERNES: Judith.

THE SERVANT: **Oh, the barbaric and inferior vile inhuman bestial and bloodsoaked monster of depravity!**

HOLOFERNES: Judith . . . !

JUDITH: **Oh, the barbaric and inferior** — (*Seeing* JUDITH *is stuck between slogan and action, the* SERVANT *swiftly resorts to a stratagem, and leaning over* HOLOFERNES, *enrages* JUDITH *with a lie.*)

THE SERVANT: He is smiling! He is smiling! (*With a cry,* JUDITH *brings down the sword.*) Goddess! (JUDITH *staggers back, leaving the sword in place. The* SERVANT *leaps to it and saws energetically.*)

        Immaculate deliverer!

        Oh, excellent young woman!

        Oh, virgin!

        Oh, widow and mother!

        Oh, everything! (*She saws in ecstasy.*)

        Fuck this! Hard going, this! (JUDITH *groans, crawling along the floor, and shaking her head from side to side like an animal trapped in a bag. The* SERVANT *ceases her labours. She takes deep breaths.* JUDITH *stops. Long pause.*)

        Have you got the bag? (*Pause*)

        Judith? (*Pause*)

        The bag? (*Pause. She sits, wearily.*)

I do apologize, I thought for — I really do — for one moment, I thought — she won't — she can't — I do apologize — (*Pause*) I will put it in the bag. You needn't. (*Pause*) Ever see it again. (JUDITH *gets up with a strange energy. She dusts off her hands.*)

JUDITH: I was silly there.

THE SERVANT: Oh, I don't know, you —

JUDITH: I was. So fucking silly. Nearly fucked it, didn't I? Nearly fucked it with my. No, I was a silly cunt there, wasn't I?

THE SERVANT: Well, you —

JUDITH: Oh, fuck, yes, a proper slag and bint there —

THE SERVANT: In your pocket I think there's a —

JUDITH: A right bitch cunt, I was, nearly bollocked it, eh, nearly — (*She staggers.*) **Oh, my darling how I** — (*She recovers.*) Nearly poxed the job, the silly fucker I can be sometimes, a daft bitch and a cunt brained fuck arse — (*She staggers.*) **Oh, my** — **Oh, my** —

THE SERVANT: The bag. Give me the bag.

JUDITH: **Oh, my** — **Oh, my** —

THE SERVANT: **Give it to me, then.** (*Pause.* JUDITH *stabilizes herself.*) We take the head because the head rewards the people. The people are entitled symbolically to show contempt for their oppressor. Obviously the spectacle has barbaric undertones but we. The concentration of emotion in the single object we etcetera. So. (JUDITH *is still.*) All right, I'll wrap it in a sheet. (*She pulls a cloth from the wall and begins with a will to wrap the severed head.*)

JUDITH: I want to fuck. (*Pause. The* SERVANT *stops.*)

THE SERVANT: Lie down. Rest for a little while, then we can —

JUDITH: No, I must fuck. I must. (*Pause*)

THE SERVANT: With who do you —

JUDITH: With him. I want to fuck with him. (*Pause*)

THE SERVANT: You are in such a state, my dear, and I do understand, but —

JUDITH: I can arouse him. He is still warm, so obviously I can arouse him. (*She moves towards the body.*)

THE SERVANT: Sit down, and count to a hundred —

JUDITH: You count to a hundred, I'll arouse him, look! (*She draws back the cloths, exposing him to herself.*) Oh, look . . . !

THE SERVANT: **Get away from him**.

JUDITH (*touching him with innocence*): It curls . . . it moves like weed in the slow current of my gaze . . .

THE SERVANT: **Vile and dishonourable** —

JUDITH: Shh! Shh! Do look, the strange and mobile nature of him here, a landscape, look, I never saw my husband so revealed, so innocent and simple, I must arouse him.

THE SERVANT (*attempting coolness*): Don't do that with an enemy —

JUDITH: An enemy?

THE SERVANT: It demeans your triumph and humiliates our —

JUDITH: How can he be an enemy? His head is off.

THE SERVANT: **Enemy. Vile enemy**.

JUDITH: You keep saying that . . . ! But now the head is gone I can make him mine, surely? The evil's gone, the evil's in the bag and I can love! Look, I claim him! Lover, lover, respond to my adoring glance, it's not too late, is it? We could have a child, we could, come, come, adored one . . . !

THE SERVANT: I think I am going to be sick . . .

JUDITH: No, no, count to a hundred . . .

THE SERVANT: I will be made insane by this!

JUDITH: You weren't insane before. Is it love makes you insane? Hatred you deal admirably with. Come, loved one . . . ! (*She lies over* HOLOFERNES's *body. The* SERVANT *is transfixed with horror.*)

        He doesn't move . . .

        He doesn't move . . . ! (*Slowly, reluctantly, she climbs off the body. She sits among the wreckage of the bed. The cry of the sentry. A long pause. The* SERVANT *looks at* JUDITH.)

THE SERVANT: Judith . . .

JUDITH: Yes . . .

THE SERVANT: I think we must —

JUDITH: Yes —

THE SERVANT: Or it'll be —

JUDITH: It will be, yes —

THE SERVANT: Dawn and —

JUDITH: Exactly. (*Pause.* JUDITH *doesn't move. The* SERVANT *kneels beside her.*)

THE SERVANT: I will find you a husband. Such a fine man and he will make you laugh but also fill you with admiration. He will have both wit and intelligence. And the wit will not demean him, nor the intelligence make him remote.

JUDITH: Difficult . . .

THE SERVANT: Difficult, yes, but I will find him. And he will give you children. He will be a child with them and a man with you. And his childishness will never mock his manliness, nor his manliness oppress the child.

JUDITH: Difficult . . .

THE SERVANT: Difficult, yes, but I will discover him. And old women will smile at your radiant delight, and silences will fall between you born of perfect understanding, so deep will be your mutuality speech will be redundant, such a bond, oh, such a union, the plants will thrive on your allotments from your tender touch, get up now. (*Pause*)

JUDITH: I can't. (*Pause*)

THE SERVANT: You can't . . . ?

JUDITH: Move. (*Pause. She stares at the* SERVANT *in horror.*)

THE SERVANT: Judith —

JUDITH: **Can't move!** (*Pause. The* SERVANT *subdues her irritation.*)

THE SERVANT: What are you saying? I'm full of patience but. All sympathy and tolerance but. A hard night this, admittedly but. **If they catch us it's wombs to the Alsatians, bitch!** (*Pause*)

JUDITH: Listen —

THE SERVANT: All right —

JUDITH: Are you listening —

THE SERVANT: Yes —

JUDITH: Because I have no more wish to be —

THE SERVANT: All right —

JUDITH: Than you have —

THE SERVANT: All right, all right —

JUDITH: I am fixed to the ground, do you follow me, I am unable to move, I have the will but not the power —

THE SERVANT: Yes —

JUDITH: I'm stuck, **I'm stuck**. (*Pause. The* SERVANT *looks around, anxiously, then with resolution, goes to lift* JUDITH. JUDITH *lets out a cry of pain.*)

JUDITH: It hurts!

THE SERVANT: What, what hurts?

JUDITH: Don't touch me, please!

THE SERVANT: Don't touch you?

JUDITH: Please, don't touch me again . . . ! (*Pause. The* SERVANT *wipes her palms on her skirt, nervously. She walks swiftly up and down, stops.*)

THE SERVANT: God's punished you. (*Pause*)

JUDITH: What.

THE SERVANT: God has.

JUDITH: Why.

THE SERVANT: Obviously.

JUDITH: Why.

THE SERVANT: For —

JUDITH: What!

THE SERVANT: Just now. With him.

JUDITH: Punished me?

THE SERVANT: You have offended Him! (*Pause*) I can't come near you, in case — can't possibly — in case — He might — (JUDITH *emits a long wail.*) Obviously, you're judged and — (*The wail rises.*) Plead! Plead with Him! (*She stares at* JUDITH. *Pause.*) All right, I will. (*She kneels.*) And if it fails, I have to go, forgive me, but —

JUDITH: No, don't do that, I —

THE SERVANT: **Have to obviously**. (*She stares at* JUDITH.)
      Take the head and. (*Pause*)
      Obviously. (*Pause*)

   You will be honoured. All Israel will. And streets will be. And parks. Great thoroughfares. Whatever you suggest. (*Pause*)

JUDITH: Plead! (*The* SERVANT *concentrates.*) Louder!

THE SERVANT: I am, but —

JUDITH: Louder, then! (*The* SERVANT *rocks to and fro on her knees, then stops. She scrambles to her feet.*)

THE SERVANT: I think you must do it.

JUDITH: He wants me to die!

THE SERVANT: I don't think we can make assumptions of that sort but — (*She finds the head, and wraps it swiftly.*)

JUDITH: Yes! Hates me and wants me to die!

THE SERVANT: I'm sorry but — (JUDITH *lets out a profound cry of despair as the* SERVANT, *clasping the head, goes to the door. She stops. She looks back at* JUDITH. *Pause.*) I say God. I mean Judith. (*Pause*) I say Him. But I mean you. (*Pause. The cry of the sentry is heard. The* SERVANT *places the head on the ground, and comes back to* JUDITH. *She kneels before her, and leaning on her knuckles, puts her forehead to the ground. Pause.* JUDITH *watches.*)

JUDITH: You are worshipping me.
      Aren't you? Worshipping me?
      Why are you doing that?

THE SERVANT: Not for what you are.

JUDITH: No?

THE SERVANT: For what you will be.

JUDITH: When?

THE SERVANT: When you stand, Judith.

JUDITH: I can't stand . . . (*Pause*)

THE SERVANT: Firstly, remember we create ourselves. We do not come made. If we came made, how facile life would be, worm-like, crustacean, invertebrate. Facile and futile. Neither love nor murder would be possible. Secondly, whilst shame was given us to balance will, shame is not a wall. It is not a wall, Judith, but a sheet rather, threadbare and stained. It only appears a wall to those who won't come near it. Come near it and you see how thin it is, you could part it with your fingers. Thirdly, it is a facility of the common human, but a talent in the specially human, to recognise no act is reprehensible but only the circumstances make it so, for the reprehensible attaches to the unnecessary, but with the necessary, the same act bears the nature of obligation, honour, and esteem. These are the mysteries which govern the weak, but in the strong, are staircases to the stars. I kneel to you. I kneel to the Judith who parts the threadbare fabric with her will. Get up, now. (*Pause. JUDITH cannot move. The SERVANT counts the seconds. She perseveres.*) Judith, who are those we worship? What is it they possess? The ones we wrap in glass and queue half-fainting for a glimpse? The ones whose works are quoted and endorsed? The little red books and the little green books, Judith, who are they? Never the kind, for the kind are terrorized by grief. Get up now, Judith. (*Nothing happens. Pause.*) No, they are the specially human who drained the act of meaning and filled it again from sources fresher and — (JUDITH *climbs swiftly to her feet.*)

JUDITH: You carry the head until we reach the river. Then I'll carry it. (*She busily goes to the sword.*) The sword I'm taking with us. (*The SERVANT, amazed and gratified, starts to scramble to her feet.*) **Who said you could get up.** (*Pause. The SERVANT smiles, weakly.*) Beyond the river, you walk behind me. Ten yards at least.

THE SERVANT: Yes. Good. (*She starts to rise again.*)

JUDITH: **Who said you could get up.** (*The SERVANT stops.*) And any version that I tell, endorse it. For that'll be the truth.

THE SERVANT: Absolutely — (*She moves again.*)

JUDITH: **Who said you could get up.** (*The SERVANT freezes, affecting amusement.*)

THE SERVANT: I was only thinking —

JUDITH: Thinking? I do that.

THE SERVANT: Wonderful!

JUDITH: In fact, looking at you as I do, I find your posture contains so many elements of mute impertinence.

THE SERVANT: Honestly?

JUDITH: Honestly, yes. Your head, for example, presumes the vertical.

THE SERVANT: I'll stoop. (*She lowers her head. Pause. JUDITH comes close, kneeling beside her.*)

JUDITH: I shall so luxuriate in all the honours, I do not care what trash they drape me with, what emblems or what diadems, how shallow, glib and tinsel all the medals are, **I'll sport them all** — (*The* SERVANT *goes as if to embrace her.*) **Don't shift you intellectual bitch!** (*The* SERVANT *stoops again, laughing with delight.*) No, I shall be unbearable, intolerably vile, inflicting my opinions on the young, I shall be the bane of Israel, spouting, spewing, a nine-foot tongue of ignorance will slobber out my mouth and drench the populace with the saliva of my prejudice, they will wade through my opinions, they will wring my accents out their clothes, but they will tolerate it, for am I not their mother? Without me none of them could be born, **He said so**. (*Pause*)

THE SERVANT: Yes. To everything. Shall I get up?

JUDITH: No, filth.

THE SERVANT: I was only thinking —

JUDITH: Thinking? I do that.

THE SERVANT (*with a short laugh*): Yes! I forgot! But it occurs to me, time is —

JUDITH: No hurry, filth. Sit still. (*Pause. The* SERVANT *stares at the ground. JUDITH walks round her, holding the sword.*) Filth —

THE SERVANT: Do you have to call me —

JUDITH: Filth, put your teeth against my shoe. (*A black pause.*) Filth, do. (*The* SERVANT *inclines her head to* JUDITH's *foot, and is still.*) I think I could cut off a million heads and go home amiable as if I had been scything in the meadow. Clean this. (*She holds out the weapon. The* SERVANT *goes to wipe the blade on a cloth.*) No, silly, with your hair. (*Pause*)

THE SERVANT: Now, listen —

JUDITH: **You listen.** (*The* SERVANT *anxiously regards the door. She takes the weapon and cleans it with her hair. She lays the weapon down, goes to stand. JUDITH's foot constrains her. Pause.*) Your hair's vile.

THE SERVANT: Obviously, I have just —

JUDITH: Cut it off, then. (*With a weary movement, the* SERVANT, *affecting patience, leans forward on her hands.*)

THE SERVANT: Judith . . .

JUDITH: **Must! Must!** (*Pause. The* SERVANT *lifts the weapon again.*) To kill your enemies, how easy that is. To murder the offending, how oddly stale. Real ecstasy must come of liquidating innocence, to punish in the absence of offence **You haven't done it yet** that must be the godlike act, when there is perfect incomprehension in the victim's eyes **I will if you won't!** (*The* SERVANT, *in an ecstasy of disgust, hacks her hair. She is still again.*) Later, we'll crop it. What you've done is such a mess.

THE SERVANT: Yes . . .

JUDITH: Well, isn't it?

THE SERVANT: Whatever you say.

JUDITH: Whatever I say, yes. (*Pause. JUDITH walks over the stage, looking at the still form of the* SERVANT. *She walks back again, stops.*)

> I'm trying to pity you.
> But it's difficult because.
> Because for you nothing is really pain at all.
> Not torture. Death. Or.
> Nothing is.

It's drained, and mulched, and used to nourish further hate, as dead men's skulls are ground for feeding fields . . .

THE SERVANT: Whatever you say.

JUDITH: Whatever I say, yes.

THE SERVANT (*seeing the slow spread of light*): There's light under the flaps. It's dawn, Judith.

JUDITH: Dawn! Yes! This is the hour sin slips out the sheets to creep down pissy alleys! Morning, cats! Did you slither, also? Morning, sparrows! Rough night? Hot beds cooling. The running of water. **Well, it has to end at some time, love!** But its smell, in the after hours . . . **Magnificence!** (*She laughs, with a shudder. A cracked bell is beaten monotonously.*)

> Israel!
> Israel!
> My body is so
> Israel!
> My body has no
> Israel!
> Israel!

My body was but is no longer
Israel
Is
My
Body!

The cracked bell stops. Sounds of naturalistic conversation, the clatter of pots, the rising of a camp. The SERVANT *gets up. She goes to* JUDITH *and kisses her hands. Taking the head in the bag, she slips out of the tent.* JUDITH *does not follow at once.*

EGO IN ARCADIA

CHARACTERS

DOVER	A Queen
SANSOM	A Revolutionary
MOSCA	A Minister of State
SLEEN	A Fugitive Novelist
LE VIG	A Fugitive Actor
LILI	A Fugitive Dancer
VERDUN	An Artist's Model
POUSSIN	A Painter
MADAME POUSSIN	The Mother of a Painter
TOCSIN	The Dispenser of Relief

A landscape of dereliction. The detritus of heroic cultures. The oppressive polyphony of flies. A raucous cry of pleasure, hysterical and brief. A thunderclap, distant. A painter of the Seventeenth century enters. He uncovers a canvas on an easel. He departs. The sound of swooping, strafing aircraft. The sounds of bickering, panicked conversations, utterances. A crowd of refugees, clutching bags and coats, enters tightly in a mob. As the aircraft sweeps low they stoop, freeze. The aircraft departs and instantly, they stagger onwards, muttering, cursing, hysterical. The Queen of a fallen monarchy enters, resplendent, dishevelled. She is attached by the wrists to a rope which leads off stage. She stares out. Silence, concluding the cacophony.

FIRST ECLOGUE

DOVER: I'm History. (*Pause*)
Flesh (*Pause*)
And History. (*Pause*)
Separate them, why don't you? (*A man is discovered, who holds the distant end of the rope.*)

SANSOM: Your tree . . . (*He indicates.*)
Awaits . . .

DOVER: The acts . . . (*Pause*)
The body . . . (*Pause*)
Part them, can't you?

SANSOM: Enemy . . . I'm hanging you . . . (*He throws the end of the rope over the branch.*)

DOVER: One more decaying corpse will hardly notice in this atmosphere —

SANSOM: **Enough wit** —

DOVER: Yes —

SANSOM: **Enough charm** —

DOVER: Yes —

SANSOM: **Enough affectation** —

DOVER: I bore myself, I promise you —

SANSOM: Ever since the city, your wit —

DOVER: And charm —

SANSOM: And affectation —

DOVER: Cleverness made me lonely, I assure you . . . (SAN-
SOM *makes the knot.*) Lonely, even among friends . . .

SANSOM: My father had a farm here. Goats he kept, and in
the evening a scent of flowers drifted in my room **find me a
flower and you can live** don't look, there are none, **it's your
government spoiled this place** the tree had leaves on, rippling
and translucent leaves — (*He bursts into song, wildly, arbitrarily.*) Loved I was by one who laughed at men / She was
sharp-mouthed as daggers / in the bower she undressed for
me / such tenderness she showed me then / (*Pause*)

A bower is a place where —

DOVER: I know what a bower is —

SANSOM: Where the foliage is thick and shelters nakedness
against the sun —

DOVER: Are you hanging me or educating me — (*She
regrets her wit.*) No — no —

SANSOM: **That was a bower there**. (*He points to a barren
spot. Pause.*)

DOVER: Be naked with me now . . . it is my last hope . . .
(SANSOM *stares at* DOVER *with contempt.*)

SANSOM: Somehow I knew you would die badly . . .

DOVER: Who says badly? Search me and you'll discover
other landscapes —

SANSOM: **Queen of vileness and corruption all the scandals
of your court are known to me**. (*Pause. He regrets his out-
burst, he is calm.*) I am not here to prosecute you, but to
carry out the orders of the revolution, stand beneath the tree
now.

DOVER: I am sorry about your father's farm, he could have
asked for compensation **look at me I'm twenty-nine and
perfect** the odd grey hair but **perfect perfect perfect woman
undress me**. (*He contemplate her.*)

SANSOM: Not while you live . . .

DOVER: My underwear took women years to make so intri-
cate it is . . . do I outrage you . . . and my hair three women
every morning laboured on . . . the perfumes cost the harvest
of ten fields that I am wearing and there was starvation we
were aware of it . . . do I outrage you . . . look at my mouth
the paint for it was brought from foreign countries at
appalling cost **undress me, idiot** . . . (SANSOM *stares.*)

I am History . . . (*Pause*)
Flesh . . . (*Pause*)
And History . . . (*Pause*)

Separate them, why don't you? (SANSOM *wavers. He kneels at her feet, embracing her hips, his face pressed into her skirts in an ecstasy of surrender. She looks coolly ahead.*) His father can turn in his grave . . . for all he cares . . . and stuff revenge back down his throat . . . I am so clever no wonder I am lonely . . . no wonder . . . (*As* SANSOM *plunges in her garments, a man appears, dark suited, elegant, but like her, spoiled by travel. He watches* SANSOM's *delirium of desire.* DOVER *puts a finger to her lips to caution him.* SANSOM *looks up at* DOVER *unaware.*)

SANSOM: I love you . . .
And all I thought obsessed me . . . is . . . abolished
. . . (*Distant sounds of aircraft strafing.*)
Justice . . .
Truth . . .
Responsibility . . .
So what
Say you love me even if it is a lie . . . (*Pause. The suited man takes silent steps towards them, stops.*)

DOVER: I love you. (SANSOM *seizes her tied hands and smothers them in kisses. With a single stride, the suited man advances on* SANSOM *and kills him with a knife, lowering his body to the ground. With profound distaste he wipes the blade on a spotless handkerchief. Pause.*) You terrible and beautiful man I thought they hanged you from a lamp post . . .

MOSCA: Yes . . .

DOVER: They said you were dissected by a mob . . .

MOSCA: Yes . . .

DOVER: And your beloved limbs paraded round the city . . .

MOSCA: My guards were minced . . . drunk women gouged their eyes and filled the little wells with urine . . . I wept for them . . . something made them keep their posts . . . honour, was it . . . habit . . . lack of imagination, possibly . . . and I had designed their uniforms myself . . . This is Arcadia . . . where nothing lives but love . . . and therefore . . . is a place of infinite suffering **do you still love me** I am sixty and a statesman with no city . . . (DOVER *smiles.*)

DOVER: Idiot . . .

MOSCA: Always you call me idiot . . . when I had the best brain of my generation . . .

DOVER: Idiot . . .
         I love you and God knows what instinct made me
         want to live when I believed you murdered
         Some dim appetite
         Some dark habit
You are more beautiful than ever and we have lost our life
of laughter, darling . . . ! (*They stare at each other. The pecu-*
liar tones of an anxious man are heard. They withdraw rapidly.)

SECOND ECLOGUE

SLEEN: **Still alive!**
         Still alive me! (*A man enters, followed by a young*
         woman and a well-made man in his thirties. SLEEN
         is loose-mouthed, and fallen.)
The planes came down! The rockets came down! The
Typhoons and the Lightnings! Bits of cattle! Bits of meadow!
Phut, Phut, Phut, the cannons tearing tracks between our
legs but
         Evil is immune!
         Still alive me! (*The man and woman look around.*)
Machine guns are the music of my life! And I am not nice,
oh, no, not nice, but who requires the nice, this woman I was
never nice to and she loves me
         I
         The
         Intolerable
         Man
         I can't stop talking so don't ask me to
         We flee the righteous
         We evade just punishment
         The howls of the vindictive echo in our ears
         Still alive me! (*The briefest pause. He casts a glance*
         around.)
         Where are we? As if I didn't know **I had a classical**
         education (LE VIG *peers indifferently at the body of*
         SANSOM, *prods it with his foot.*)
         And this woman craves the bidet and the room service

Some hopes this is Arcadia (*A cry off, a melancholy tone. A man enters with an easel, he erects it, watched by the others. Pause.*)

I shall like it here.

No drugs.

Down I go with the next bout of angina but.

And no lipstick.

Razor blades?

I'm thinking of Lili's legs.

LILI: Shut up . . .

SLEEN: **Still alive, me**! (POUSSIN *ignores them.*)

This woman

Whom I love

This woman

Is so relentlessly shallow and banal so intransigently trivial and

LILI: Shut up . . .

SLEEN: Mundane no imbecilic horror ever cast a shadow on her life

Do paint her

As a nymph perhaps her life as an actress was to put it kindly, situated in the penumbra of fame and she blames politics

LILI: **It was politics**

SLEEN: But actually she moves badly

LILI: **It was politics and you**

SLEEN: But who would know that in a painting? Do put her in, are you Poussin? (*The painter ignores him.*) As for Le Vig here, he merely thought the uniform went well with his eyes, he can't be blamed

It was I who swallowed the message (*Pause*)

You are Poussin, aren't you?

I

The

Criminal

Betrayer

Of

His

Own

Great

Gifts . . . (*Pause. Suddenly* SLEEN *weeps, staring ahead all the time.* LILI *wipes his eyes.*)

LE VIG: He betrayed people, too, but that's less important to him. . . .

SLEEN: It's less important in any account . . . (*He recovers, spontaneously.*)

> **How quiet it is**
> **No Typhoons**
> **No Lightnings**
> How they will miss their favourite target
> How they will pine
> The cannon-firing youth
> The teenage pilots of America (*He turns to* POUSSIN.)
> Put me in if you can't find space for Lili
> As some gargoyle
> As some fallen idol toppled in the grass
> I know the style
> I know the manner
> Monsieur Poussin
> S'il vous plait . . . (*Pause*)

POUSSIN: I lie . . .

> I lie supremely . . . (*He looks at* SLEEN.)

SLEEN: That's your job . . .

LILI (*staring in horror at* SANSOM): He's not dead . . .

POUSSIN: The function of the artist is to make you hate your life. . . .

SLEEN: All the more reason to put Lili in. Let Lili glimpse what she can never be . . .

LILI: **This man's not dead!** (*She turns on them.*)

   Are you listening? Look. . . . (*She points to* SANSOM's *moving arm.*)

POUSSIN (*mixing paint*): No one dies in Arcadia . . . That is the horror of the place . . . (*They look at him.*)

> You'll want to, obviously . . .
> Oh, how you'll want to . . .

   And Death is here. Certainly, he's here, but so discriminating, you will hate him for his impeccable disdain . . . (*He smiles, drawing down his brush.*) I am so fashionable it hurts . . . (SANSOM *sits up. He stares at them.*)

SANSOM (*to* SLEEN): If you were a god, I'd worship you . . .

LILI: Worship him, anyway! I do!

SLEEN: Ha!

LILI: I do! I do! You are my religion!

> **Pity**
> **Pity me**

   Any man who suffers as he does must be a god surely! I mean, let's not be fussy who we worship as long as we

worship somebody! A life without abasement, imagine it!
Nothing to revere, nothing to stoop to, horrible! And he has
no rules. He is governed by nothing but
> **Blood**
> The speed of it
> Some days sluggard
> Some days
> **Whoosh!**

You can't predict! (SLEEN *looks at her*.)

SLEEN: Oh, the bedrooms we have clashed in . . . oh, the
scattering of jewellery and make-up jars she cut me down like
a sapling, and like a sapling, up I shot again . . . she is a child
. . . but so am I . . .

LE VIG: **Not a very nice child** . . .

SLEEN: Not a nice child, no . . . and this childishness is the
source of our inveterate union . . .

SANSOM: I love . . .

SLEEN: Do you?

SANSOM: Advise me . . .

LILI: My advice is —

SLEEN: Shh —

LILI: If you want my advice —

SLEEN: Shh I said —

LILI: **He wants some help poor man** —

SLEEN: **What help can you give**
> **What mundane**
> **What arid**
> **Comfort**
> **All your ideas are scooped from magazines** . . .
> (*Pause*)

LILI: Oh, it is so awful to love you . . . so relentlessly and
unremittingly . . . awful . . .

SLEEN: Yes . . .
> And I am undeserving, obviously . . . (*He looks into
> the clouds*.)
> If love was earned. . . . ! If love was deserved . . . !
> But no, it is a bacillus . . .

POUSSIN: Arcadia has wolves . . . You cannot have sheep
without wolves . . . We don't paint the wolves, however . . .
(SLEEN *laughs*.)

LE VIG (*looking at* POUSSIN's *canvas*): I wish I painted . . .
I would however, only paint myself . . . I am a narcissist.
Sleen says that is why I am unhappy, but he is also unhappy,

and he hates himself. The fact is I find myself both more attractive and more interesting than anybody else. Why pretend otherwise? Maybe I am merely honest.

SANSOM: I love the Queen. I love the Enemy . . . I so desired the honour of being her executioner — after all she's bad, no doubt of that, badness — emanates from her, it comes with every syllable, every word she said confirmed the absolute necessity of her death and yet — hardly were we in Arcadia but — the reasons failed . . .

LILI: Oh, that's so — (SLEEN *looks at her.*)

So —

Don't look at me like that it's lovely

Yes

Lovely I said (*Pause*)

LE VIG: When you look into another's eyes, what do you see? I ask you, what do you see? **You see yourself re-flected**. Admit it! When their pupils dilate the pleasure you feel is nothing but **aggrandizement**. No one wishes to admit this. It spoils the cherished fallacy of love. But you must admit, there is intellectual courage in the very articula-tion of —

SLEEN (*leaping off his chair*): **Look out, the RAF . . . !** (*With instantaneous reactions, LE VIG dives to the ground and covers his head.*)

Rat — tat — tat — tat —

Get the fascist bastards!

Another thousand in spent ammunition! (LILI *gig-gles*. SLEEN *looks into the sky.*)

It's all right, it was only a Typhoon . . . better target somewhere else . . . (*He sits again.* LE VIG *gets up, dusts off his knees.*)

LE VIG: You don't like me because I tell the truth . . .

SLEEN: **The truth! Spare us the truth!** There goes the truth! (*He points to the imaginary aircraft.*) Truth in the eyes! Truth in the testicles!

LILI: We won't stay here, will we? As soon as the peace is signed and the enemies of the people have been gaoled, and their property confiscated and the water pipes repaired we'll go back, won't we? Sleen? Go back to Vienna? (*Pause*) Cairo? (*Pause*) Amsterdam or something! (*Pause. A wind blows.*)

LE VIG: I tempted brides from their beds —

LILI: Shh . . .

LE VIG: I did, and they said, come to the room where I am
waiting, prior to my wedding —

LILI: Shh . . .

LE VIG: And lifting my clothes, sink your body in mine, you
gorgeous actor . . . (*Pause*)
It's true!

LILI: We know, Viggy, we know it is . . . (*She shrugs.*) No, I
can take it . . . (*She looks boldly at* POUSSIN, *walking
around his easel.*)
I can take —
Ar — ca — di — a . . . (*She sings.*)
Oh, my lover, forgive me if
My intelligence is thin . . .
Ignore a soul that's destitute . . .
I stood on your step one morning
With nothing but my body of bent tin . . .
If I give my whole life in your hands,
My lover, will you take me in . . .? (*Pause*)

SLEEN: She doesn't sing well . . . but then . . . she never
danced well, either . . .

LE VIG (*enraged*): **Leave her alone you — leave her — just —**

SLEEN (*in despair*): **Can't help it can't help it can't help it . . . !**
(LILI *lights a cigarette.*)

THIRD ECLOGUE

*The easel and the picture. A young woman enters. She looks at
it, with love and hatred. She takes out a knife and proceeds to
slash the canvas. Sounds of sheep and rooks. She weeps. She
recovers.*

VERDUN: No, he is *such* a good painter!
          I don't think
          Honestly
          And I know art
          I do not think there is another like him
          Plenty similar
          Heaps of imitators

Some catch the style
Some borrow the content
But none who have his
I am not blinded by love
Who have his
**I am capable of discernment even if my body screams
with pain**
His
Absolute
Selfishness . . . (*Pause. She laughs, madly, stops,
shakes her head.*)
And what a life of unrelenting and numbing
banality! What a life of!
But only in such circumstances can genius appear
It can't be bred
It can't be smothered
I revere him
The
Inert
And
Gutless
Bastard . . . (*She sobs.* DOVER *enters, tattered.*
VERDUN *looks at her.*)

DOVER: Yes . . .
How poor they are . . . how promising and tepid . . . the
genius class . . . nauseating mortality grips even them . . .

VERDUN: I love the scum . . . the filth . . . I could . . . die
for . . . ! (DOVER *laughs, encouraging her.*) Yes, oh yes . . .
and decent men adore me . . . !

DOVER: Oh, yes . . . !

VERDUN: Trainloads of decent men any one of whom could
give me —

DOVER: **Happiness!** (*She smiles at* VERDUN. *Pause.*)

VERDUN: Please don't smile like that. I have no intention of
putting up with this, I have my dignity to think of — please
don't smile like that — I am a beautiful woman of consider-
able intelligence and I refuse to be — **it's not funny I can't
sleep!** (*Pause*)
Or breathe, for that matter . . .
I will kill him one day. I'll kill him because there's nothing
else to do . . . (*Pause*)

DOVER: Yes . . . (*Pause*) I was going to say — to utter —
such mundane sentiments, such lame and bloodless, crippled,

stumbling, phrases of anaemic kindness **time heals all wounds** and similar articles of a numbing futility no
Kill him do
It's the solution . . . (VERDUN *looks at her, deeply.*)

VERDUN: Is it . . . ? Is it the solution . . . ?

DOVER: Yes. It so often is. I should know! I am the remnants of a queen and always we were organizing murders! I don't hide in words, I don't describe them as necessitites, expediencies, no, they were murders and how efficacious it could be! Believe me, whole crises disappeared into their graves! (*Pause*)

VERDUN: But . . . he's a genius . . .

DOVER: Anyone can see that . . .

VERDUN: So many paintings of . . . brilliance . . . society will never get to see . . .

DOVER: Never mind . . .

VERDUN: Never mind? **Never mind he is —**

DOVER: **Always another genius. They pile behind each other like logs at the sawmill gates!** (*Pause*) When the war began . . . one war . . . I don't know which . . . I conscripted geniuses for the infantry . . . and the Minister of Culture said — said? — **pleaded** — please place them in the hospitals as orderlies or gardeners, we dare not squander talent . . . but I ignored him, knowing if they did not die, how wonderfully they would be transformed. Sometimes five died out of six, but the sixth who had endured hell, his work was worth all the others in their undamaged states . . . **Yes I am so cruel** . . . which is to say . . . I love life . . . I hold it by the throat . . .

VERDUN: You are so beautiful . . .

DOVER: Yes . . . why shouldn't I be? (*Pause*)

VERDUN: I'll kill him. Then I can mourn . . . and mourn . . . and he'll be mine . . . am I not mourning him already? (*She swiftly kisses* DOVER *and hurries out.* DOVER *raises her hand.* MOSCA *enters, kisses it.*)

DOVER: Oh, the pleasures of intrigue . . . what can fill minds as preposterous as ours . . .
Oh to be common, undistinguished and the colour of earth
But no
Not
Our
Destiny . . .

Let me undress you . . . let me remove your body from the cladding of a routine life . . . (*She kisses him, removes his clothes.*) You are not young, you are not young . . . ! Nothing mundane, hopeful or ambitious, clings to you . . .

MOSCA: I never was . . .

DOVER: Never young, no . . . I do believe you, never . . . so serious among your books . . . a young priest already old among the spired cities . . . who walked beneath my window, where I lay newly born, raising my little fist up to the booming of the midday bell . . . I knew you . . . even then, I knew you . . . (*She kneels to him, taking him in her mouth with adoration.* SANSOM *witnesses this, from a remote corner of the stage. He is drawn, inexorably, by pain and love, towards them. He stands, silent, tortured, behind* MOSCA, *as* MOSCA *had stood behind him. As he writhes, an old woman enters, watches.*)

MME POUSSIN: Love me instead . . . (SANSOM *turns. A look of horror crosses his features.*)

> The incredulity . . . ! (*She laughs, kindly.*)
> The incredulity . . .
> Is
> Just
> A
> Screen . . . (SANSOM *shakes his head.*)
> I know
> And you know
> How
> You
> Need
> To
> Look . . . (*She undoes her clothes,* SAN-SOM *writhes.*)
> You are not looking
> Where
> You
> Want
> To
> Look . . . (SANSOM *drags his eyes from* MOSCA, *to* MME POUSSIN, *half-horrified. Pause.*)
> Look!
> Look!
> **It is also beauty**

> **This** . . . (*She extends her breast to him.*)
> **And this** . . . (*And her belly. He stares. Pause* . . .)

SANSOM: And I once cared about
> **Long hours in rooms of smoke and argument**
> Once cared about
> **Cascading resolutions and consipiracies**
> The poor
> The blind
> The ugly
> The growing gap between societies
> The urgency of institutional reform
> The squandered promise in the urban gaols
> **My hands reached out to every supplicant**
> Dishonest hands perhaps . . .

MME POUSSIN: Love me, I am rinsed by time of every indignation . . . (SANSOM *hesitates, then strides swiftly to her taking her head between his hands.*)

SANSOM: Is this a good place?

MME POUSSIN: Good . . . ?

SANSOM: Arcadia . . . ! (MME POUSSIN *smiles, draws him down to her. The sound of* DOVER's *gratified and sweet laughter.* DOVER *rises to her feet. She is still, staring at* MOSCA. *The smile leaves her face, by degrees* . . .)

DOVER: Time to part, surely . . . ? (MOSCA *is aghast.*) Oh, darling, teasing you . . . ! (*She sweeps out, stops, turns, extends her hand.* MOSCA *goes to her, takes it. They go off.* POUSSIN *enters, with his brush and palette. He sees his mother and* SANSOM *making love. He watches, uncritically.*)

POUSSIN: Her arse goes
> Her handled, shaped and still fecund arse goes
> Ploughing the land of men
> Beating
> Pulping
> Life away
> **Oblivion**
> **Oblivion is it**
> You found there . . . ?
> Mother? (MME POUSSIN *neither hears nor heeds him. He turns to the canvas, to work. He sees its damaged state. He looks, as if dispassionately* . . .)

VERDUN (*entering, watching*): Sorry . . . (*Pause*)

POUSSIN: How cold we are, and distant from each other . . .

　　　　　　Archipelagoes of loneliness . . .
　　　　　　Through which storms rage and then . . .
　　　　　　Still days of such lucidity . . .
　　　　　　The islands almost seem to touch . . . (*Pause. He
　　　　　　looks at* VERDUN.)
　　　　　　Almost . . .
　　　　　　Trick of the light, perhaps . . . (*Pause*)
VERDUN:　There is a better version. I know there is.
POUSSIN (*shaking his head*):　This is Arcadia . . . (*He turns to
　　　attend to the canvas. VERDUN *strides to him and thrusts her
　　　knife into his back. A scream of birds.* POUSSIN *staggers
　　　under the blow.* VERDUN *seizes him in her arms kissing him
　　　fervently.*)
VERDUN:　Oh you darling oh you beloved you perfect and
　　　impeccable fragment of my life I love you I adore you and
　　　will hold these days in such religious ecstasy my whole life
　　　through I'll hold your picture in my arms darling darling you
　　　showed me perfection blinding blinding light . . . ! **Help him
　　　somebody**! (*An effect of light.* POUSSIN *rises, goes back to
　　　the easel . . .*)

FOURTH ECLOGUE

POUSSIN *at the canvas, which is whole.* VERDUN *lies silently
weeping in a corner of the stage.* SLEEN *enters, looks at*
POUSSIN, *then at* VERDUN.

SLEEN:　Pity . . .
　　　Pity, this impossibility of death . . . I never liked him either,
　　　but did I ever like myself? **All my hatreds were unjust**, they
　　　said so at the tribunal, **my hatreds were the product of a
　　　fevered mind**, most unbecoming in an intellectual, **the gro-
　　　tesque excrescence of a toxic personality**, I quote, those
　　　lawyers were poets, they dripped with metaphors, I like
　　　Arcadia, but Lili and Le Vig . . . ! There are no mirrors . . . !
　　　Whole days pass and they cannot see themselves, she is a
　　　child, why did I marry her, it should have been illegal, a man
　　　of my appalling knowledge and her a perfectly blank sheet,

there was a subject for the legal mind, Odysseus had more communication with Nausicaa than I have with her, but then did I converse with anyone? To tell the truth I don't think I. (*He is silent.* MOSCA *enters.* SLEEN *recovers.*)

MOSCA: They have stopped looking for us.

SLEEN: Yes . . .

MOSCA: No tracker dogs . . . assasins . . .

SLEEN: Or spotter planes . . .

MOSCA: I hate to admit it . . . but we have been consigned to History . . . and books already on the shelves describe my days of power as unutterably **dark** . . .

SLEEN: Were they not dark, then?

MOSCA: Dark for somebody. All days are dark for some.

SLEEN: Only so much light in the world . . . ! Only so much space beneath the beam . . . and then it moves . . . arbitrarily . . . I was under the beam . . . not for long, however . . . the only other light I saw was cast by burning books . . . my own . . . what did it matter? I was exhausted by success . . . I was vomitting in restaurants . . . and they so enjoyed themselves . . . ! The public . . . ! They were wild, the young . . . the savage young . . . auto-da-fe of my disgusting works . . . the planet cleansed of filth . . . (DOVER *enters. She is still. She looks profoundly at* MOSCA.)

DOVER: Oh, this is hard . . .

MOSCA (*going to her*): Beloved — (*She stops him with her hand.*)

DOVER: So hard . . . (*She prepares herself.*) I want to speak the truth — (MOSCA *starts to smile. She stops this also.*) **Don't smile** . . . ! (*Pause*) You always disparaged truth, which was a mark of your sophistication, but . . . we are not sophisticated any more . . . and must learn simple things . . .

MOSCA: Simple? You?

DOVER: Yes . . . (*Pause*) Our world went, darling man . . . and though I have lived years of ecstasy in the power of your gravity . . . we are not stars, are we? Our orbits aren't eternal . . . ? (*Pause*)

MOSCA (*gravely*): The moon . . . is quitting . . . the sun . . .

SLEEN: Oh, Count, she aches for your disintegration.

MOSCA: No moon without the sun . . . his light . . . reveals her . . . in the staggering dark . . .

SLEEN: She wants you shredded at her feet . . . They do! They do love that!

DOVER (*to* SLEEN): **Be quiet you ranting idiot**. (*Pause*)

MOSCA: You are nothing without me.

DOVER: I don't know that yet . . .

MOSCA: I am reluctant to exaggerate, but without me you
are —

DOVER: I don't know yet! (*Pause*)

MOSCA: Anna, the world is a map of our encounters . . .

DOVER: Yes . . . but this is not the world . . . this is Arcadia
. . . (MOSCA *stares at her.*)

SLEEN: Oh, she is consigning you to her biography . . .
chapters two and three . . . not bad . . . some are only foot-
notes . . . (MOSCA *weeps.* DOVER *watches.*)

DOVER: I want to hold you, but I must refrain . . . (MOSCA
laughs derisively through his tears, shaking his head.) Don't
be sarcastic, please . . .

MOSCA: **Sarcasm was the music of our life!**

DOVER: Yes . . .

MOSCA: **Sarcasm**
Irony
Disdain

DOVER: Yes . . .

MOSCA: The pillars of our ecstasy!

DOVER: Yes . . . but pity . . . no . . . (*Pause.* MOSCA *wipes
his tears on a fresh handkerchief.*)

MOSCA: Pity? No, that rarely put in an appearance. What
was there to pity? We were too magnificent for that **leave me
and I'll hang myself** I don't threaten you I merely state I
don't bend you to my will I only inform this man is my
witness life was hell to me and you redeemed it sunsets and
the smell of flowers choirs of infants faithful hounds etcetera
no it was barren to me the governing of states was tedium
except to have you show your arse for my eyes only in the
chancellry my bitch my loved one **Death yes no horror there's
the tree**. (DOVER *stares, swaying, then resolutely marches
out.* SLEEN *looks after her.*)

SLEEN: I do so love the survivors, they are so —

MOSCA: Please —

SLEEN: Utterly — impervious to pain —

MOSCA: Please —

SLEEN: How else can they survive? In the end, nothing
separates them from the prison guards they affect to hate —
(*He sees* MOSCA.) Forgive me, you only want to weep . . .
(*Suddenly,* DOVER *rushes back, seizing* MOSCA *in her arms,
smothering him with kisses, then hurrying away again.* SLEEN

is moved . . .) Oh, all your arguments . . . that kiss . . . makes sheer futility of . . . the finality of it. (*Pause*) The rope's over there . . . (MOSCA *is utterly still. A distant sound of animals, in aggression.*) And she is not shallow . . . there's the misery.

POUSSIN: If it's any comfort to you . . . she will also want to die . . . she also will crave some smothering oblivion . . . no luck however . . . this is the land of uncommitted suicides . . . and murders which bring no relief . . .

SLEEN: It's hard to like you, Monsieur Poussin . . .

POUSSIN: Yes . . .

SLEEN: Not that I've tried . . . I submitted to a prejudice . . .

POUSSIN: Another one . . .?

SLEEN: Yes. They are the only sentiments I trust. (*He goes out. MOSCA looks at POUSSIN.*)

MOSCA: What lies . . . the other side . . . of undone death . . . Monsieur? (POUSSIN *ignores him.* MOSCA *looks at the pitiful crouching form of* VERDUN.) I decline to be mad . . . and dignity . . . which I have studied every crease and colour of **I will not repudiate** . . . no dribbling . . . no flowers in the mouth or clothing back to front . . . **I decline to be mad I decline** . . . ! (POUSSIN *laughs, quietly . . .*)

FIFTH ECLOGUE

LE VIG, *alone.*

LE VIG: Some days the postman could not stagger up my steps. Postcards, parcels spilling lurid infatuations, preposterous proposals for liaisons of the most degraded sort, children, animals, all with photographs, the pathetic invitations of suburban wives demented by desire, and I say demented with a clinical precision, they were unhinged with an insatiable hunger for my flesh, and pleading for relief! The postmarks were of every hamlet and colonial possession, plastered with scent and exotic stamps, obviously you grew accustomed to it, you were blasé, indifferent, after all, the

contents were repetitive, but the volume! That I studied with
a nervous eye, and if the postman was not sweating I began
to fret and run to mirrors, yes, I am not exaggerating, one
sackful less and I was the victim of an inquisition — my own
— my whole appearance was dragged through a court of
scrupulous examination, was my face a little more, was my
voice a little less, oh, hell, oh hell, and heaven . . . ! (*Pause*)
There are no mirrors here. Nor any soap . . . (*Pause.* MME
POUSSIN *enters. She looks at* LE VIG.) Undress, but please
don't tell . . . (*Pause. She makes no move.*)

I beg you, take your clothes off, but don't tell! (*Pause*) You
see, I have this reputation — I have this female following all
of whom — in some way — fatuous, of course — idolize me
and — it is imperative I am seen only with the most
conventionally and — fatuous, of course, routinely glamor-
ous women, please say you understand my tortuous predica-
ment, I —

MME POUSSIN: This is Arcadia . . . (*Pause*)

LE VIG: Yes . . . ? (*Pause*)

MME POUSSIN: Come here . . . (LE VIG *hesitates. He
walks, and stops.*)

LE VIG: Even my walk is false . . . (*He looks down at his feet.*)
And how I walked before the films . . . I really can't remember . . . (*He shakes his head.*)

MME POUSSIN: I'll walk. And you can be . . . as motionless
. . . as an idol . . . (*She goes to him, she kneels to him.*
MOSCA *passes singing a song of self-parody . . .*)

MOSCA: How painfully inflexible
He lacks the courage to adapt
How pitifully stiff his manner is
An idiot's rebuke to circumstance
But look
His will is wounded
And his pride is sapped
His elegance is comic as the indignation
Of a stabbed aristocrat . . .
How ludicrously honourable
He perseveres in habits of antique regimes
How ill-judged his demeanour is
Thinking it commands respect
But look
We jeer to see
His coat come undone at the seams

His cruelties are no more than dreams
In the skulls of senile women . . .

MOSCA *goes out*. LE VIG *crawls away from* MME POUS-
SIN *on all fours, humiliated . . . he lies in a distraut posture*.
POUSSIN *enters, observes his mother's state, goes to his
canvas*.

POUSSIN: I love Arcadia . . .
                    Whether I love you is another matter . . .
MME POUSSIN: I embarass him . . .
POUSSIN: Embarassed? Me?
MME POUSSIN: My nakedness. My age. My appetite.
POUSSIN: No, do disintegrate, I love disintegration, it is the
    visible confirmation of existence, how else could we know
    beauty if the spectacle of its disintegration were not trailed
    before our eyes? Fuck on, philosophy demands it . . . !
MME POUSSIN: You are such an unhappy and inveterate
    prig . . .
POUSSIN: Yes. I hate life. Ever since I was a child I knew it
    could only fail me.
MME POUSSIN: Perhaps it's you who's failed —
POUSSIN: Oh, no
                    Oh, not that
                    Oh, please resist
                    This reiteration of meaningless rebukes
                    You don't affirm life you make it twice as melan-
                    choly
                    I never failed
                    I never have
                    What is failure
                    What
                    The word
                    Absurd
                    Have you not failed? (*Pause, he relaxes.*)
    Now you have irritated me . . . now I am . . . distracted . . .
    and . . . (*He covers his face with his hands. With infinite self-
    awareness, he removes his hands and picks up his brush
    again.*)
MME POUSSIN: My poor. My so poor and stricken son . . .
    (POUSSIN *ignores her. She turns. She sees* VERDUN, *rolled
    in a corner*.) Do you love him? (VERDUN *merely looks at*
    MME POUSSIN . . .)

Why?

Impossible, surely...? (MME POUSSIN *goes out. It thunders, distantly.* LE VIG *stirs, sits up,watches silently.*)

LE VIG: Can we... (*It thunders again...*)

Leave here... (*Pause*)

Or not...? (*Pause*)

POUSSIN (*not removing his eyes from the canvas*): Leave...? Why? It's ecstasy, surely...? (LE VIG *shrugs.*)

LE VIG: I'm not an intellectual, I —

POUSSIN: Oh, don't say that —

LE VIG: Actors very rarely have much judgement, we —

POUSSIN: Oh, come, now —

LE VIG: Respond, in the first instance, purely emotionally, and —

POUSSIN: Surely not —

LE VIG: That is the explanation for my — looking back the only possible explanation for my — brief flirtation with the fascists, we —

POUSSIN: Mmm —

LE VIG: The atmosphere, the music, it was —

POUSSIN: Mmm —

LE VIG: Infectious —

POUSSIN: Mmm —

LE VIG: Infectious and corrosive at the same time, though now it seems so long ago — I hardly recognize the person I was then —

POUSSIN: I don't criticize —

LE VIG: It seems incredible — the uniforms — the candle-light —

POUSSIN: Really, I don't criticize... (*He looks at* LE VIG *for the first time. Pause.*)

LE VIG: I don't like it here... (POUSSIN *merely looks into him.*)

It's —

I'm being emotional again — its —

Peculiarly —

Like being —

Dead...

POUSSIN: Forgive me, but you are new here...

LE VIG: Well, yes...

POUSSIN: And so much of the film actor still clings to you...

LE VIG: Yes... I admit that... I...

POUSSIN: I think, quite soon, you will come to see — (*He stops, irritated with himself.*) No! No! The tone of that! The patrician tone of that! The audible disdain, as if my genius entitled me —

LE VIG: Well —

POUSSIN: Perhaps it does? Entitle me? (LE VIG *is uneasy.*) Dead, you say? No, you were dead. This is life. (*Barking of dogs, distantly.* LE VIG *gets up, anxiously.*)

LE VIG: I must find Lili and — talk with Lili and — (*Pause*)

POUSSIN: Yes, do find Lili and. (*He smiles,* LE VIG *turns to leave.*) My mother — (*He stops.*) That was my mother, incidentally — she — becomes addictive, you will find ... (LE VIG *hesitates, then hurries out.* VERDUN *stares at* POUSSIN.) Fascism? What's that?

VERDUN: A word ... (*She looks at him. She smothers her face.*) No, not a word ...! A thing ...! The opposite to democracy ... which ... Please ... please ... let me go ...

POUSSIN: Democracy? What's that?

VERDUN: Let me go, will you ...! (*Pause*)

POUSSIN: It's true I've lost a certain inspiration with the years, and yet, even if the landscape is routine, I bring to it new polish, which is not facility, I fervently deny it is facility, it is rather, mastery, which is not corrupt, as facility might be. If the focus is smaller, the powers are more concentrated, surely that is ... (*He looks at her.*) Why confide in you? (*Pause. They lock. He grapples with emotion.*)

> I love you ...
>
> I love you ...
>
> And you may not leave ... (*Pause. She stares at him.*)

VERDUN: I'll love another.

POUSSIN: Will you? Excellent.

VERDUN: And fuck all nights into a pulp of pleasure —

POUSSIN: Yes —

VERDUN: His fluid will run down my thighs, a lazy and slow finger stealing from my skirt and sparkling in the morning sun —

POUSSIN: Good —

VERDUN: What is the matter with you, are you mad?

POUSSIN: You picture things so well, you should be the painter, possibly ...

VERDUN: **Are you mad I said I knew decent men before you
and some of them what lovers oh what persistence oh what
skills in —**
POUSSIN: Skills?
VERDUN: **Skills yes in handling flesh I —**
POUSSIN: Skills . . . !
VERDUN: Erupted in such — oh, my cries, they might have
lifted tiles and sent the bookshelves spilling!
POUSSIN: Formidable men, how I envy their powers, but
now I must —
VERDUN: **You don't envy. You don't envy anything**. (*She
stares at him. Pause.*)

> I don't know what to do . . .
> I don't know what to do . . . (*She goes out.* POUS-
> SIN *swiftly leans against the easel in despair. Dogs
> bay.* DOVER *is discovered, observing him. He is
> made aware of her, slowly. He does not move.*)

DOVER: Obviously, you are the master here. Obviously you
govern. And equally obviously, I am your natural partner.
(*Pause.* POUSSIN *is motionless.*)

> Mate. (*Pause*)
> Spouse. (*Pause*)
> And concubine. (*Pause*)
> Shall I undress? (*Pause*)

I go straight to the point. Sometimes this causes anxiety.
But not in you, surely? Shall I undress? Why are there so
many dogs here?
POUSSIN: They quit the cities in pursuit of sheep. They ate
the sheep. And now they eat each other. (*Pause. He looks at*
DOVER.) Arcadia . . . !
DOVER: I have to be the queen. (*Pause. She laughs loudly.*)

> I am so frank with you! I just say what comes into
> my — (*Pause*)
> Something in you compels. Not the truth, exactly,
> but — (*Pause*)
> I sense life is cruel here, and decorum something
> absurd, redundant and irrelevant . . . (*Pause*)
> I am not shallow, incidentally . . . (*She goes closer
> to* POUSSIN.)
> And I know you are full of fear . . .

DOVER *reaches out, and places her hands on* POUSSIN's *face.
The dogs bay louder, until at last even her concentration on*

POUSSIN *is broken. Her hands fall, irritably, as she turns to see*
SLEEN *stagger in.*

SLEEN: **Not dead yet!**
         Even the animals hate me
         The strays the rabid half-breeds all teeth all saliva
         Not dead yet however!
         They ressemble human beings I find once one is
         clobbered the others turn and devour it
         Never mind the original quarry
         Easily diverted
         So human oh so
         Am I interrupting I was driven here . . . (*He looks at*
         DOVER, *who looks witheringly at him.*)
    I am certain Death is here. It is a graveyard after all. A
graveyard of convictions . . . But where? Monsieur Poussin
knows, it is the single source of his authority **why I do not
share this fascination I can't think** why do I resent his powers
I am not competitive God knows the instinct was beaten out
of me years ago **Sleen competitive he took his superiority for
granted** am I interrupting you you want to be alone but
one never is here for all the pastoral the idyll and the
oily waterfalls every murmur's shared by somebody give
me the city every time **I never loved another never** . . .
(*Pause*)
         Let me watch, therefore . . .
         Let me witness . . . (POUSSIN *goes to* SLEEN, *who
         shakes his head in despair.*)
         Oh, dear . . .
         After all I've been through . . .
         Oh, dear . . . (POUSSIN *touches him lightly.*)
         What's that, kindness?
         Oh, dear . . .
         Oh, dear . . . (*The dogs bark, distantly.*)
DOVER (*to* POUSSIN): You frighten me . . . and I was fear-
    less . . . (*She walks out.* LILI *enters, sees* SLEEN *in collapse.
    She points, limply.*)
LILI: He —
         He never — (*She is puzzled, knits her brows, then turns
         her back, thoughtfully.*)
         If he is — (*She turns back.*)
         What have you done to him! (SLEEN *is sobbing.*)
         Sleen never weeps . . . ! (*Pause*)

I don't like this place for one thing there are no mirrors and the ponds are filthy a girl can look at herself can't she I have to see my face what I wouldn't give for a radio set a little music a quiz programme some news **I never thought I'd see the day Sleen weeping** why don't I go to him I could no more go to him than kiss a lizard **love what's that** . . . ? (*Pause*) Come on, Sleen . . . please . . . (*He doesn't move. She walks out.*)

SLEEN: Give me to the dogs . . . I don't like the world . . . give me to the dogs . . .

POUSSIN: Silly . . .

SLEEN: **Life more life no thank you Monsieur Poussin** . . .

POUSSIN: Silly . . .

SLEEN: Days and more days . . . skies and more skies . . . every one different so what . . . as if variety could compensate a man of my profundity . . .

POUSSIN: Your mistress, I think, has ceased to love you, Mr Sleen . . .

SLEEN: Obviously, since I have ceased to love myself.

POUSSIN: The climate here . . . rots . . . everything . . . it's no one's fault . . . no cause for shame . . .

SLEEN: Let an old man die, will you . . . ? (POUSSIN *smiles*.) I said that — sweetly, didn't I? I said that without a trace of — irony . . . (*Pause. He stares at* POUSSIN.) Go on . . .

POUSSIN: But you're not old, Mr Sleen . . .

SLEEN: I am old. I was born old. And I've suffered. Surely that entitles me? (POUSSIN *shakes his head*.)
           More to endure, then?
           More points to earn? (POUSSIN *walks slowly away*.)
           Of what order?

A wind blows anxiously. SLEEN *remains on his knees. It darkens. A squall.* SLEEN *is slowly made aware of a figure watching him, brushed by a faint light. A deep gurgle of laughter comes from* SLEEN.

SIXTH ECOLOGUE

SLEEN: Oh, dear . . .
Oh, dear . . .
You've come to prick my conscience . . .
I never had one . . . !
No
No conscience
Ego yes
Sensation
But
And as for shame
That merely was the irritation born of knowing I
had opted for the wrong side
History
Yes
But
Conscience . . . ! (*He shakes his head. The figure is
still.*)

A typical day! I was in the restaurant **are you Death** my
favourite restaurant a stone's throw from the railway sta-
tion on the first floor window seat they kept it for me
whether I turned up or not no writers artists none of that
sort honest businessmen crooks without apologies all
round you sordid deals and tinkling glasses mirrors red-
mouthed tarts skirts up underneath the linen it was home to
me fingers roaming in their hair and peculiar old women
selling stocks you know the atmosphere home to me no moralists no world-shatterers just the rhythms of unadulterated
greed **are you Death** and on the forecourt deportees an
ordinary day taxis buses hooting newsboys I took my mail in
slit it with the fish knife oh my phone bill oh my royalty
cheque coquilles Saint-Jacques is their speciality and what a
wine list those crooks are just like politicians and on the
forecourt deportees the socialists the communists the impor-
ters what a head for wine home to me the police did not
require to use a single truncheon rather they were gentle
strangely gentle merely tapping them with one finger on the
back I sometimes ate four courses sometimes one or
even smoked there with a brandy I was not conspicuous
say if you're Death and in a minute at the most I looked
away I couldn't say I turned to call a waiter they were

gone the deportees ushered marshalled children and old
women handsome men too some in decent overcoats
gone it was home to me the company of moralists I
never could it made me ill my head swum their ambition
dwarfed the dreams of dictators I thought no more of it do
you like restaurants a typical day I oozed prosperity
they bombed the place the English airforce not deliberately ... (*He is silent. The figure moves in, hands in pockets.
Pause.*) It's angina and the pills I lost three weeks
ago ... (SLEEN *suddenly experiences an excruciating attack. He is racked by pain, falls forward, crawls, draws up
this knees in a paroxysm, slowly recovers, breathes deeply
on his back. Light pierces the sky.*) Come on, that's not
funny ...

TOCSIN: Sing us a song, Mr Sleen ...

SLEEN: That was a song ... (*Again he is seized in an attack.
He rolls. He froths. He recovers.*) You are Death ... and how
pitiful ... even you ... are a fucking moralist ... (*He goes
down again.*) Sorry I swore! Sorry! Sorry! (*He crawls, he
gnaws, he rolls, and recovers. Pause*) I never swear ... ask
Lili ...

TOCSIN: I'm not sophisticated. What I like in a song is
melody and words that I can follow ... of few syllables ...
modern words ... jingles ... and if I like the song ... who
knows ... ? Maybe the next attack will be your last ...

SLEEN: I'll put my mind to it — **no sarcasm intended
honestly** — (*He hesitates, expecting an attack.*) Honestly ...
funny words we use ...

TOCSIN: It is the land of song, you see ...

SLEEN: Is it ... ?

TOCSIN: Arcadia ... and the best song ... wins ... (*Pause*)

SLEEN: Wins ... ?

TOCSIN: The prize, of course! (TOCSIN *goes out, leaving
SLEEN on his knees. SANSOM enters, looks at him nervously, then hurries to him, seizes his hand and kisses it
quickly.*)

SANSOM: Master!
        May I call you master?

SLEEN: Why not?

SANSOM: And I thought I would never call a man my
master!

SLEEN: Indulge yourself ... there is a lot to be said for
stooping ... genuflection ... arse-licking and the like ...

SANSOM: It is not arse-licking. It is respect. Some are worthy of it. Most are not. I respect you. All the others I hold in contempt. What do you know about women?

SLEEN: Nothing.

SANSOM: Liar! (*He regrets his temper.*) You must help me . . . I have been so . . . all my little life I've been — drunk — on — theory — manifestoes — programmes — what is it they like? (*He grabs* SLEEN's *hand and kisses it again.*) And I called you a liar! I am in such a state I am in such a torrent of confusion! As if you could lie!

SLEEN: Well, I might just —

SANSOM: Never! Never lie I'm certain of it! (SLEEN *looks at* SANSOM *intuitively* . . .)

SLEEN: She is not nice . . .

SANSOM: No.

SLEEN: On the contrary, she is —

SANSOM: Vile and selfish. And though I am ignorant of women I can tell she only pretends to love . . .(*He looks at* SLEEN.)

SLEEN (*puzzled*): That's obvious, is it?

SANSOM: Absolutely obvious! The make-up and so on . . . the vanity . . . she hates to be touched . . . and her posturing, her swagger . . . the only satisfaction she obtains comes from humiliating men . . . (*Pause*)

SLEEN: I can see why you adore her . . .

SANSOM: If I don't make love with her I'll kill myself . . .

SLEEN: Easier said than done round here . . . (*He looks round in sudden fear.*) **No sarcasm intended**! (*Pause. He looks at* SANSOM.) You're wrong . . . She's . . . (*He hesitates. He reflects. A wind.*)

SANSOM: Advise me, then . . . ! (SLEEN *looks up, into* SAN-SOM's *eyes. Pause.*)

SLEEN: Absurd ambition . . . yours . . .

SANSOM (*defiantly*): I'll teach her love . . . and kindness will be shining in her eyes —

SLEEN: Absurd I said —

SANSOM: **Why do you say that, Master! Why!**

SLEEN: What could you teach, but the necessity for others? **Am I cruel?** You appointed me your teacher **I teach your hopelessness** you don't want to make love to her you want to save her from herself **no woman wants that** that's all for today you rebels are so sentimental you kill art you murder the imagination bombs rockets self-sacrifice so what and banners

flying you hate life barricades and pamphlets how you hate
the untamed animals of love how unheroic you are goodbye
I must take some precautions for myself you milk my brain
you want everything in cultivation goodbye you little farmer
of the heart . . . ! Goodbye . . . (*He turns away and looks into
space.* SANSOM *is stricken, patient. Pause.*)

SANSOM: Master . . . (SLEEN *is adamant.*) Master . . . (*He
drifts away, stops.*) I'll have her . . . and bring her to you . . .
sweet . . . and her head tilted . . . for your blessing . . . (*He
skips away.*)

SLEEN: Tilted for my what . . . ! (*He laughs, but it is false,
and ceases. His brow is furrowed.* MOSCA *is discovered
watching him.* SLEEN's *head turns slowly towards him.*)
　　　　Oh, dear . . .
　　Oh, dear, Count . . . in talking of the woman . . .
I have . . . fallen for her . . . and **I am arid with cynicism,
surely?** (*He covers his face with his hands.*) God — help —
me . . .

MOSCA: Arcadia is barren, Mr Sleen . . .

SLEEN: I've noticed . . .

MOSCA: In the heart . . . (*He looks at* SLEEN.)

SLEEN: I wasn't thinking of pursuing —

MOSCA: I was not dissuading you —

SLEEN: At my time of life —

MOSCA: Please, I have no rights —

SLEEN: Some impossible —

MOSCA: No rights at all —

SLEEN: And ludicrous infatuation —

MOSCA: Infatuation, well —

SLEEN: For which no doubt I should be utterly humiliated —

MOSCA: Possibly —

SLEEN: Self-respect I find can be dredged up from some
bottomless sump of the soul to save even a man like me from
absolute — (*Pause. He looks into* MOSCA.) You're encouraging me . . . (*Pause*) And I thought I was dissolute . . .
what's in it for you . . . ? (*Pause*) Oh, you are such an
immaculate aristocrat . . . in the marrow . . . in the veins . . .
The spectacle of us floundering . . . our pitiful ambition . . .
our painful aches . . . lends you the comfort that comes from
having parted with the struggle to make sense of life . . . I do
admire you . . . I do . . . I was a baker's son myself . . . **Yes I
will throw myself at her stupidity and pathos notwithstanding
I have never seen a woman like her she can dribble her**

contempt and still I'll advocate my passion stupid word I
thought I'd stifled it ten years ago oh, for your coolness oh,
for your deadness but that's only a pretence she whipped
blood out your heart I saw it, forgive me, Count, I like you
very much no doubt all things that make her wonderful came
from her nights with you . . . (*Pause*) Forgive me, I am in for
a terrible time . . . watch . . . and be . . . comforted . . . (*He
gets up, goes out.* MOSCA *listens to the distant sounds of
human riot, borne in on a wind. He strains.* LILI *enters
dragging a massive, broken mirror of which some glazed parts
remain.*)

MOSCA: Shh! (LILI *stops.*)
        That sound . . . (*She drags it.*)
        Shh! (*She stops.*)
        That sound . . .

LILI: I found one! (*She poses, pouts.*)
        Me!
        So much junk here, surely I thought — (*She peers.*)
        Me! (*Pause. She looks sadly at herself.*)
        Me in Arcadia . . . (*Pause*)
        Dump . . .

MOSCA (*listening*): It's riot . . .

LILI: Hag . . . in a dump . . .

MOSCA: Riot . . . what is riot . . . ?

LILI: Bitch . . . in a hole . . .

MOSCA: I know the sound . . . I know the word . . .

LILI: Slag . . . in Slagland . . .

MOSCA: But the thing . . . ?

LILI: First I wanted the mirror! Mirror, mirror, **craved the
        thing** and now . . . no . . . one should know oneself, shouldn't
        one, one should familiarize oneself . . . with one's . . . **debili-
        tation deterioration and decline** . . . Sleen thinks I'm stupid
        but that's my game, I have two degrees but he prefers it if I
        clad myself in ignorance he has a horror of the educated
        woman but Sleen is in a state, have you seen him, I mean ill
        or something, I couldn't look . . .

MOSCA: Yes . . . he's ill . . .

LILI: You should look in here because I don't think you are
        quite aware how ludicrous you look, and don't say it doesn't
        matter in Arcadia everybody says that and standards are
        slipping right left and centre Le Vig is **horrific** even when the
        reds were after us he found time to shave . . .

MOSCA: You can't leave here, Mademoiselle . . .

LILI: No? You see, that's just the attitude that — (*Pause*) Can't leave . . . ?

MOSCA: It's not a sentence, it is a state of mind . . . you cannot serve it . . . it is a sickness . . . no, gaol is simple by comparison . . . walls, doors, chains and so on . . . banal . . . (*He smiles.*) And yet the world is near . . . (*He listens again. Sounds on the wind.*) What was a riot? (LILI *looks, dimly* . . .)

LILI: Something to do with politics . . .

MOSCA: Politics . . .

LILI: **Get a grip on yourself, Count . . . !**

MOSCA: Yes, I must do . . . (LILI *turns to go, stops.*)

LILI: Look after Sleen . . . I can't . . .

MOSCA (*calling after* LILI): **The vocabulary is going what next the language slipping what next . . . !** (*She ignores him, he turns, defiantly.*)

> No
>
> No

I am quite capable of accommodating myself to the new conditions after all what is sophistication but the knowledge of inevitable decay the certainty of degeneration not to be shocked not to be surprised not to be prostrated by the inevitable that is sophisication surely

> **Anna**

What's unpredictable to him who's mentally prepared, who has rehearsed in dead of night all possible calamities including

> **Anna**

The rotting of the single passion that gave you breath

I am an idiot slobbering in a restaurant yes I saw him once in my most golden year a toothless lover whose despairing tears fell into a bitch's hands even his collar was too large for the rotting landscape of his neck I could not look I winced I saw in him the terrible absurdity of love that outlasts flesh

> Oh
>
> And I was the cleverest man in the world
>
> Never
>
> Clever
>
> Enough
>
> However . . . (TOCSIN *is discovered in a poor light.* MOSCA *is aware of him.*)

Yes I am working on my song I know your tastes are simple which exercizes me who is not simple but urgency inspires me . . . ! (MME POUSSIN *enters, looks at* MOSCA.)

MME POUSSIN: The actor loves me . . .
MOSCA: Yes . . .
MME POUSSIN: And I never asked for love.
MOSCA: Quite.
MME POUSSIN: Silly boy but.
MOSCA: Very.
MME POUSSIN: Powerful.
MOSCA: Is he.
MME POUSSIN: An engine.
MOSCA: Really.
MME POUSSIN: Striving. Striving for what can't be won.
MOSCA: Oh?
MME POUSSIN: Energy. Not subtlety, however.
MOSCA: Ah.
MME POUSSIN: Whereas — (MOSCA *swiftly takes* MME POUSSIN *by the neck.*)
MOSCA: No more (MME POUSSIN *grunts, choking.*)
        No more of your (*She frantically mutters.*)
        The very articulation of (*Her arms flutter.*)
        Is like irons (*She grunts.*)
        In the bowel (*She suffocates.*)
        Which I have witnessed, incidentally
        Oh yes
        The governors see too much . . . .

MOSCA *releases* MME POUSSIN. *She gasps, silently, on her knees. He looks at her.* TOCSIN *laughs in the gloom, and disappears.* MOSCA *stares at the kneeling form of* MME POUSSIN, *for a long time. A wind rises, whipping rubbish across the stage.* MOSCA *goes to* MME POUSSIN, *unbuttoning himself. He presses himself on her from behind. The light goes.*

SEVENTH ECLOGUE

POUSSIN *is painting, raised on a scaffold.* DOVER *stands beneath.*

DOVER: You are stupid. You are irrational. You are a threat
to your own sanity and consequently to mine. You deny me
for reasons of the most absurd kind none of which stand up
to examination. We are made for each other everybody says
so and I insist you come to me unencumbered I absolutely
insist and come down from there when I am talking! (POUS-
SIN *paints. Pause.*) I have never once in my life failed in
what I earnestly desired I warn you . . . (*He stops. He looks
at her.*)
POUSSIN: Love can be commanded, can it?
DOVER: Yes. (*She looks at him, for a long time.*)
           No
           Not exactly that but
           Yes it can and in any case you do desire me
           Beauty alone compels you
           Beauty
           Curiosity
    What you would not give to see me naked I know your
eyes betray you I overwhelm you very well I will be softer I
can be soft I long to be your animal I long to be your
murmuring thing **stop smiling I do long** I am so exasperated
I could (*Pause*) It is a good thing you are up a ladder I would
beat you . . . (*Pause*) When I had power I should certainly
have had you killed . . . (*She smiles. She shakes her head. Her
eyes close.*) Everything I say is wrong . . . everything I have
is not required . . . I could rip my face with broken glass . . .
POUSSIN (*stopping*):   Oh, now that is beauty . . .
DOVER (*her eyes still closed in despair*):   Is it . . .
POUSSIN: That . . .
           Almost . . . (*Pause*)
           But not quite . . .
DOVER: You thrive here . . . don't you . . . you thrive . . .
(*Pause*) What must I do . . . ?
POUSSIN: It is the absolute of love . . . that you would turn
yourself inside out . . . and maim your very perfect parts . . .
and hack your soul . . . for another who remains . . . implac-
able . . .

DOVER: Yes . . .

      I've lost my pride . . .

POUSSIN: There's none here, Anna . . .

DOVER: **I never pleaded never**

      Not for breakfast

      Not for dinner

      And never for a man

    I must sit in the sun I must expose myself to rain and all my qualities will crack and chip and wash away like ancient temples in the sand you are the sun you are the rain I will submit to every weather of indifference I shan't know myself but you will witness it I do not pester I merely decay . . . (*She is still.*)

      I love you. (*She sits, cross-legged.*)

      Silently. (*A storm breaks.* SANSOM *enters with a cloth. He casts it over* DOVER, *to shelter her. She is still.*)

SANSOM (*to* POUSSIN): This pleases you, does it?

POUSSIN: I don't know. Possibly.

SANSOM: This gratifies some —

POUSSIN: I don't know, Mr Sansom —

SANSOM (*to the indifferent* DOVER): Don't let him spoil you . . . !

POUSSIN: You would prefer to do it yourself, I assume?

SANSOM: **I am not the same man that I was**

POUSSIN: Who is? Who is?

SANSOM: You are vile and even your own mother detests you —

POUSSIN: Her particularly —

SANSOM (*to* DOVER): You will be ill . . . you will be spoiled . . . look, her make-up is running down her face in little rivers . . .

POUSSIN: Shh . . . Shh . . .

SANSOM: **No you be quiet** . . . ! And she is not eating . . .

      I adore you . . .

      I adore you . . . (*He puts his head in* DOVER's *lap.*)

    We used to sing . . . before they spoiled Arcadia . . . everybody . . . singing . . . ! (*He sits up suddenly.*) If she dies I will kill you . . . !

POUSSIN: But why? I'm not responsible. Perhaps you are the guilty one.

SANSOM (*horrified*): Me? Why?

POUSSIN: For failing to inculcate in her the love that might have warmed her life . . . (*Pause*)

SANSOM: I try.

POUSSIN: Yes . . .

That's it, of course . . .

You try . . . (SANSOM *stares bitterly at* POUSSIN.)

SANSOM: You are so — so lean with coldness and contempt — so — barren and —

POUSSIN: You know that isn't true —

SANSOM: So — dry and sharp like —

POUSSIN: Unfortunately —

SANSOM: Rusting razors left in —

POUSSIN: Not true at all, you merely compensate yourself for my —

SANSOM: **What is it, then?**

POUSSIN: Gifts. Which appall you. As gifts do appall the ungifted. (*Pause*)

SANSOM: I want to kill you. But I can't. So . . .

POUSSIN: You will have to love me instead . . . (SANSOM *stares.*) **I only tell the truth** . . . (*He laughs, for the first time.*) Really . . . ! Even I am sentimental . . . off and on . . . (*He goes back to his brushes.*) Truth . . . !

SANSOM: Yes . . . (*He kisses* DOVER, *chastely as one might reverence a statue, and covers her.*) Yes . . . (*Dogs bark. The storm breaks.* POUSSIN *sweeps his brush in a massive blue arc across the sky. The voice of* MME POUSSIN *can be heard singing as the sound of fury stops, a pure tone. She enters.*)

MME POUSSIN: Simple

Simple

Pleasure

Spare me your imagination

Simple

Simple

Pleasure

My heart is sky

Blue aether and I love no one

That's liberty (*She stops.* LE VIG *is discovered watching her. Pause.*)

And laughter . . . ! I am the only one who laughs now . . . and I say laugh most specifically . . . much ironic rumbling but that's pain settling to the bottom of the jar no I possess the last real laugh believe me . . . I demonstrate . . . (*She produces a laugh.*)

It rings . . . !

Unspoiled by —

LE VIG: You've met someone.

MME POUSSIN: You're not listening —

LE VIG: You've

Met

Someone . . . (*Pause*)

Oh, isn't that the saddest sentence in the world? **In any language . . . !**

Oh, doorway to such corridors of torture . . . !

Aren't I all you require? I must be! (*Pause*)

No, no, that's silly, no, nobody is, are they, no one can be, no one can satisfy in every single solitary regard the

Nevertheless (*He gasps, snorts.*)

Please . . . I am not accustomed to . . . much less than . . . utter . . . devotion . . .

If this was not Arcadia I would not even notice you

Straight in the bin your begging letter

No

No

You sit in my brain and pluck like an idle child all my free thoughts . . . none left which are not in your basket . . . and you . . . are the antithesis of beauty . . . (MME POUSSIN *laughs.*)

Yes

Yes

Silly word . . . beauty . . .

One which I will not ever use again . . . (*He bawls.*)

All right Monsieur Poussin! (*She laughs again.*)

That laugh contains another man

Quite right

What am I after all

An actor

A sham

A mockery of —

SLEEN (*limping in*):   Shut up . . .

LE VIG: The preposterous product of accountancy . . .

SLEEN (*shaking his head*):   Le Vig, they do not like abjection, women . . . (*To* MME POUSSIN.) Do you, Madam, like this kind of thing? Their wombs go cold.

LE VIG: Can't help it . . .

SLEEN: No . . . no . . . perhaps you can't . . . (*He stares at* DOVER. MME POUSSIN *goes to* LE VIG *and touches him affectionately.*)

MME POUSSIN: I live for pleasure . . .

SLEEN: Rubbish . . .

MME POUSSIN: And keep my soul light and airborne as a
cloud . . . (*She smiles, goes out.*)

SLEEN: It isn't true, she's barmy for the count —

LE VIG: What —

SLEEN: Mosca —

LE VIG: What —

SLEEN: Oh yes —

LE VIG: She —

SLEEN: Sixty years so what they kill at seventy for love I've
seen it —

LE VIG: I want to walk with her in Paris —

SLEEN: You can't —

LE VIG: **And show her body to the world its full and mobile
shape** —

SLEEN: Le Vig . . . your juvenile infatuations — (*He stops.
Pause. He shakes his head.*) are no worse than anybody else's
. . . (LE VIG *sees that* SLEEN *is gazing at* DOVER.)

LE VIG: Are you —

SLEEN (*glancing back at* LE VIG): Ill, yes . . . now leave us
alone . . . (LE VIG *goes out.* SLEEN *is silent for a long time,
preparing himself to speak.*)

> Nothing I say
> Nothing
> Can affect
> Nothing move or alter
> Words were never more transparently absurd than
> now and yet (*Long pause*)

Still force the lips to serve me though humiliation lies in it
all kinds of things I've stooped to being without faith
nothing I'd not confess to just to keep the righteous off the
angry or the vengeful words with me became the sabres of a
champion but love (*Pause*)

> That rarely appeared except to ridicule (*Pause*)
> Flesh
> And
> Greedy
> Copulations . . . (*Pause*)
> The spectacle of instinct . . . (*Pause. A wind.* POUS-
> SIN *ceases painting and moved leans on the scaffold*
> to hear SLEEN's *appeal.*)
> So this is — (*He falters.*)
> What?

> The foredoomed and futile statement of a faith . . .
> Pure
> Pure
> Arcadia . . . (*He laughs, dimly, shakes his head.*)
> I reverence
> I discard every weapon of contempt
> Which leaves me naked
> Naked and absurd
> Old
> Fatuous

But not so full not so replete with knowledge that I stand back from my hopelessness that would be death, surely?

> Ex-Queen of somewhere
> I am not actually ashamed
> The first time
> Possibly
> To
> Adore . . . (*Pause. He sways very slightly. His eyes rise to meet* POUSSIN's, *of whose presence he was unaware. He smiles.*)
> Feel stupid . . .
> Years since I felt stupid . . . (*Long pause*)

DOVER: Go away, now . . .

> I am in such pain . . .

> Go away, now . . . (*Pause.* SLEEN *rubs his hands through his hair. He is inundated with hopelessness and lacks the power even to move.* TOCSIN *is visible in a half-light.*)

TOCSIN: How's that song?

SLEEN: Coming along . . . (*Pause*)

TOCSIN: Okay . . . (*A cheerful chorus on the wind. At last* SLEEN *moves, but stops.*)

SLEEN: Moved, but why . . . ? To go where . . . ? (MOSCA *enters, looks at* SLEEN.)

MOSCA: I was a suicide. Quite right. How excellent it is. Draw down the curtain. The very mark of sensibility. **And now I am a madman** talk them out of it why, the suicides are perfect in their judgement **jump, sir, slash, sir, kick the chair away** it's a tiny horror in comparison with what awaits the **undone act**. (*Pause*) As long as I was loved I was civil cynical but civil not burdened with the ideal but mildly tolerant and capable of kindness on and off — (*He leans to* DOVER.) **You are the cause of such degeneracy I hate myself** . . . (MME

POUSSIN *enters, looks at* MOSCA.) You deliver me to wolves, Anna . . . there are wolves here . . . (*He points to* MME POUSSIN.)

> **That's one!**
> **Here's another!**
> Don't ask me back I couldn't speak our language any more . . . .
> Don't ask me back . . .
> No, no . . .
> Don't ask me . . . (LE VIG *strides in with a shuddering vigour. He seizes* MOSCA *from the back and futilely attempts to strangle him.* TOCSIN *laughs out loud. They stagger in a peculiar dance. As he fails,* LE VIG *begins to weep. They falter, stop.*)

LE VIG: I hate myself . . . I hate myself . . . !

SLEEN: So do we all, apparently . . . (*The dogs bark distantly.*)
> Except for Monsieur Poussin, who loves, and loves and loves his life . . . (*He drags up his eyes to* POUSSIN.)
> I must say, I do like you, Monsieur Poussin, oh, I do . . . (POUSSIN *covers his face with his hands and silently weeps.*)

DOVER: I have reduced great men to tears . . . which once . . . I will admit . . . delighted me . . .

MOSCA: It's not because of you . . .

MME POUSSIN: Shh . . .

DOVER: They wept . . . and I . . .

MOSCA: Anna . . . it's not because of you . . .

DOVER: I experienced appalling satisfactions . . . as if I had not power in abundance . . . ! I thrived on their despair . . . I wore their tears like sashes . . . (*She shakes her head.*)
> Not now, though . . . (*Pause. To* POUSSIN.)
> Please love me . . . I will attend on your life as a maid cleans a room . . . and with the lightest touch, turn down the starched sheets of your unhappiness . . . (*Pause.* LILI *enters. She looks at them.*)

LILI: Listen, this place is — (*Pause. They ignore her.*) I walked to the edge of it and — (*They ignore her.*)
> There is an edge but — (*She looks at them.*)
> I think if we tied things together . . . ropes and so on . . .
> (*It is as if she were invisible, inaudible to them.*)
> **Don't you want to live a life**? (*She looks around.*)

Viggy?
Sleen . . . !
Life . . . ! (*Distant machine guns, mixed with the sounds of restaurant interiors. No one moves . . .*)

EIGHTH ECLOGUE

Applause. A point of light reveals the head of TOCSIN. *The applause is relentless, monotonous. The light spreads. The applause stops.* TOCSIN *is seen to be standing at the head of a table along which the characters are seated. A single dog barks.*

TOCSIN: I'm loved . . . ! (*Pause*)
                And I — could not care less . . . ! (*Pause*)
     Now, that is typical. That is life all over. Don't you find? That is the human condition? (*Pause*)
     I, the focus of desire — am supremely — what's the word — indifferent! Blasé! Anodyne!
SLEEN: That's not the word . . .
TOCSIN: Not the word? He knows, he is the author of a dozen books —
SLEEN: At least —
TOCSIN: At least a dozen — he is culture itself — whereas I —
SLEEN: Just get on with it . . . (*His eyes meet* TOCSIN's.)
                No offence . . . (*An unpleasant pause.*)
TOCSIN: Culture itself, whereas I possess **I am not charming** the single thing **not very seductive in myself** you all aspire — to . . . (*Pause*)
                Oblivion. (*Pause*)
     No wonder you love me . . . only I can give relief . . . ! No wonder you fawn and flatter me. I am the solitary doctor in the house of plague
                Plead now, plead! (*They all wail with piercing cries.*)
                Stop!
                Stop! (*Silence*)
                I call that love . . . it's . . . (*He shrugs.*)
                Dishonest but . . . I'm gratified . . . (*He shakes his head.*)

Poor me . . . (*He sits abruptly, then puts his finger to his lips.*)

Shh . . . ! (*A sound of distance. The whine of planes.*) The real world, ladies and gentlemen, is so well-attended to . . . all the best brains there . . . (*He laughs. They are attentive to the sounds.* POUSSIN *walks in, stops, looks.*)

POUSSIN: First the sheep died . . . then the shepherds . . . and with the shepherds . . . song . . . so asking you, so very urban, so very poor in personal resources, to stand up and sing is — (*Pause. He looks from one to another.*)

　　　　　　Cruel —

　　　　　　Humiliating —

　　　　　　But — what else do you suggest? Reciting, possibly —

SLEEN: No, I like to make a fool of myself, Monsieur Poussin. I always did —

LILI: Sleen, you are a horrible sight —

SLEEN: Aspire to the ridiculous —

LILI: **Am I the only one with any dignity round here?**

SLEEN: Yes, of course you are . . . for what it's worth . . . (DOVER *stands abruptly*)

DOVER: I can sing. (*Pause*)

　　　　　　And play the piano. (*Pause*)

　　　　　　Dance. (*Pause*)

And every fucking thing not one of which earned me your love so all my childish hours were fatuous and futile silly infant I believe these things were called **accomplishments**

　　　　　　Thank you father

　　　　　　Thank you mother

Who kept me at the piano and the harpsichord they might at least earn me a peace if death is peace I so dislike my life . . . (*She breathes.*) May I go first, then?

TOCSIN: Yes! I love your eagerness! The eager are my favourites, though I must warn you, I have a habit of frustrating them . . . the ones who jump off cliffs, for example . . . are often hooked on branches . . . (*He grins.*)

DOVER: I would expect nothing less from you . . .

SANSOM (*standing, wildly*): I love you.

MME POUSSIN: Oh, shut up —

SANSOM: I love you . . . !

MOSCA: Sit down. Nobody wants your affirmations now. (SANSOM *reluctantly sits.* DOVER *sings.*)

DOVER: I was born to authority

How hard it comes to plead
And even foolish
Love I know does never yield
To goodness
I was born to beauty
How impossible to look in mirrors how
Without self-hatred
Face you have failed me
You poor ally to betray me how
My looks concealed
A greater power to offend
Oh, useless wit, oh, absurd thing
What I would not surrender to be somehow
Even liked by him
And that miserable hope
Is my pride's end . . .

Pause. TOCSIN *is leaning back in the chair looking into the sky.*
DOVER *resolutely stays standing.* TOCSIN *pushes back his chair, walks a little, turns.*

TOCSIN: Well . . . the trained voice is a lovely thing . . . of course I am not sophisticated —
SLEEN: Oh, you always say that —
TOCSIN: I do, do I —
SLEEN: Always on about simplicity, I don't believe him —
TOCSIN: I'm boring, am I?
SLEEN: No offence, but —
TOCSIN: Boring and repetitive —
SLEEN: I never said that — I just —
TOCSIN: You are full of compliments tonight, Mr Sleen —
SLEEN: **All right I'm stupid but she** — (*Pause*) Broke my heart again . . . (*Pause*)
TOCSIN: Yes . . . it was good . . . in many respects . . . (SLEEN *bangs the table with his fists.* MOSCA *puts a hand on his arm.*)

And you may say —
I'm sure you do say —
That such a one as me should arbitrate is really an offence against — (*He emits a scream appalling, inhuman.*)
But
That

Is
Me

A gale drives leaves hurtling over the stage. They cling to the table. Loose sheets of rusty iron flap, rattle. MME POUSSIN *cries over the noise.*

MME POUSSIN (*standing*):   I sing!
                     I sing! (*The gale and sounds subside.*)
                     Not very well, perhaps . . . but with feeling, and —
DOVER: I had feeling —
MME POUSSIN: I wasn't saying you lacked feeling —
DOVER (*sitting abruptly*):   Good —
TOCSIN: Shh . . .
DOVER: Yes . . .
TOCSIN: Shh . . .
DOVER: I am so — utterly —
TOCSIN: Yes . . .
DOVER: Contemptuous of my life . . .
TOCSIN (*to* MME POUSSIN):   Please, don't be distracted by the pain of others . . . (MME POUSSIN *prepares.*)
LE VIG: **Certainly not mine** (*He laughs.*)
SLEEN: Le Vig —
LE VIG: **Don't let my misery impinge, will you, I'd hate to think you —**
SLEEN: Le Vig —
LE VIG: **Might suffer the inconvenience of my existence —**
SLEEN: You are —
LE VIG: **A child? Yes, I am a child and always was one . . . !** (*He sobs.*) Pity you're not childish . . . pity everybody isn't . . . we could . . . play . . . until the sun went in . . .
MME POUSSIN (*singing*):   Kiss me
                     I am not critical of men
                     Kiss me
                     This way we might forget our pain
                     But then comes one who
                     Won't allow us to be still again

                     Torture me
                     I am not ignorant of men
                     Torture me
                     This way my life was set on fire

And you who care so little
Have roped me with desire

Lie to me
Oh, let me hear more of your lies
Lie to me
I shan't be free again
Believe me I was never critical of
men
Smother me now
Smother with your eyes . . . (*Pause*)

MOSCA: Nothing
Nothing so bad
As passion where you asked for none
Really it is exquisite in its refinement
An embarassment akin to God's . . . (MME
POUSSIN *looks at* MOSCA. LE VIG *turns to
him.*)

LE VIG: That's *your* song, is it? **That's your song**?

MOSCA: No, I am not singing —

TOCSIN: Not singing, your excellency? But —

MOSCA: Which is not to say I do not wish to die, I certainly
wish to die, I merely thought to spare you the discomfort of
watching a man disintegrate before your very eyes —

LE VIG (*cruelly*): Got to sing!

MOSCA: Instead, I propose —

LE VIG: **Got to sing, hasn't he**?

LILI: Le Vig, you are so full of malice, really it is —

LE VIG: **Everybody has to sing**. (*He looks at* TOCSIN.)
That's the rule, isn't it? I thought?

TOCSIN: Count Mosca clings to dignity like a drowning man
clings to a lobster pot . . .

MOSCA: I thought I'd read a poem.

LE VIG: No! (MOSCA *shrugs*.)

MME POUSSIN (*to* MOSCA): Make a fool of yourself.
Everybody else has. (*She sits*.)

MOSCA: That's hard . . . for me . . . worse, I think, than
being ripped in pieces by a mob . . .

MME POUSSIN: Yes . . . you prefer to degenerate . . . in
solitude . . .

MOSCA: Evidently . . .

MME POUSSIN: You prefer to keep your vileness under
cloths . . .

MOSCA: Yes. I call that manners . . .

MME POUSSIN: Ha!

SANSOM: Please . . . it's obvious we all hate each other . . . why therefore —

MME POUSSIN: You know nothing. (*Pause*) Nothing at all. (SANSOM *shrugs*. MOSCA *stands*.)

MOSCA: No, the actor's right. Sometimes, the poorest motives stimulate unwelcome truths. It is perfectly obvious I should humiliate myself, and not simply for his satisfaction.

DOVER: Don't. (*Pause*)

MOSCA: No?

Oh, Anna . . . you hate to see me . . . ridiculed . . .

DOVER: Yes . . .

MOSCA: And is that — (*Pause*) A little, lingering love?

DOVER: I don't know . . .

MOSCA: I don't think so . . . much as I wish it might be . . . rather I think it is . . . oh, Anna . . . self-regard . . . **was that idiot, mine** . . . ? (*He laughs, a resigned laugh.*) Ego . . . in . . . Arcadia . . . (*He falls forward, leaning on his hands on the table and sings, crudely, tunelessly.*)

> I found nothing
> I found nothing
> Gratification eluded me
> Cunt
> Cunt
> A corridor of self again
> What hangs on the womb's wall but mirrors
> I walked through men
> I rode through men
> Autumn leaves
> Autumn showers
> A Queen found me
> And shaped the formless hours
> Axeman
> Axeman
> The years have stripped bark from my tree
> Naked wood
> All naked wood
> Axeman
> Deliver me . . . (*He ceases. A silence. At last* SLEEN *speaks.*)

SLEEN: There . . . (*Pause*) I do have competition . . . and I thought I would romp home . . .

POUSSIN (*to* MOSCA):   I drew you . . .
           I so rarely draw from life. . . .
           But I drew you. . . .
           Pure
           Pure
           Arcadia . . .

MOSCA (*still leaning*):   Yes . . . well, you love it here. (*He turns to* DOVER, *with a peculiar triumph.*) She's dead . . . ! (*He looks around.*)
           Dead . . . !
           No, if I say dead it implies — existence!
           No, not dead, she —
           N'existe pas! (*He puts his hands to his face in a struggle to comprehend and express.*)
           Oh, words . . . !
           Oh, shapeless approximations . . . !
           She
           Went
           With
           The
           Wind . . . ! (*He laughs, shaking his head. He turns to* SLEEN.)
     Say you understand . . . you . . . surely . . . of all . . . have some notion of philosophy?

SLEEN (*shrugs*):   Forgive me, Count, I've none at all . . .

MOSCA (*to* TOCSIN):   I withdraw my song. (*He pulls his coat round him.*) I have no desire whatsoever to be parted from this life. Old, yes. So what? And teeth, they frequently betray me. But I have overcome Arcadia. I throttled it. When she left me she left the world. It is that simple. Lili, we can leave. (*He extends a hand to* LILI.)

TOCSIN: Too late, Count, you have sung your song now.

MOSCA: You don't understand. In singing the song I —

TOCSIN: That's what songs are for! (*Pause. He smiles.*)

POUSSIN: I spent rather little time in life class. I was perhaps, never much in love with flesh . . .

MOSCA (*turning to* POUSSIN):   **I withdraw my application!** (POUSSIN *is indifferent*)

SANSOM (*to* MOSCA):   You may not win. It is so — arrogant of you — to think that you will win. Perhaps I will. And Sleen . . . The man's a poet, he will obscure you.

MOSCA: No . . . they want to kill me . . . because I have
  throttled love . . . I have thought love to extinction . . . (*He
  sits, depressed.* LE VIG *stands.*)

DOVER (*reaching a hand to* MOSCA *over the table*): Please
  — (*Pause. He looks into her.*)

MOSCA (*ignoring her gesture*): Gone . . .

LE VIG (*standing*): I'm singing. (DOVER *stares, hollow.*) I'm
  singing because, even if it isn't my turn — (*He looks at*
  MOSCA.) **I am nauseated with your vanity**.

LILI (*anxious for him*): Viggy . . .

LE VIG: Don't Viggy me. (LILI *shrugs.*) Even at death's door
  . . . he claims precedence . . .

MOSCA (*to* LE VIG): You delight them . . . you give them so
  much satisfaction, hating as you do . . . for love . . . you
  utter, born Arcadian . . . Monsieur Poussin is perfectly
  charmed by you . . .

LE VIG (*pressing on, as if to silence him*):

> I loved myself
> And my reaching hands were like the gestures
> Of bad actors
> Only claiming light
>
> I loved myself
> And my yearning eyes were like the
> Moon in water
> Brief as the night
>
> This love makes my soul ring
> Like the ribs of dead aristocrats
> Caught in the heels of dancers
> Worthless thing
>
> She walks through me
> She treads the poverty
> Of my —

MOSCA (*to* DOVER, *violently*): No!
> You only want it neatly stowed in memory
> **Too bad madam**!

LE VIG (*bursting into tears*): **He's ruined my** — (POUSSIN
  laughs out loud.)

MOSCA (*indifferently, to* LE VIG): Forgive me —

LE VIG: **Ruined my** —

SLEEN: Forget it, Vig, it was mawkish —

LE VIG: **It was not mawkish it was** —

SLEEN: It was, it was mawkish and like everything you do, another advertisement for someone called Le Vig —

LE VIG: **Not true!**

POUSSIN (*delighted*): The Count has shown himself! For a moment I believed he really had — I did believe him that he had **conquered pain**, Count, I was sunk in admiration —

MOSCA: **I detest life I detest all life** —

POUSSIN: Yes
           Yes
           You perfect human being
           Embrace me, please
           You are so human you are a god
           Kiss me!
           Kiss me!

POUSSIN *closes his eyes. His arms open. The wind blows.* MOSCA *silently sobs in his arms. A gun thumps miles away. Others slump in their seats, broken by despair.*

TOCSIN: That isn't everyone. (*Pause*)
          Is it, gents? (*Pause*)
          Ladies? (*Pause*)
          Don't be shy . . . !

DOVER (*to* POUSSIN): Why do you — why —

TOCSIN: No, this is not the moment for your inquisitions —

DOVER: Is it because —

TOCSIN (*savagely*): **I said.** (*Pause*)

POUSSIN: These landscapes . . . are made from . . . solitude . . .

DOVER: Then let me —

TOCSIN: **Time to sing**
          Time to
          Time

VERDUN (*standing*): My song is not a song at all. (MOSCA, *freed from* POUSSIN's *embrace, slumps in a chair.*) It's a dagger.

TOCSIN: Not a blunt one, I hope! (*He laughs.*) I am so shallow! I am completely unaffected by your feelings, which are beautiful feelings, they are perhaps the finest any of you ever had and yet. How do I do it?

SLEEN (*looking at* DOVER): 'Then let me — ' (*He looks up, into the sky.*) Aren't those the finest words a woman ever said?

LE VIG: Now who's being mawkish?

SLEEN: **It is not mawkish you poor minded you utterly**
No I'm being cruel
No I'm being savage
I heard the gate of Heaven turning on its hinge
Her voice is like a (*He coveres his face with his hands.*)
Carry on
Carry on

VERDUN (*proceeding*): I've ceasèd to love
It's done
The pain has fled loved one
And I can look at you

I've ceased to live
Existence yes
But so much less
Than even pain gave me to bite

I breathe so shallowly
You failed
To be necessity

**And life can drive through
Sentiments even of this complexity** (*She ends, but stays, hand to mouth.*)

Find me a poor husband somebody just to sit with
**Just
Sit
With** . . . (*Pause*)

TOCSIN: A dagger . . . ? In what way a dagger . . . ? I —

SLEEN: **In her own flesh** . . . (*He glares at* TOCSIN.)
The blade . . .
Mundane idiot . . . (*Suddenly*)

I take a chance here but — I risk the most appalling but — all circumspection has deserted me and obviously if Death takes me it will be with such a festival of diabolical agony I predict, such refinement of cruelty **the worst death yet recorded** and I include the martyrs, no, I am piling up a spectacular departure but even I cannot hear beauty bludgeoned by Mr Tocsin's cretinous sensibility, even I, God help me, **is it my turn now** . . . ? (*His eyes are shut.* TOCSIN *looks at him, long and coolly.*)

TOCSIN: How offensive you are, Mr Sleen . . .

SLEEN: Yes . . . I deserve all I get . . .

SANSOM: You are a great man!

SLEEN: Shut up, that doesn't help . . .

SANSOM: **A great man I said** . . .

SLEEN: Please, you are contributing to my punishment . . .
(*Pause*)

TOCSIN: So unkind . . . (*He shakes his head.*)

SLEEN: Yes . . . life's short . . . and I thought nothing was
worth dying for . . . I like Arcadia, Monsieur Poussin . . .

POUSSIN: Yes, and how good Arcadia is, for you . . .

SLEEN: It is, is it . . . ?

POUSSIN: Whereas you — (*He turns to* VERDUN) will
never be beautiful again. (*She looks at him.*) Pain-free, but
never beautiful . . .

TOCSIN: Next!

POUSSIN: Love

How glad we are when we get over it
Love
How quickly we convert it to domesticity
Love
Was there any subject on which so many were
thrusting their advice?
Everyone's an expert
Not here, however . . .

TOCSIN: Next!

POUSSIN: Here, it makes Death even, bland . . . (TOCSIN
looks at POUSSIN, *resentfully.*)

SLEEN: It must be me...
Did I sound reluctant on the contrary

DOVER: Please . . . (*Pause*) You cannot hate yourself more
bitterly than I do. If you love me don't sing . . . (*Pause*)

SLEEN: If I love you . . . (*He shrugs, smiles.*)
Lili . . . she wonders if . . . (*Pause*)
It's that absurd to her . . . (*Pause*)
The very fact you wonder if . . . makes me so anxious to
be out of it! **Deliverance, Mr Tocsin!** (*He rises, kicks his
chair over.*) What a way to go but I was ever short on
dignity! (*He stops.*) I want to die. And Monsieur Poussin
is correct, always, so correct. Who wants to recover from
love? It rots the thing to recover from it. It makes us
ludicrous as planets, on their routine trips . . . (*He smiles,
thinly.*)

'I grew out of it.'
'I smothered it.'
'I saw through it.' (*Pause*)
No. (*Pause*)
It killed me. (*He sings, in a voice dignified by pain, but inexpert.*)

I exaggerate
It is one of my triumphs
Exaggeration
Nothing in proportion
And illogical in all respects
I don't want truth I only want effects
I exaggerate

I lie
It is one of my greatnesses
Mendacity
Reality was never satisfactory
And I hated how I hated niceness
Nothing I liked better than pure prejudice
I lie

I cringe
It is one of my accomplishments
Cringing
And done properly
It gratifies the soul of man
I so wanted to live you understand
I cringe

And now I find I've nothing in my hand
Not even abuse
To penetrate indifference ... with ... (*He falters, looks around him. Pause.*)

Come on, Mr Tocsin, that's the best yet ...
MADAM POUSSIN: Well, that's open to —
SLEEN: **I claim it** —
MADAME POUSSIN: Obviously you think you —
SLEEN: **I claim it**. (*Pause. He defies them to challenge him.*)
SANSOM: Yes, and I shan't sing mine because —
SLEEN: That's right, don't bother.

A profound silence fills the stage. LILI, *overcome with pity for* SLEEN, *goes to him and takes his hands in hers.* DOVER *leans face down on the table.* LE VIG *stands, as if to act, fails to, stares into a distance.* POUSSIN *examines them, almost surreptitiously.* TOCSIN *waits on* POUSSIN. *The hiatus extends, and extends . . . they become stiller, and stiller. At last* POUSSIN *utters.*

POUSSIN: Arcadia . . . is . . . beauty,   then?   Intolerable beauty . . . ? (*Pause*)
        Believe me, nothing follows from fulfilment but the most mundane . . . (*Pause*)
        And . . . fultile . . . (*Pause*)
        Happiness . . .
TOCSIN: It's what they want, Monsieur . . . (*He takes a rope from his clothing. He tosses one end with practised skill over a branch. No one has moved.*)
POUSSIN (*to* TOCSIN): Who is it to be, then? (TOCSIN *adjusts the lengths.*) Obviously in choosing Mr Tocsin I could not have done better. He brings to his task such simple sentiments. Perhaps there are more sophisticated men, but who would want them? It's a job for no one in particular . . . (*Pause*)
        Well? I have my favourites, but . . . (*Pause.* TOCSIN *looks at him.*)
        You choose . . . (*Pause.* POUSSIN *is aware of every nuance of a changed atmosphere.*)
  I did not invent Arcadia! No, and who did invent it? We don't know! Perhaps it did not require invention. Perhaps it **struggled to be born with every infant soul!**
MME POUSSIN: My little son . . . (*She shakes her head, pitifully.*) It's you . . . (POUSSIN *looks into her. The dogs of Arcadia quarrel, distantly. It darkens on his gaze.*)

NINTH ECLOGUE

The wind. They are all still.

POUSSIN: No one so desired can be killed, can they . . .
        I wear their adoration
        I wade in their esteem

My enemies even suspect they suffocate a longing
when they hate
Aren't I immune
How can I die
Your very hope of life runs in my veins
I mean
I mean (*He stops. He is peculiarly innocent . . .*)
It never occurred to me . . . (TOCSIN *takes a
step.*)
Don't come near me (TOCSIN *stops.*)
The way he
His repulsive
And the artificial bonhommie, really I
Mother

MME POUSSIN: Yes —

POUSSIN: Stand between me and that man —

MME POUSSIN: I will do but —

POUSSIN: His mouth —

MME POUSSIN: Yes —

POUSSIN: Particularly offends me —
Stay where you are I said (*Pause. He laughs.*)
No, it's funny, it is . . .
Because . . .
The spectacle of a man squirming with his destiny
is —
It is
I will admit
Hilarious
The stratagems the tortuous manoeuvres
And the loss of dignity
No
There comes a point (*Pause. He goes to* DOVER.)
Did you know I never slept?
Less and less until
I watched the entire night turn by a wheel of stars
My love was certainly the moon
Who when she hid herself ached for me
In forbidding me
Injured herself
We are all like that aren't we?
And self comes up through love like the sailor's
body through the sands . . . ankle . . . elbow . . .
rib . . .

> **No I've never seen one**
> **I've seen nothing**
> But dreamed it all ... (*He holds* DOVER *in his arms.*)
> Sufficient, surely ... ? (*They kiss.*)

DOVER: Don't die ... you are in love with me ...

POUSSIN (*in despair*): **Am I**
> **Am I**
> Is that what it is ... ?

DOVER: In love ... and terrified ...

POUSSIN: Is that what it is ... ? (*Pause. He looks deeply into her.*)
> If you hate the world ...
> You must invent another ...

DOVER: Yes ... ! (*The distant cry of frenzy.*)
> Invent me!
> Please! (*Pause.* TOCSIN *picks up a chair.*)

TOCSIN: Sometimes I feel I am a barber ... (*He routinely places it under the rope.*)
> My conversation —
> Is —
> Of the barbering sort —
> Some would call in insincere —

But no, I promise you, its mutedness ... the miserable lack of speculation that distinguishes it ... is ... the best that I can do ... (*He waits by the chair. He laughs, weakly, looking at the floor. His eyes rise to* POUSSIN.)

MME POUSSIN: Nicholas ... !
> Don't keep the man waiting ... (*She claps her hands to attract* POUSSIN's *attention.*)

POUSSIN (*to* DOVER): If I love ... love dies ...
> If I die ... love lives ...

DOVER: No, it need not —

POUSSIN (*indicating* MOSCA's *tortured expression*): Look at him!

DOVER: That was ... that ... was —

POUSSIN: Perfection, yes ...

POUSSIN *moves from* DOVER, *as if to yield himself to* TOCSIN, *but suddenly flings himself upon him. The chair falls.* TOCSIN *laughs in pure amazement. The others rise like a crowd at a match. They shout. The cacophony of Arcadian sounds rises as the struggling pair manoeuvre in a dance. On the sound of a*

*percussive note they cease. The stage is still. The sound of glass
cascading from high windows.*

TENTH ECLOGUE

The body of TOCSIN *hangs from the rope. It revolves slowly in
a breeze, to the sound of pan pipes.* POUSSIN *sits astride a chair
at the feet. A plane swoops low, firing cannon. It fades.*
POUSSIN *is unmoved.* SLEEN *enters, bawling in despair.*

SLEEN: **Still alive, me!**
        Oh, Monsieur Poussin, I do not like you . . .
        Still alive and she . . . ! (*His mouth gapes.*)
        Can't say the word . . .
POUSSIN: Can't say it, why? (DOVER *enters, radiant.*)
SLEEN (*contemptuously*): **Happy**. . . . ! Is it not a rebuke to
    life, Monsieur Poussin, that love never destroyed a soul? (*He
    looks at* DOVER.) In pain you were magnificent, but in
    prosperity . . . (*He shrugs, opens his hands.*) Love on . . . !
DOVER: I'm unforgivable.
SLEEN: Love on. . . . !
DOVER: Unforgivable because in all things I succeed. And
    yet of all things, only this was wanted.
SLEEN: So it seems . . .
DOVER: Only **this**
SLEEN: Today . . .
DOVER: **Solitary man** . . . (*She looks at* POUSSIN.) Who is a
    mystery to me . . .
SLEEN: Take me away, Monsieur Poussin. Show me a grotto
    or a hermitage. I like to be disposed of. You dispose . . . of
    me . . . (DOVER *kisses* SLEEN *on the cheek.* SLEEN *is
    still.*) What's that? Pity?

A plane swoops. POUSSIN *goes off a little way, stops, waits for*
SLEEN. SLEEN *joins him. They go out. A second plane passes.*
SANSOM *is discovered watching* DOVER *from a distance.*
DOVER *is gradually made aware of him.*

SANSOM: I so admire Mr Sleen . . . (*Pause*)

DOVER: Yes . . . Me too . . .

SANSOM: And you, of course, I admire also . . .

DOVER: I know that very well. (SANSOM *advances a little.*
She is apprehensive.)

        Arcadia . . . !

        Sometimes the light is such that —

SANSOM: And I am not a mystery, I suppose . . . ? (DOVER
looks at him. Pause.)

DOVER: You can see why people want to paint here —
(Swiftly, SANSOM *is beside* DOVER *and has her in a tight
grasp, a hand on her mouth. A pause.*)

SANSOM: I am not a mystery. (DOVER *tries to speak under
his hand.*)

        How many mysteries would you want? (*She
mumbles again.*)

        No

        No

        It's as well some of us are so (*Pause*)

        Legible . . . (*Pause, then he frees her mouth.*)

DOVER: I could

        I'm sure

        Attempt

        Some

        Trick or

        Some

        Manoeuvre

SANSOM: Yes . . . !

DOVER: You know me —

SANSOM: I so admire you!

DOVER: How I —

SANSOM: Yes —

DOVER: But —

SANSOM: No hatred —

DOVER: No —

SANSOM: No, none —

DOVER: So better if I — (MOSCA *is discovered, observing.*)
This time

        Merely (*Her eyes are fixed on* MOSCA, *who this
time does not move.*)

        Oh, let me have some happiness. . . .

SANSOM *suffocates* DOVER *with his hands. She moves in his
arms.* MOSCA *does not stir from his place.* SANSOM *lowers*

her body to the ground, gently, lovingly. Only then does MOSCA *kills* SANSOM *with a knife. With a shudder of disgust, he tosses the knife away. He sits in the chair* POUSSIN *had occupied. For a long time he is still, then he tosses back his head and emits a long laugh, which stops . . . Sounds off of* LILI *and* LE VIG *searching for* SLEEN.

MOSCA: As if she lacked happiness . . . ! Did anyone have more? (POUSSIN *enters, sees, stops.*) Did anyone?

LILI (*off*): Sleen is in a cave . . . !

LE VIG (*off, a tone of disbelief*): What?

LILI (off): A Cave! and won't come out! (*Other voices.* POUSSIN *is quite still.*)

MOSCA: I killed the fool who did it . . . (*Pause*) Obviously . . .

POUSSIN, *with a supreme effort of will, recovers and looks at* DOVER's *body with an artist's eye. He goes to her and changes the disposition of a limb.* MOSCA *gets up, and walks out, uncritically. The sound of feet rushing down iron stairs, flight after flight, which* POUSSIN *hears, and is fixed by. It stops.* VERDUN *is discovered, watching him.*

VERDUN: Not drawing it . . . ?

POUSSIN (*alerted*): Yes . . .

        Drawing it . . .

        Of course . . . (*He goes to his sketch book but the sound recurrs, breaking his concentration. He stops. It stops.*)

VERDUN: Draw it . . . (*He shrinks. He shakes his head.*)

        Dear friend . . . (*He looks up, pitifully.*)

        Oh, dear friend . . . (*She puts out a hand.*)

        Less . . .

        Less . . .